THE ILLUSTRATED PRACTICAL ENCYCLOPEDIA OF
RUNNING

THE ILLUSTRATED PRACTICAL ENCYCLOPEDIA OF

RUNNING

FITNESS • JOGGING • SPRINTING • MARATHONS

EVERYTHING YOU NEED TO KNOW ABOUT RUNNING FOR FITNESS AND LEISURE, TRAINING FOR BOTH SPORT AND COMPETITION, AND THE GREATEST RACES

STEP-BY-STEP INSTRUCTION, INDIVIDUAL RUNNING PLANS AND EXPERT ADVICE, SHOWN IN OVER 550 FANTASTIC PHOTOGRAPHS

ELIZABETH HUFTON

HERMES HOUSE

CONTENTS

This edition is published by Hermes House,
an imprint of Anness Publishing Ltd,
108 Great Russell Street, London WC1B 3NA;
info@anness.com

www.hermeshouse.com;
www.annesspublishing.com;
twitter: @Anness_Books

Anness Publishing has a new picture
agency outlet for images for publishing,
promotions or advertising. Please visit
our website www.practicalpictures.com
for more information.

A CIP catalogue record for this book
is available from the British Library.

Publisher: Joanna Lorenz
Project Editor: Amy Christian
Photographers: Mike King and Phil O'Connor
Designer: Nigel Partridge
Illustrator: Peter Bull illustration
Copy Editor: Wendy Horobin
Production Controller: Pirong Wang

Page 2: Usain Bolt runs in the men's 200m final,
2008 Olympic Games.

Cover illustrations: Main image shows (L-R) Kim
Kum Ok, Paula Radcliffe, Constantina Tomescu
and Zivile Balciunaite in the 2008 Olympic
women's marathon final (Michael Steele/Getty
Images). Top row (L-R): Beginners jogging; Usain
Bolt wins the men's 2008 Olympic 200m final
(Fabrice Coffrini/AFP/Getty Images); cross-
country running; men's 400m hurdles winner
Angelo Taylor (R) of the USA with compatriots
2nd placed Kerron Clement (L) and 3rd placed
Bershawn Jackson (C), 2008 Olympic Games
(EPA/Franck Robichon/Corbis).

Introduction

Running is a natural activity. Almost as soon as a child can walk, he or she will try to run. Thousands of years ago, this natural instinct was born out of a need to run to survive, but these days many people have no need to run and, once we reach adulthood, no desire to. Perhaps it is because of this, and the complications of modern life, that the last 50 years has seen a gradual growth in the number of people choosing to run; the simplicity and naturalness of the action appeals to people with otherwise cluttered lives.

Ironically the surge in participation and interest has made running more complicated. An entire industry has grown up around running, with fierce competition to develop more technical running shoes, clothes, and computers to analyse running data. At the same time, for all the millions of people running today, there are millions of different reasons for doing so, and someone who starts with one goal in mind soon finds their motivation has changed. A recreational runner who starts out to lose weight becomes faster; he wants to race, then to race well, then perhaps to try to win. At the competitive end of the spectrum, the days of the have-a-go amateur athlete are long gone, and training, nutrition, racing and recovery have become finely tuned scientific processes.

This is not bad news. As the runner becomes more involved in the finer details of the sport, he finds he has a better understanding of and connection with his own body. As a sport, running is perhaps the purest means of pushing the body to its very limit and finding out what you can do, since the basic technical ability is in all of us. This is as true for the elite athlete, pushing to find out whether the marathon can be run closer to the two-hour mark, as it is for the everyday runner curious to see if he can break three hours for a marathon or just make it to the end of his first 10K race.

Once these goals have been achieved, there are plenty of other directions for runners to take. Some choose to branch out into specialist fields, to become fell runners or ultra-distance runners. Some choose to explore other sports at the same time and become adventure racers or triathletes.

No matter what your running origins or future, this book aims to help you make the most of the sport you love, from beginners to advanced runners, children to veterans, sprinters to marathon runners and beyond. It contains all the information you will need to fine-tune your running and, hopefully, the inspiration you will need to enjoy running for pleasure.

Right: Running is the perfect sport for connecting with your body and with the world around you. You don't need any special equipment to get going.

GETTING STARTED

Despite its simplicity, running is a misunderstood
form of exercise. Start out on the wrong foot, and
you could be turned off immediately. This chapter
looks at how thousands of people have found
the right way to run over the last few decades,
and how and why you can and should join them.
It provides all the information you need to get
from no exercise at all to being able to run for
30 minutes, five times a week, and to build the
foundation for more advanced running later on.

Above: Your first runs should be fun and energizing, so keep them easy.
*Left: It's hard to take your first steps as a runner – starting out with a friend will
keep you motivated.*

The First Running Boom

Running is one of the most natural activities a person can do. Nowadays it may seem that people have always run for fitness and enjoyment, but this is not the case. It was only in the 1970s that recreational running as we know it really took shape.

Go to almost any park at any time of day, and you will spot at least one runner faithfully putting in miles. First thing in the morning, at lunchtime or straight after work, there are often more people out running than you can count.

Yet if you were able to visit that same park in the 1960s, the scene would be very different. Few people ran for fun or fitness; those who did so were considered eccentric. The changes that have taken place since the early 1970s can be broadly categorized into two running booms, driven for the most part by a rise in marathon and distance running.

Passing the baton

Today there are two types of runner: the serious, competitive runner; and the fitness or recreational runner. The two are not completely distinct, however,

Above: Recreational runners were rarely seen in parks before the great running boom of the 1970s.

with the Olympic Games providing the spark that ignited the running movement in the USA and, a few years later, Europe. In fact, the first boom can be traced almost as a relay from event to event.

The first boom started with an Olympian, the American distance runner Frank Shorter. From modest success as a college athlete, Shorter trained hard and won a number of national titles.

However, it was not until the 1972 Olympic Games in Munich that Shorter became a national hero by winning gold in the marathon. Four years later, after winning silver at the next Olympics, he took part in the revamped New York City Marathon, the race that is credited with bringing marathon running to the masses.

Jim Fixx: the father of jogging

Though Frank Shorter had inspired thousands of Americans to take up running, the idea of running purely for fitness was made popular by a former gas-pump

attendant called James F. Fixx, who had turned around his own health through running. Having taken up the sport at the age of 35, he had gone from being an overweight, heavy smoker to a marathon runner, and he wanted to show others what running could do for them. His first running book, *The Complete Book of Running*, was a bestseller, and he went on to write *Jim Fixx's Second Book of Running* in 1980.

However, the odds were stacked against Fixx, whose family had a history of premature death from heart problems. His father had died at 42 from a heart attack. In July 1984, on a favourite running route, Fixx succumbed to the same problem and died at the age of 52.

Left: Jim Fixx showed a generation of Americans how to love running.

New York: the people's marathon

The New York City Marathon started in 1970 but, like most marathons at the time, was a very low-key event, with just 55 runners finishing the race. In 1976, the race's co-founder, Frank Lebow, redesigned the marathon course so that it ran through all the five boroughs: Staten Island, Brooklyn, Queens, the Bronx and Manhattan. By the time Frank Shorter lined up for the race, it was a completely different event, with 2,090 runners at the start with him, television crews and thousands of spectators lining the route.

The marathon was seen by people all over the world, and the community in New York was united by the street-party atmosphere; suddenly the marathon had gone from being the preserve of the mad or the immortal to being a much more accessible challenge. As well as the goal of racing, the benefits of running to people's health and fitness were becoming more widely accepted, especially following the publication of Jim Fixx's classic running manual, *The Complete Book of Running*, in 1977.

In 1979, one of the thousands of runners drawn to New York was the British Olympic athlete Chris Brasher. Brasher was so impressed with the spirit of the race that he set

Above: The New York City Marathon brought elite athletics and mass participation together in 1976.

Below: Dick Beardsley (USA) and Inge Simonsen (Norway) won the first ever London Marathon together, cementing the good nature of the event.

about trying to organize a similar event in London. In March 1981, his plans came to fruition and 6,255 runners finished the first race, again with many thousands of spectators and huge media interest. Though Britain was already experiencing an upsurge in running, the birth of the London Marathon made it into a real national pastime.

The end of the first boom

Despite the massive increase in the numbers of people – mostly men – running in both the UK and the USA, by the late 1980s running had become a victim of its own success. During the first part of the decade, races were set up in almost every town;

every major city had its own marathon. The number of events and the rate of growth were not sustainable, and while the biggest races continued to draw crowds, many smaller events had to downsize or stop altogether. The drop in interest was not helped by the death of Jim Fixx while running in 1984, leading to negative press coverage suggesting that the sport was to blame. However, it was only a few years before a second, bigger running boom began to take hold as the idea of running for everyone truly took off.

Running Today

From the streets of New York and London, running has now reached a peak in the USA, Europe and around the Western world. In a movement described as the second running boom, the sport has reached a wider base of participants with varying reasons for getting involved.

It is impossible to give an accurate figure for the number of runners worldwide – or even in any one country – because the very simplicity of running that draws so many people is such that there is no need to register or tell anyone that you run; in fact, many who do so may not consider themselves to be 'runners' at all. Nevertheless, it is safe to say that the second running boom is even bigger, more encompassing and more prolonged than the first.

Running the numbers

The only thing that can be said for certain about the typical runner today is that he or she could be anyone. However, there is no doubt that the face of marathon running has changed.

	1980	1995	2006	2014
Women as % of runners	10%	26%	40%	43%
Men as % of runners	90%	74%	60%	57%
Masters (over 40)	26%	44%	46%	48%
Average marathon times: Men	3:32:17	3:54:00	4:15:34	4:19:27
Average marathon times: Women	4:03:39	4:15:00	4:46:40	4:44:19

(Figures for USA, source: Running USA Road Running Information Center annual marathon report)

Keeping pace with change

While the first running boom was inspired (at first) by the performances of elite athletes such as Frank Shorter,

Below: The Paris Marathon is the second biggest in Europe, attracting runners with its wide streets and flat course.

and focused on the challenge of running a marathon as quickly as possible, the second surge has a different focus – or lack of focus. Runners in the 70s and early 80s were usually male, under 40 years of age, and ran to compete, but there is

now a roughly 50:50 gender split, with more masters (or veterans) running, and reasons for running range from a means of losing weight, to raising money for charity, or a way to beat stress.

The second running boom has been driven by a number of factors. The most noticeable has been the increased involvement of large charities setting up their own running events, with an emphasis on taking part rather than fierce competition. This change in atmosphere has drawn more women to the sport. In particular, women-only charity races such as Race for the Cure in the USA and the Race for Life series in the UK have created a new type of event, encouraging participants to run to improve their health and fitness while raising vast sums of money for charity. Over 3.4 million women have taken part in the Race for Life, raising over £200 million for Cancer Research UK – an event which began with a single race with just 680 runners in 1994.

A sport for everyone

This 'taking part' ethos has flowed through to more established events, such as the big city marathons that started the first running boom. Where runners may once have given

Above: The Real Berlin Marathon was the setting for the men's world marathon record in 2008, 2:03:59.

up at the age of 40, frustrated that they could no longer compete at the front of the field, many of them now continue, choosing to compete against their age-group peers, creating the phenomenon of Masters (or Vets) competitions. Running has also benefited from increasing concern about public health: with rates of obesity, diabetes

and lifestyle-related conditions increasing, exercise is seen as part of the solution. Running is cheap, accessible and perhaps the most time-efficient form of exercise available, and public health bodies recognize its importance particularly for those whose socio-economic backgrounds put them most at risk of lifestyle-related health problems.

At the same time, a running industry that helps to support newcomers has grown with the second running boom. Never has so much specialist running equipment, information and so many resources been available to people thinking of taking up running. Where once athletics clubs only catered for those willing to train extremely hard for top-three race places, clubs now cater for all ages and abilities, and a new type of informal running network has sprung up.

Professional race organizers stage huge events in countries all over the world, creating 'destination' events, to which people are willing to travel great distances for the experience of visiting a place rather than a fast finishing time.

World's largest marathons: 2014 (finishers)	
New York City Marathon	50,386
Chicago Marathon	40,595
Paris Marathon	38,575
London Marathon	35,878
Tokyo Marathon	34,097
Boston Marathon	31,932
Berlin Marathon	28,984
Osaka Marathon	28,076
Honolulu Marathon	21,814
Los Angeles Marathon	21,508
Naha Marathon	20,027
Marine Corps Marathon	19,689
Walt Disney World Marathon	19,201
Kobe Marathon	17,027

Now the process has gone full circle. With participation at an all-time high, more people are discovering a talent for running and hunger for competition that they didn't know they had, so the traditional athletics clubs are benefiting from a new influx of fast runners.

Below: The Chicago Marathon is a loop course that is mostly fast and flat, thereby giving rise to a number of world records.

How many runners are there?
The only country to carry out a census of runners is the USA where, in 2005, 37.8 million people reported running at least three times a week. Elsewhere, a reasonable estimate of the numbers of regular runners can be made from the circulations of different countries' specialist running magazines (figures shown here are from 2006):

UK	1,670,000
Germany	1,200,000
France	1,040,000
Netherlands and Belgium	760,000
Sweden	100,000
South Africa	360,000
Spain	560,000
Japan	2,400,000
Australia and New Zealand	160,000

Why Run?

Running often comes under attack as being more damaging than other forms of exercise, but the truth is that just about every aspect of a person's physical and mental health will benefit from moderate running.

Apart from the sheer enjoyment and satisfaction you will gain from running, here are just some of the proven benefits that you can acquire by running three or four times a week for 20 to 30 minutes each time.

Healthy heart and lungs

Running reduces your risk of heart disease, lowering blood pressure and levels of 'bad', artery-clogging LDL (low density lipoprotein) cholesterol, while raising levels of 'good' HDL (high density lipoprotein) cholesterol, which helps keep blood vessels clear. Your heart is a muscle, so working it harder at safe levels will build its strength and size; as you become fitter, your heart rate will gradually drop slightly, showing that the heart has

Below: You don't need to run particularly far or fast to start feeling the benefits of regular running.

become more efficient. Meanwhile your body's ability to transport oxygen improves as capillaries (tiny blood vessels) develop in working muscles. Not only will running become easier, but everyday activities will seem to take less effort.

Reduced body fat

Of course, running helps people lose weight and maintain a healthy body weight, decreasing the risk of obesity-related conditions. Even if you are a healthy weight to begin with, you will benefit: research has shown that excess body fat around internal organs is a risk to your long-term health no matter what your overall size. Regular exercise is the best way to reduce your body fat levels.

Reduced stress levels

Going out for a run may be the last thing you want to do at the end of a hard day, but it will help you to relax. When we become stressed, whatever the reason, our bodies react as though faced with danger and produce what is known as the 'fight or flight' response, developed in early man to fend off or escape from

Above: No matter what your age, you can use running to become fitter and, more importantly, happier!

Below: Moderate exercise – such as a track session – helps to use your body's 'fight or flight' hormones.

predators or other humans. Stress hormones called catecholamines are released in to the bloodstream, raising the heart rate and blood pressure and speeding up breathing, to prepare the body for physical activity. Running provides a release for these chemicals, thus reducing the more unpleasant symptoms of stress such as anxiety, shaking and wakefulness.

Better bones and joints

Many people avoid running, believing the impact to be bad for their joints and bones. However, running improves bone density, helping to fend off osteoporosis (brittle bones). While often cited as a cause of osteoarthritis, particularly in the knee, there is no evidence to suggest regular runners are more at risk than anyone else. In fact, regularly activity can help to maintain joint mobility as you get older.

Improved mental health

Once you have been running a few times, you will understand why people become runners for life. Moderate

Below: Women are more prone to osteoporosis, but running can help to decrease the risk.

exercise produces a 'high' feeling that can last for hours afterward. Scientists are unsure why, but exercise has been linked to the release of endorphins, natural painkilling chemicals that are released during prolonged and intense activity. More recent research has shown an increase in levels of another substance, anandamide, in the bloodstream of runners and cyclists after exercise, which makes them feel relaxed and 'high'. There are longer-term effects, too. Anecdotal evidence shows that running improves the symptoms of depression, and many doctors now recommend exercise to help depressed patients.

Better gut health

It may not be an obvious benefit, but running also helps to keep your bowel movements regular. It is thought

Above: Over time, your body fat will reduce through running, so you'll look good as well as feel great.

that increased levels of stomach acid, improved blood circulation and muscle tone, and the repeated impact of running could all contribute to this effect.

Improved muscle tone

As well as these largely unseen health benefits, one of the main reasons people run is simply to look good. Running increases muscle mass and improves tone, and not just in the obvious areas (your legs). If you maintain good form, running will help improve your posture, tone up your stomach and back muscles and, as a consequence of reducing your level of body fat, your new-found muscle tone will be all the more visible.

Before you Run: Basic Health Checks

We have seen that running has many health benefits, but only if it is done properly. Before you head out on your first run, it is important to consider some of the risks – though usually small – involved in taking up exercise.

Being aware of the impact exercise can have on the different parts of the body is particularly important if you generally lead a sedentary lifestyle. Rushing into a demanding exercise regime is inadvisable – you could do yourself some real damage. Before you start running, visit your doctor for a thorough health check and to discuss with them whether more in-depth tests may be necessary to ensure you get the most from your running.

Below: Start training very gradually to avoid over-stressing your body, even if you feel perfectly healthy.

Pregnant pause

If you think that you may be pregnant, you should take a test before you start any intense exercise programme. Running is no longer considered unsafe during pregnancy and can be beneficial for women who already exercise regularly, but pregnancy is not a good time to start running (or any other form of strenuous exercise) from scratch as your body will be unused to the extra strain of the activity.

Right: If you are new to running, wait until after your baby is born to start; try gentle walking instead.

Family history

Talk to older relatives about any conditions that run in your family. These may be anything from heart problems, high blood pressure and cholesterol, to early osteoarthritis. Some allergic conditions may affect your sport – for example, asthma can be triggered by exercise and often runs in the family. The information you uncover about your family's health history will enable your doctor to test for particular conditions.

Blood pressure

All exercise helps to lower blood pressure, but if your blood pressure is very high to start off with, you may require regular check-ups and medication to control it.

Blood pressure measurements show systolic pressure (the maximum pressure in your blood vessels as the heart pumps blood around the body) and diastolic pressure (the minimum pressure, between beats). Normal values may be anything from 100/70 to 130/90. Some people suffer from white-coat syndrome, where the

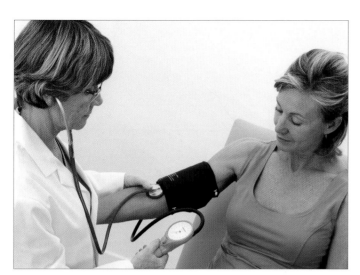

Above: Regular exercise will keep your blood pressure down, but check it before you start.

doctor's surgery setting causes stress and raised blood pressure. In this case an electronic home blood pressure gauge can give a more typical reading.

Exercise ECG

An ECG or EKG (electrocardiogram) measures the electrical activity of heart muscles, which can show irregularities and help to diagnose any heart problems. This test involves exercising on a treadmill or stationary bike with electrodes attached to your chest. The electrodes pass information to the ECG machine, which produces a printed representation of your heart's activity. It is arranged through your doctor and would usually only be carried out if you had experienced chest pains or had a genetic risk of heart problems.

Current level of fitness

There are many ways to test your fitness, but many health centres use heart rate during and after exercise as a simple starting point.

Wearing a heart-rate monitor – a chest strap with an electric transmitter that sends signals to a computer – you will be asked to exercise at increasing

intensity for a few minutes. After you stop, the time taken for your heart rate to return to normal helps a fitness instructor, or your doctor, to determine your starting level of fitness and advise you on how to progress your training.

Body Mass Index (BMI)

A standard measure of whether you are a healthy weight for your height, BMI is worked out as your weight in kilograms divided by your height in metres squared, for example $68/(1.74 \text{ squared}) = $ BMI 22.5. A healthy BMI is between 20 and 25. If your BMI is high, you may need to start your exercise programme more gradually; you will have an increased risk of high blood pressure and cholesterol so should have these checked. If it is low, you will need to ensure you eat more to fuel your exercise.

Biomechanics

Visiting a specialist podiatrist or biomechanist before you start running could save you painful injuries later on. While obviously there is no such thing as a 'perfect' gait, if you have any particular problem such as a leg-length discrepancy, it could have a serious knock-on effect once you start running.

A podiatrist or biomechanist can perform a full gait analysis by examining your standing posture, walking and running gait; using slowed down video footage or electronic pressure plates to show the finer points of your running cycle. If potential problems are spotted, they can be dealt with using exercises or special insoles for your running shoes (orthoses).

Below: An exercise ECG makes sure that your heart is as ready to run as you are.

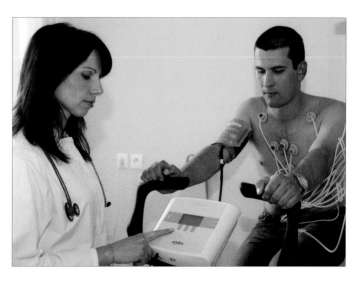

Starting a Walk/Run Programme

It will take time for your body to adapt to the unique stresses of running, so you need to ease in gently, build your fitness gradually, and learn to walk before you can run. This six-week plan will help you adjust to new levels of exercise.

Your first jogging sessions should be exhilarating, but for many the experience of taking up exercise is marred by trying to do too much, too soon.

If you are completely new to exercise, or coming back from a long break, build up time on your feet by walking at first. Slowly introduce periods of running, which can become longer as you become fitter, until you can run comfortably for 15 minutes. Some people choose to continue using walk breaks and never switch to continuous running; this can be a particularly effective strategy for longer sessions as the walk breaks allow you to recover. In fact, some athletes have been known to complete sub-three hour marathons using this technique.

Below: Follow a walk/run programme to help you build your fitness steadily and enjoy making progress with your running.

Below: Walk confidently and briskly in between run segments to stretch out your body and freshen up.

Above: Using a walk/run method could one day help you to conquer a race; maybe even a marathon.

Walking tall

In a walk/run programme, your walk breaks should provide recovery time from running, but do not be tempted to relax so much that you begin to slouch. You will find the transition from walking to running much easier if you walk 'tall'; this will also help to stretch out your muscles as you go and to encourage good posture as you speed up. Imagine a string attached to your head, drawing you up tall. Keep your shoulders back, dropped but relaxed, and your neck relaxed. Make sure you look forward, not up. Take long, fast but relaxed strides and swing your arms from the shoulder, breathing deeply. Keep your spine neutral, so that your pelvis is neither tucked right under, nor tilting back.

How to use this plan

Treat the sessions as a guide and choose days on which you know you will be able to exercise. Decide in advance which days you will do your walk/run sessions, write these sessions in your diary and treat them as 'unmissable' appointments. If possible, try to fit your session in early on in the day – before work or any other commitments – to prevent anything getting in the way. Don't be tempted to push yourself too early by running for longer periods than stated in the plan, as you will run the risk of injury. It's also important to remember that the sessions described should be in addition to any activity you already do. You may feel more tired than usual at first, especially when you're adding run intervals to your walks, but by the end of the six weeks this should wear off and you'll find you have more energy, rather than less.

Below: In just six weeks you can build up to a daily 30-minute walk/run, a precious half-hour to yourself in a busy day.

	Six-week walk/run programme
Week one	Session one: Walk for 15 minutes
	Session two: Walk for 15 minutes
	Session three: Walk for 15 minutes
Week two	Session one: Walk 20 minutes
	Session two: Walk 10 minutes; run 1; walk 10, run 1
	Session three: Walk 10 minutes, run 2; walk 8, run 2
Week three	Session one: Walk 8 minutes, run 2; walk 8, run 2
	Session two: Walk 8 minutes, run 2; walk 5, run 2; walk 3, run 1
	Session three: Walk 8 minutes, run 3; walk 4, run 2, twice
Week four	Session one: Walk 5 minutes, run 2; x 4
	Session two: Walk 5 minutes, run 2; walk 5, run 3; walk 5, run 2
	Session three: Walk 5 minutes, run 3; walk 5, run 4; walk 5, run 3
Week five	Session one: Walk 5 minutes, run 4; x 3
	Session two: Walk 5 minutes, run 5; x 3
	Session three: Walk 5 minutes, run 5; x 3
Week six	Session one: Walk 4 minutes, run 6; x 3
	Session two: Walk 4 minutes, run 6; walk 3, run 7, twice
	Session three: Walk 4 minutes, run 10; walk 3, run 5

Running for Fitness: Six-week Plan

You will be amazed at what you can achieve in six short weeks. Even if you don't see yourself as a 'sporty person', a little application and a structured plan will take you from just a few walk/run sessions per week to becoming a real runner.

Once you have become used to regular exercise, you will be surprised how fast you can progress. This plan aims to bring you from walking and running three times a week to the recommended minimum of 30 minutes of moderate exercise, five times a week.

While any physical activity improves your health, building up to and then maintaining this level will keep you at a good level of fitness. Research has shown it will reduce your risk of developing heart disease by 50 per cent, as well as reducing your risk of obesity and several forms of cancer. It is also a good basis for moving your running up to the next level, should you choose to do so.

Building up slowly

When you have come from no activity at all to regularly managing three sessions per week, you can feel as though you're ready to tackle anything, but try to hold

something back. It is right that you should feel stronger and stronger as your sessions build up, but the way to maintain this feeling is not to let it fool you into doing more than you intended. Keep to the planned sessions, leaving your walk breaks in as scheduled, to make sure your body becomes fitter and

Above: Follow the plan and by the third week you will be ready to try some harder run-only sessions.

doesn't breakdown due to early overuse. Similarly, while it's useful to get in to a routine, don't be tempted to exercise every day. Even at the early stages of

Making the most of fitness

You should think of 30 minutes of exercise as a bare minimum. Research shows that it doesn't matter if your total exercise time is broken up, so take every opportunity to boost your fitness. Walk up stairs, give yourself lunchtime errands that require a ten-minute walk; even ten minutes of housework counts toward your total.

Right: The more active you are generally, the more energy you'll have – even housework helps!

	Six-week plan				
	Day one	**Day two**	**Day three**	**Day four**	**Day five**
Week one	Walk 5, run 10 x 2	Rest	Walk 3, run 12 x 2	Rest	Walk 5, run 10 x 2
Week two	Walk 3, run 12 x 2	Walk 3, run 12, walk 5	Walk 3, run 12 x 2	Rest	Walk 5, run 10 x 2
Week three	Run 5, walk 2 x 4	Run 7, walk 3 x 3	Run 12, walk 3 x 2	Run 7, walk 3 x 3	Run 13, walk 2 x 2
Week four	Run 5, walk 1 x 5	Run 8, walk 2 x 3	Run 13, walk 2 x 2	Run 5, walk 1 x 5	Run 13, walk 2 x 2
Week five	Run 5, walk 1 x 5	Run 20	Run 15, walk 2, run 10	Run 5, walk 1 x 5	Run 20
Week six	Run 5, walk 1 x 5	Run 25	Run 5, walk 1 x 5	Run 10, walk 1 x 3	Run 30

your fitness-building regime, your body needs rest days to adapt to the training you've done. Watch your speed as well – getting fitter makes you feel more energetic but throwing that extra energy into bursts of fast running before you're ready could jeopardize the work you've done, leaving you injured.

How to use this plan
If it seems daunting, think of this six-week plan as having three two-week phases. In the first phase, you are gradually building up the total amount of running you do each day. In the second phase, you are becoming used to exercising five times a week. Finally, in the third phase, you will introduce some more difficult run-only sessions.

In weeks one and two, focus on your posture as you run, carrying your tall walking frame into your running and keeping your strides long and relaxed. As you run for longer periods, it can be easy to allow yourself to slouch, but this can lead to injuries.

In weeks three and four, you should start to feel fitter. At this stage it is really important to keep your running pace even, as you may feel ready to speed up; make sure you are able to chat or sing as you go.

In your continuous run sessions in the final two weeks, maintain the steady pace you have learned through most of your run, but as you near your finishing point – say when you are 100m (330ft) from your front door – imagine you are racing someone and give yourself a sprint finish.

Below: After a few weeks of building up your training, you'll be able to speed up to run home.

Above: Take a friend with you so you can talk as you run, a great way to keep your pace steady.

Running and the Human Body

One of the joys of running is that it increases your appreciation of the human body. Although your legs may appear to do all the work, almost every part of the body is involved in or affected by the act of running.

Learning about the basic processes involved will not only give you a better understanding of what happens when you run, but will also help you to develop your training over the months and years to come.

Heart

The resting heart rate of an average man is around 70 beats per minute (bpm), and slightly faster for a woman. When you run, the rate increases to pump blood to the working muscles. Your resting heart rate will go down with months of training, and your heart rate will not go up as much during runs; your maximum heart rate (calculated using the formula 214 – [0.8 x age] for men, and 209 – [0.9 x age] for women) will also stay level as you age if you continue to train, where it would usually drop for people with a more sedentary lifestyle.

Lungs

You will become more aware of your breathing as soon as you start to run and, like your heart rate, your lungs respond to training over time. Your lung capacity (the volume of air you are able to breathe out in one breath) will increase. The oxygen you take in is essential for powering your running, as it reacts with sugars, fats and proteins from food to create energy that enables your muscles to contract. Efficient expulsion of carbon dioxide is also key to running well.

Blood and blood vessels

It is blood which transports the oxygen and fuel your muscles require to run well, and the waste products that need to be removed to keep running for long periods of time and to recover afterward. Your blood volume increases with regular exercise, as does the number of oxygen-carrying red blood cells.

Immune system

Any moderate exercise increases the body's resistance to minor ailments, though intense training such as marathon running blocks the action of some types of white blood cells, lowering immunity. You can counteract this by consuming higher levels of carbohydrate before and during running.

Digestive system

Your body requires higher levels of most nutrients once you start training regularly, from carbohydrates, proteins and fats for fuel to vitamins and minerals that help keep your muscles and nerves functioning well, and help metabolize the food you take in.

Brain

Since the brain controls all movement, it is the starting point for all your running, but you can train your mind to help improve your performance in less obvious ways. Elite athletes use a technique known as neuro-linguistic programming (NLP) to prepare for events, and ordinary runners can use exercises such as visualization – seeing a successful outcome – to build confidence. The more intense your training becomes, the more important the power of your mind will be.

Muscles

Your working muscles respond to training and will develop differently depending on the kind of running and cross-training you do. There are two broad types of muscle fibre: fast-twitch and slow-twitch. Good sprinters have a higher percentage of fast-twitch muscle fibres, while endurance athletes have more slow-twitch fibres (the average person has roughly a 50:50 split). Whether you are better at fast or long running depends on your natural starting level of fast or slow-twitch muscle fibres, though specific training can have some effect on the size and action of the fibres. Most recreational and fitness running uses slow-twitch muscle fibres. Your muscles are able to store a small amount of energy as glycogen (a type of glucose), which is the first and most accessible source of fuel for exercise. More glycogen is stored in your liver; around 2,000 calories in total, enough to fuel around 32km (20 miles), or three hours of running.

The human body: main systems

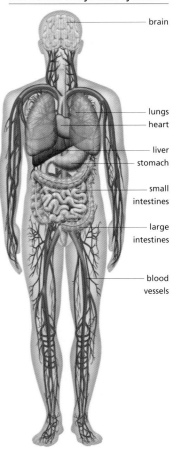

- brain
- lungs
- heart
- liver
- stomach
- small intestines
- large intestines
- blood vessels

Main muscle groups: front and back

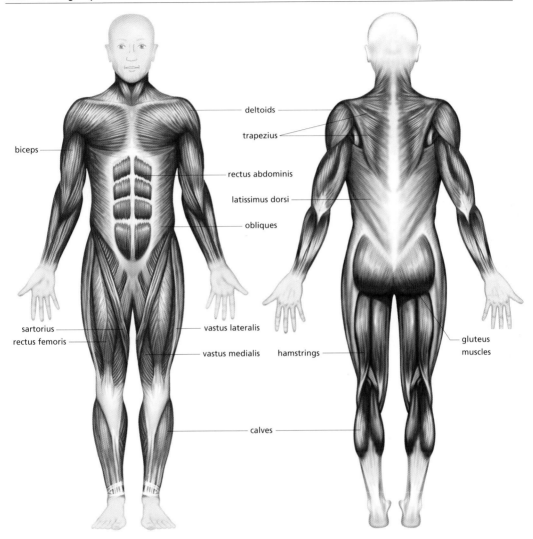

deltoids

trapezius

biceps

rectus abdominis

latissimus dorsi

obliques

sartorius

rectus femoris

vastus lateralis

vastus medialis

hamstrings

gluteus muscles

calves

Muscle groups

Throughout this book, and as you train more, you will learn more about how different muscle groups work to create a smooth, strong running action. Some of the muscles you might strengthen are:

Gluteus muscles and hamstrings: the 'glutes' run around the pelvis, and the tops of the thighs; the hamstrings run down the backs of your upper legs. They provide forward propulsion when you run.

Quadriceps: the muscles down the front of the thigh, which extend the legs and stabilize you when running downhill.

Calves: the muscles at the back of your lower leg, which help with forward propulsion while running.

Back and shoulder muscles: the latissmus dorsi (lats) and rhomboid muscles in your mid and upper back, and the trapezius and posterior deltoid muscles in your

shoulders, help you to stay upright and maintain good form, especially when running longer distances.

Abdominal muscles: these work with the muscles in your back to stabilize your trunk, allowing for more efficient driving movements with your legs. The deep stomach muscles, together with some deep muscles in the lower back, are sometimes called your core.

Basic Stretching for Runners

Stretching is a vital part of any runner's training routine. It helps get the muscles moving easily and eliminates the risk of injury during a run. Running and stretching go hand in hand, but still many runners neglect flexibility, particularly at the start of their career.

Even though you may not feel like it after a run, it is important to spend a few minutes stretching. You will feel the difference if you don't. Stretching is attributed with reducing muscle soreness after running, decreasing the risk of injury, and improving performance by enhancing the range of motion in joints. Complete these eight basic stretches wherever you finish your run – you don't need any special equipment. Hold each stretch for 20 seconds before swapping to the opposite side and repeating.

Gluteals

Raise one leg and bend the knee, drawing it in toward your chest. Wrap your arms around your raised leg and pull it in to your body; hold for 20 seconds. Draw the leg toward the opposite side of your body to stretch the smaller, deeper gluteals muscles.
Watch point: *make sure you bring your leg up to your chest, not the other way around; keep your back straight or the stretch will be less effective.*

Hamstrings

Stand with your feet hip-width apart. Step forward, place the heel of your front foot on the ground and bend your back leg, with the front leg straight. Lean forward from the hips, with your back straight, holding your front leg. Feel the stretch along the back of the straight leg.
Watch point: *you may find the hip on your supporting side will swing out as you lean forward, but keep your hips level to focus the stretch on your hamstring.*

Iliotibial bands

Cross one leg in front of the other, with the outsides of your feet together. Raise the arm on the side of your back leg and lean from the hips in the opposite direction. Feel a stretch along the outside of your back leg, from hip to knee.
Watch point: *the iliotibial band is difficult to stretch, but do not be tempted to overcompensate if you are unable to feel it by twisting your back. Make sure your torso faces forward.*

Stretching rules
• As a beginner, save your stretching for after exercise. You only really need to stretch beforehand if you are going to run very fast
• Before each stretch, take a deep breath, and perform the movement of the stretch as you exhale
• Try to relax when you are in each stretch; it should pull, but not hurt
• Do not bounce or jerk. Go in to each stretch slowly, then stay still

Right: Stretch well after exercise.

Quadriceps

Stand with your legs together, holding on to a chair or wall for support. Bend one knee and bring the heel of the foot toward your bottom. Use your free hand to pull the foot farther in, keeping your hips level and facing forward.
Watch point: *point your knee down toward the floor against the action of your hand pulling the foot back, rather than pulling your entire leg backward.*

Calves

Stand with your feet together and take a step forward. Lean forward keeping your back straight, so that your front leg is bent while your back leg remains straight (you may need to hold on to a support for balance).
Watch point: *make sure your back heel stays on the ground throughout; push it into the floor to feel the stretch more.*

Lower calves

After stretching the upper calves, bring your back leg in slightly. Again, bend your front leg, but allow your back leg to bend, which will bring the heel off the floor. Push the heel down to feel the stretch in the bottom part of your calf.
Watch point: *this may not feel as intense as the main calf stretch, but resist the urge to put all your weight on the back leg.*

Lower back

Stand with your feet hip-width apart. Stretch up, lengthening your spine, then bend forward from the hips, gradually allowing your back to relax down as though trying to touch your toes (don't worry if you are unable to do this!).
Watch point: *do not force this stretch, as you may damage your back; it should be relaxing.*

Hip flexors

Kneel on the floor and bring one leg in front, so that your foot is flat on the ground and your knee is at a right angle. Stretch your other leg behind you, and point your toes so the upper side of your foot is on the floor. Lean forward, feeling the stretch at the front of the opposite hip.
Watch point: *if you cannot find any soft ground, don't flatten your back foot, instead keep your toes tucked under. The stretch will be less intense.*

Above: You will often see more experienced runners stretching; it is a good habit to form early on.

Basic Strength Training

All-over body conditioning is not just about looking good. Strengthening the major muscle groups with these eight simple exercises will soon help you to become a more comfortable, efficient and faster runner. No special equipment is needed; they can be done anywhere.

There is no need to join a gym or buy any equipment to begin with, as your own body weight will provide all the resistance you need for a simple but effective workout. Between runs, perform these basic exercises in the order given here, and as you become stronger, and the exercises begin to feel easier, run through the same sequence twice in a row.

1 Wall Squat

Works: Gluteals, calves, hamstrings, quadriceps
Watch point: keep your knees pointing forward.

Stand against a wall with your feet hip-width apart and about a foot in front of you. Keeping your back straight against the wall and looking ahead, bend your knees to lower yourself toward the floor until your thighs are parallel to the ground, so that you are 'sitting' as if in a chair. Hold for a count of 10, then slowly push back up. Repeat 5 times.

2 Push-up

Works: Arms, shoulders, pectoral muscles, back muscles, core abdominal muscles
Watch point: keep your abdominal muscles tensed throughout to protect your back.

1 Start on your hands and knees. Raise your feet and cross them over, and slowly walk your hands forward so they are level with your shoulders.

2 With your weight forward over your hands, lower your body until your elbows form right angles, then slowly push back up. Aim for 10 to 15 repetitions.

3 Lunge

Works: Quads, hamstrings, gluteals, calves, hip adductors and abductors
Watch point: keep the movement controlled; do not jump forward or back up. If necessary, use your arms to balance.

Start with your feet hip-width apart and your hands on your hips. Step forward so that one leg is in front, then lower yourself toward the floor until both knees form roughly a right angle; keep your back straight and look forward. Push your front heel into the floor and push back up again. Repeat with the other leg and do 10 on each side.

4 Chair squeeze

Works: Hip abductors and adductors
Watch point: keep the rest of your body relaxed through the exercise; it can be tempting to twist your back, but avoid this.

Sit on the floor facing a sturdy chair (not a folding chair) or small table. With your legs straight, squeeze the legs of the chair together using the inside edges of your feet; hold for five seconds and repeat 10 to 15 times. Then switch so that the outsides of your feet are pressing the chair legs outward.

5 Bicycle

Works: Abdominal muscles, obliques
Watch point: avoid rocking from side to side during the exercise. Your back and pelvis should stay still throughout.

1 *Start in the crunch position. Lift your legs off the floor, keeping your feet side-by-side and your knees bent at right angles.*

2 *Tense your stomach muscles to pull your shoulders off the floor, then pull your right shoulder up toward your left knee, bringing the knee in to meet it.*

3 *Then repeat the exercise on the other side. Do 15 to 20 repetitions on both sides. Do this without resting in between repetitions if possible.*

6 Standard crunch

Works: Abdominal muscles
Watch point: do not tense your neck or use jerking movements to pull yourself up. Breathe out as you pull up to keep your neck soft.

7 Lower-back raise

Works: Erector spinae, gluteals
Watch point: do not jerk. If you feel pain, stop – you are overarching your back.

1 *Lie down on the floor with your knees bent and feet together, flat on the floor. Bend your arms at the elbow so that your hands are lightly touching your ears.*

2 *Tense your stomach muscles, keeping your pelvis in a neutral position, and draw your shoulders up, pulling your ribs toward your hips and with your stomach flat. Slowly lower. Repeat 20 to 30 times.*

Lie on the floor on your stomach, with your hands touching your ears. Slowly raise your shoulders and upper back so that you are looking up and ahead, then lower the body to the floor again.

8 Tricep dip

Works: Triceps, abdominal muscles
Watch point: keep your legs straight and steady throughout; if you are wobbling, practise with your legs and bottom on the floor.

1 *Sit with your legs straight out and your hands on the floor behind you. Draw your abdominal muscles in, pushing up. Your body should be in a straight line, with your arms supporting your weight.*

2 *Bend your elbows to slightly lower your torso toward the floor, then push back up. Repeat 10 to 15 times at first, increasing the repetitions as your arms become stronger.*

3 *To make the exercise harder, use a step to raise your hands off the ground. Lower your torso toward the ground in the same way, then push back up, repeating 10 to 15 times.*

Tracking Your Progress

Running brings fitness gains quicker than any other recreational sport. There are no technical skills to master, at least in the first few months of training; all you have to do is go out and run and you will see the results fast.

Get in to the good habit of keeping checks on your overall fitness early on in your running career and it will serve you well in future. You don't need any special equipment to carry out a quick check on how you are doing, although if you have access to a gym or personal trainer it makes sense to ask for a full fitness assessment to be carried out every six to ten weeks.

Your training diary

To see how well your fitness is progressing, you will need to keep some kind of record of your running. Even without specific fitness tests, writing a training diary and reviewing it from time to time will tell you a great deal about what you are doing right and, when problems arise, what has gone wrong.

How much detail you record in your training diary is up to you, but a basic diary should show how far you ran

Below: Keeping a training diary can help you analyze why your runs go well – or not so well.

that day, how long it took you, and how you felt during the run. You might also want to record your resting heart rate, your weight before and after the run, what you ate and drank before and during exercise, and the route you took and who ran with you. All of these details can have a bearing on your performance that day and may help you to spot useful patterns in successful or unsuccessful training periods.

Your training diary should not be just a list of numbers. Some general guidelines to help are:

Go into detail. At first it may seem obsessive, but try to be as precise as possible with your measurements: time your runs with a watch, and measure your routes on a map or using a speed and distance monitor. When describing your feelings about

Above: Your gym instructors should be able to give you full fitness checks every six to ten weeks.

the run, make notes of how you felt: physically strong, fast, sluggish, heavy footed, any aches or pains, and emotions. If you think anything may have affected your run, make a note of it.

Take measurements at the same time each day. Always record your resting heart rate as soon as you wake up and before you get out of bed, which is when it will be slowest. If you track your weight, do it first thing in the morning before eating or drinking, and ideally unclothed.

Be honest. You may not have been able to run quite as far or as fast as you had planned to, but make sure your diary entries reflect this and include any reasons why that might have happened, even if you simply did not feel up to it. This is bound to happen from time to time. If you are not completely honest with yourself then the diary stops being useful.

Simple fitness tests

The following tables contain very simple fitness tests. These four tests are all measures which can help you to track your improvements over time. These tests will only provide very rough guidelines to

your overall fitness but after just a few short weeks of training you should start to see a real improvement in all of these different areas. Take the tests regularly to keep track of how you are progressing.

(Source: American Council on Exercise)

Cooper test

This test was designed by Kenneth H. Cooper in 1968 for US military use. Run as far as you can in 12 minutes, and measure how far you have run.

Sex/age	Very poor	Poor	Fair	Good	Excellent
M20–29:	1,600m	1,600–2,199	2,200–2,399	2,400–2,800	2,800+
F20–29:	1,500m	1,500–1,799	1,800–2,199	2,200–2,700	2,700+
M30–39:	1,500m	1,500–1,899	1,900–2,299	2,300–2,700	2,700+
F30–39:	1,400m	1,400–1,699	1,700–1,999	2,000–2,500	2,500
M40–49:	1,400m	1,400–1,699	1,700–2,099	2,100–2,500	2,500
F40–49:	1,200m	1,200–1,499	1,500–1,899	1,900–2,300	2,300
M50+:	1,300m	1,300–1,599	1,600–1,999	2,000–2,400	2,400
F50+:	1,100m	1,100–1,399	1,400–1,699	1,700–2,200	2,200

Heart-rate recovery

On a treadmill in the gym, begin running at a comfortable speed. Increase the gradient by 1 per cent every minute, until you reach your maximum effort. Record your heart rate (ideally using a heart-rate monitor, otherwise take your pulse). Stop exercising, and record your heart rate after two minutes rest. Note the difference between the two numbers.

Very Poor	Fair	Good	Excellent
Drop of less than 12 beats per minute	Drop of 15–25 beats per minute	Drop of more than 25 beats per minute	Almost complete recovery (within 10bpm of standing heart rate)

Body mass index

Weigh yourself, then divide your weight in kilograms by your height in metres squared. The best time to weigh yourself is first thing in the morning.

Very poor	Poor	Fair	Good
Below 18.5 (underweight) or above 30 (obese)	25–29.9 (overweight)	18.5–20 (slightly overweight)	20–24.9 (within a healthy weight range)

Body fat

Have a personal trainer measure you with callipers to work out your body fat percentage, or use a pair of body fat scales, which you should be able to find at your gym. Alternatively, you can buy a pair of scales for home use.

Very poor	Fair	Good	Excellent
25%+ (men)	18–25% (men)	14–17% (men)	6–13% (male athletes)
32%+ (women)	25–31% (women)	21–24% (women)	14–20% (female athletes)

Troubleshooting Early Problems

The best laid plans go awry, and your training schedule is no exception. Don't be disillusioned if you suffer setbacks after a few weeks' running, as a few simple measures will get you back on track in no time at all.

Upper back and shoulder pain. This is probably a result of poor posture. Pull your shoulders back while running and make sure you are looking straight in front of you, not down at the ground.

Calf pain. This is also a very common problem for new runners, particularly for women who wear shoes with high heels most of the day. Loosen your calf muscles by stretching them after every run and strengthen them with calf raises: stand on a low step with your heels hanging off the edge. Slowly lower yourself down then push up until you are up on your tiptoes. Repeat 10 times.

Left: You'll be full of energy as your fitness grows, but listen to your body to make sure you keep running strongly.

Below: Calf pain can be a problem for women who wear high heels, so stretch your calves regularly.

For the first few weeks of your running life, every run will be a pleasure as you find you can run farther and faster than you ever thought possible. Then one day you pull up with a calf pain, it happens again the next day and then you feel like giving up.

Teething problems are likely in any new exercise regime and can leave you feeling disheartened and demotivated after all the hard work you have put in. Thankfully these niggles are usually very simple to fix, leaving you free to continue on your journey toward becoming a runner.

Aches and pains

Generalized aching is an accepted part of taking up exercise and is a good sign that you are working your muscles hard enough. However,

localized pains should not be ignored as they could be early signs of long-term injuries. Some common problems for new runners include:

Shin splints. This is a general term for pain in the shins, often caused by running on very hard surfaces. Make sure you are wearing well-cushioned shoes and switch some of your running to softer surfaces such as grass; stretching your calves will also help. For instant relief, kneel on a carpet and sit right back on your heels.

Foot pain. This is usually the result of poor footwear. If you are wearing old trainers (sneakers), these can cause pain underneath the foot, while over-tight lacing can cause sharp pain over the top of your foot.

Above: Vary the surfaces you run on. Training on hard surfaces all the time can contribute to shin pain.

Restlessness

Though regular exercise generally promotes good sleep, some people find they become wakeful the more they run. Try to avoid running within three or four hours of bedtime – switch your run to lunchtime or early morning – and develop a relaxing bedtime routine, such as having a warm bath then stretching. If you run in the afternoon or evening and are hungry afterward, avoid foods that contain a lot of sugar or caffeine, as these may keep you awake.

Digestion

Most runners are affected at some point by 'runner's trots' – stomach cramps and diarrhoea brought on by running. If it has become such a regular problem for you that you are afraid to run, try experimenting with your food. Avoid eating for two to three hours before you run and cut down on high-fibre foods. Caffeine can exacerbate the problem, so stick to water or sports drinks. If this fails, you should investigate whether you have a food intolerance – many people find that gluten and dairy products can cause diarrhoea, so speak to your doctor if you think this may be the case.

Above: Sometimes the cause of pain can be as simple as the way you tie up your shoelaces.

Fitness plateau

If you have stopped seeing big improvements in your fitness – perhaps you are slowing down, or your breathing is more laboured – then you

Below: Shin splints are painful enough to stop you running, but this stretch gives instant relief.

may have hit a fitness 'plateau'. If you are running three to five times a week for an hour or less, and have been doing so for some time, then it is time to pick up the intensity of your running with one or two faster sessions per week. If you are not ready for that, simply changing your route or finding a new running partner could provide the lift you need.

If you have been training particularly hard – for more than an hour each day – then your plateau could be the result of overtraining. Other symptoms include fatigue, lack of motivation and mood swings. In this case have a few weeks of easy running and build back up slowly.

Finding time

The more you train, the more you will want to train, but fitting it in can become a problem. Set your alarm half an hour earlier and run first thing in the morning, or arrange for a long lunch hour two or three days a week in which you can run. Try running all or part of the way to work – a great timesaver, which means you beat the rush-hour traffic, too. In time you will find that running makes time for itself.

Below: Running to work saves time and money, and is a great way to avoid rush-hour stress in the morning.

Staying Motivated

No matter how much you grow to love running, there will be times when it's hard to keep your momentum going. Learning to overcome the barriers between you and your favourite activity will make the difference between a passing phase and a lifetime of fitness.

Even the most committed runners will suffer from dips in their motivation. During your first few months of running it can be especially hard to keep going, as you readjust to your new routine. As you continue running, though, you will find that it is as much a mental exercise as a physical one, and consciously working on your drive to run is one of the keys to a long, successful running career.

There are many reasons for loss of motivation. Perhaps you are frustrated at your slow progress, or are not seeing the radical changes you had hoped for. Maybe you feel that running means making too many sacrifices in other areas of your life. Even a spell of bad weather can sap your will to go out and run.

Below: Arrange to meet up with friends so you don't skip a run.

The first thing to remember is that missing one or two runs is not necessarily a problem. It is good to allow your body to recover from all the hard work you have put it through. At the same time, it is important to stop yourself from drifting into a habit of making excuses. A good place to start is revisiting the reasons you took up running in the first place, whether that was losing weight, getting fit or relieving stress. If running is not helping you meet those targets, ask yourself why – for example, if you wanted to lose weight but are failing to do so, perhaps you are eating more to make up for training without realizing it. Think about the other, less tangible benefits of running, such as its effects on your long-term health (if you are short of inspiration, re-read 'Why Run?').

Instant motivation
- Run with others
- Set an immediate goal – for example, beating yesterday's time
- Give yourself a reward – maybe your favourite dessert, or a long bath
- Buy new kit – you will want to try it out straight away
- Run with music
- Go for a short run – the chances are that you will keep going once you are out

---

Finding solutions

If external factors are giving rise to excuses for not running, think about solutions that will deal with these problems permanently. For example, if your family or partner is resentful of the time you spend running, try to get them

Above: Remind yourself why you started running, whether it was to get in shape or to reduce your stress levels.

involved by having them cycle with you along the route; if they don't want to be involved, plan to spend quality time doing something they enjoy. You could also encourage work colleagues to run with you; set up a lunchtime running club and show your boss how running can make the team more productive.

At the same time you may find that applying some of the techniques you use at work to your running will help your motivation. Review your running goals at regular intervals as you would those at work. If you find that they have gone stale – or were unrealistic in the first place – set new goals. For example, if an original goal was to lose 5kg (11lb) and that has been achieved, look at setting a goal to improve your running instead. If your goal was to lose 10kg (22lb) and you have only lost 2kg (4½lb), find a more achievable target. Make sure your running goals are SMART: specific, measurable, achievable, realistic and timely.

Forge good running habits by setting yourself golden rules that will last all of your running life, so that lack of motivation never stops you. For example, change into your running kit as soon as

you get up or get home from work; make the rule that once you are wearing the kit, you have to run. Have an answer ready for every excuse, and tell yourself that you are only allowed certain treats on the days that you run.

Managing expectations
Often people lose motivation to run because it fails to live up to the expectations they had when they started out. In most cases there is a reason that running has not fixed a particular problem or given you a desired outcome, and in some cases the problem is just that your expectations were too high. Common reasons for disillusionment are:

Failing to lose weight. If you took up running to shift a few pounds and it's not working, first of all ask yourself if you're doing enough. Remember that to lose 450g (1lb) per week you need to burn an extra 3,500kcal (14,700kJ) – that's equivalent to running for 50 minutes, every single day! Try being more active in other ways (such as walking more or cycling to work), and keep a food diary to make sure you're not eating extra to 'make up for' running.

Not feeling fitter. Though you should feel some benefits after just a couple of runs (mainly because of the feel-good chemicals released in to your bloodstream when you exercise), it will take six to eight weeks of regular running before you find it more comfortable, as your heart, lungs and muscles need time to adapt.

Being 'bad' at running. Perhaps you were a great runner at school, or maybe you thought you were naturally athletic – either way, being slower than you hoped is disappointing. Again, you need to give your body time to adapt to training before it can run fast – even the best athletes take years to reach their peak, so be patient.

Feeling stressed out. Aside from the physical benefits of running, you may have heard that it's good for stress relief, only to find that it's another thing on your 'to do' list, leaving you feeling even more

Above: Music can be a powerful motivator – use your favourite songs to inspire you to run again.

strung out. Reorganize your timetable before you commit to running regularly, so you can always fit it in easily. For most people the simplest way to do this is to run early in the morning – then it should help to relieve stress about the day ahead and it's one thing off that 'to do' list before you've even reached the office.

Group support
The best way to tackle lack of motivation is to run with other people – often the idea of letting someone else down is more powerful than the thought of letting yourself down. If this is impossible, you can still share your training with others: try setting up a blog, or visiting forums on running websites for support. Showing your training diary to a friend regularly can also help, as you will be embarrassed by any skipped sessions. Try being your own coach, too. Remind yourself how much you have achieved since you started, and give yourself pep talks – if you find yourself thinking 'I can't face a run this evening,' tell yourself 'I always feel better after running. I've done this in the past and know I can do it again.'

Gear Basics: Shoes

One of the best things about running is that it doesn't require lots of equipment, but the one essential piece of kit is a good pair of running-specific shoes. Learn a little bit about them, and you won't need to spend a fortune.

The one piece of running equipment you need to invest in before even taking your first step, is a good pair of running shoes. These will help to correct problems in your gait, in turn helping you to avoid any injuries and to run faster and more comfortably.

The key factor that determines which type of running shoe you need is the degree to which your feet pronate – that is, roll inward – when

Below: Shoes help prevent gait problems such as overpronation (where your feet roll too far in) as seen here.

your foot hits the ground during a run. Pronation is your natural shock absorption. In a normal runner, the heel hits the ground first, then your weight rolls through the foot and the foot falls inward slightly, so that you finish each step with the inside of the front of your foot to push off again.

When buying your first pair of running shoes, it is best to have your gait analysed by a podiatrist or by experienced staff in a running store. Tests you could have might include the following:

Video gait analysis. You are filmed running on a treadmill, then the film is reviewed in slow motion to analyse the movement of your foot.

Pressure plate analysis. You are asked to run over a mat which is fitted with pressure sensors. Readings from these sensors are used to produce an accurate diagram showing where your foot places most pressure through each stride.

Running outside. At specialist running stores, you will often be asked to run up and down outside the store while the

Buying the right shoes
The best place to buy your running shoes is from a specialist running store (rather than a general sports store). If at all possible, ask experienced runners in your area where they buy their shoes from. When you find a good shop, take the time to talk to the staff; the best advisors will be experienced, enthusiastic runners themselves. Avoid buying very cheap shoes, but do look at shoes in the sales: these are usually just last season's models and will be just as effective as the newer, more fashionable versions.

Below: Take your time choosing trainers and make sure you get expert help in the store.

assistant watches your gait. You may feel self-conscious doing this, but this test has the advantage that your run will be more natural on the pavement than on a treadmill or over a pressure plate.

Static examination. Podiatrists may examine the range of movement and natural stance of your feet, ankles and legs while sitting and standing.

Following any type of gait assessment apart from a static examination, if you're then trying on shoes, the store assistant should ask you to repeat the test in different pairs of trainers to look at the effect they have on your gait. They should be able to demonstrate how the shoes are correcting any problems – remember, if you are not convinced by what you're told, you should always try to get a second opinion.

The wet foot test

The wet foot test is a quick and easy way to find out about your degree of pronation. Wet your feet and walk over a piece of cardboard, then look at the shape of your footprint.

1 Neutral/normal foot. The heel and forefoot are clear and even; the outside of the foot will have made a wide band connecting the front and back of the foot. Runners with a normal degree of pronation usually need stability shoes.

2 Flat/overpronating foot. Almost the entire foot makes contact with the ground, so the band between the front and back of the foot will be much wider and straighter. Runners with this type of footprint will need a motion-control shoe, which is usually heavier and firmer.

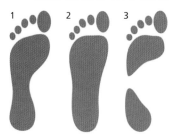

Above: Your degree of pronation will affect the way you run; it is easily detected by looking at a wet footprint.

3 Supinating foot. Runners who supinate have high arches, so there will only be a thin line, if any, between the rear and front of the foot. Neutral or cushioned shoes are best for these runners.

Running shoes inside out

Different brands have their own technologies, but there are some features which most shoes have in common.

Upper: the fabric part of the shoe, usually designed to be as light and breathable as possible, though in motion control shoes this may be firmer or more fitted to help provide support.

Midsole: the cushioned interior of the sole, between the outsole and insole, containing most of the shoe's motion control and comfort features.

Insole: the removable sole inside the shoe, which may be shaped to support the arch and help prevent pronation. If you need orthoses, these will go in place of your insole.

Forefoot: the wider front part of the shoe. Generally, the wider the forefoot, the more stable the shoe.

Heel counter: a hard cup in the heel of the shoe used to provide stability and prevent pronation from the rear foot.

Midfoot shank/arch bridge: plastic supports built in to the midsole to support the arch in flat-footed runners.

Medial post/rollbar: a firmer piece of foam in the midsole of the shoe used to force the foot upright, and prevent excessive pronation.

Outsole: the tough outside of the underneath of your shoe, with lugs of varying depth for different terrain (the bigger the lugs, the more grip the shoe has).

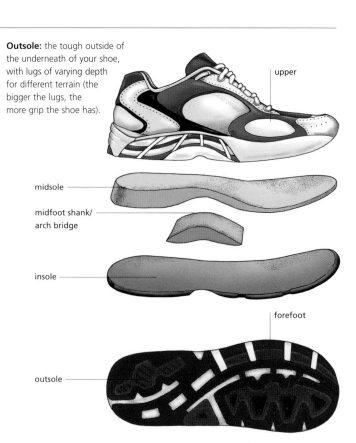

upper

midsole

midfoot shank/
arch bridge

insole

forefoot

outsole

Gear Basics: Apparel

Running kit may look simple, but behind the humble-looking shorts and T-shirt is a host of technologies designed to keep you cool, comfortable and confident while you're exercising. It may not make you run faster, but it will help you enjoy the experience a lot more.

For many people the bold step of a first run is a spontaneous decision, so an old cotton T-shirt and basketball shorts might stand in for technical running kit. After returning home weighed down in a cold, clammy top and rubbed raw from chafing shorts, you will realize why it is worth treating yourself to some proper apparel.

Spring and summer kit

T-shirts. A summer running T-shirt should control moisture, wicking sweat away from your skin and drying quickly, to help keep you cool. The cut of the top is also important: it should be fitted to allow ease of movement, and may even feel odd when you are standing still, as some tops are cut for a running motion. Other features to look for are flat or welded seams, to avoid chafing, and venting down the back and under the arms to keep you cool.

Below: Traditional split-leg shorts.

Below: Long, loose trail shorts.

Smart kit

Running apparel is becoming more technical and might include:

Odour control: Silver yarn (X-Static) woven into the fabric helps reduce odour; sometimes material is treated with antibacterial chemicals to prevent odours developing. The best T-shirts might include self-refreshing odour technology, which uses sugar molecules to catch sweat as it forms.

Temperature regulation: Increasingly, manufacturers are using fabrics that react to moisture and heat. The weave of the fabric changes shape to change the flow of air around the body.

Sun protection: Most summer kit has a loose weave, which means you can get sunburnt through it, but some manufacturers now make kit that offers protection up to factor 50.

Singlets may keep you cooler but can chafe under your arms, so be sure to try them on first.

Shorts. Again, these should ideally be made from wicking material. Traditional running shorts are cut very short with a split up each side, so your legs are able to move as freely as possible, and have a supportive inner mesh. If these make you feel too self-conscious, go for trail shorts instead, which are slightly longer and looser. Look for features like a flat waistband with a drawstring to adjust the fit, and an internal, secure key pocket.

Above: Summer T-shirt, or mid-layer.

Autumn and winter kit

Tights. The best and most effective winter tights will incorporate several panels of different materials: water resistant areas on the thighs and shins, thermal material down the calves, and cooler mesh panels in the inner thigh and back of the knee. Calf zips help to give a better fit, but make sure that the leggings are the right length, or the zip will chafe on your leg. If you expect to be running at night-time, in the dark, look for reflective flashes winding diagonally around the calf, as these will be much more visible than stripes or flashes on the upper leg.

Tops. In sub-zero temperatures, you may need three thin layers: a wicking layer against your skin, a light insulating layer in the middle, and a windproof and waterproof layer on the outside. If the weather is slightly warmer, leave out the middle layer. Remember that even when it seems incredibly cold outside, you inevitably warm up when running, so don't wear bulky layers.

Accessories

Hats. These are useful in winter, though really only necessary in sub-zero temperatures. Go for a hat made from wicking material with a brushed

Right: Light waterproof jacket.

Above: Long-sleeved winter base layer.

Above: Crop-top style sports bra.

Below: Shock-absorbing sock.

Above: Wicking winter hat.

Above: Moulded, underwired sports bra.

Right: Long, warm winter tights.

Supporting acts

Sports bras are as essential a piece of kit for women as running shoes. Breasts are naturally supported by the Coopers ligament which, once stretched, cannot regain its original shape. Research has shown that during running, breasts move in a figure-of-eight motion, but a good sports bra can reduce this movement by up to 80 per cent. Crop tops are fine for A to B cups, while larger-sized women should look for high-fronted, moulded bras with thicker, non-elastic straps.

interior that will not irritate your forehead. In the summer months, wearing a cap can be a good idea to keep the sun off your head and shade your eyes; try to find one with a folding peak so you can carry it easily in your pocket if you want to take it off.

Sports socks. These are becoming increasingly complex and can add extra shock absorption. Some manufacturers even claim that they can add support for your feet by using different weaves and thicker pads in key areas of pressure. Double-layered running socks can help to prevent blisters forming on long runs.

Gloves. These are another useful item in very cold weather. Avoid wool and go for light, wicking gloves. Useful features are rubber pads on the fingers, so you won't need to remove them to undo zips or use keys, and towelling on the outside of the thumb for mopping your face.

BUILDING FITNESS

Regular running transforms your health, but
once you are running a few times each week you
will find you want to know and do more.
This chapter will help you to make the step up
from running for health to improving your running
for the extra fitness gains this will bring. Your
running will become more technical, but more fun, too.
This means not only running faster, but also adding
strength training, reviewing your diet, and bringing
other forms of exercise into your life.

Above: Push yourself with faster sessions and you'll reap the benefits.
Left: Building up the distance you run is the first step to increasing your fitness.

Building Up Miles

A solid base of mileage is the foundation on which all good running is built, but be careful: try to take a shortcut to extra miles and the cracks will start to show. This simple guide shows how to increase your training volume the right way.

In an easy week, the British marathon world record holder Paula Radcliffe runs 160–190km (100–120 miles) – ten times as much as someone running for fitness. Unless you are training to challenge her in a marathon, your weekly mileage is unlikely to reach three figures, but gradually building up your distance will improve your fitness and give you an invaluable base should you decide to start training for events. For beginners, building up running volume is the simplest way to keep enjoying fitness gains. It helps your body to become used to the action of running. You will develop more capillaries (tiny bloody vessels) in your working muscles, helping your body to deliver oxygen to power your running. Once you have built

your base, adapting to more intensive training will be easier, with a lower risk of injury or overtraining.

Building frequency
A good rule of thumb when increasing your training is to do so by no more than 10 per cent a week, so if you run for 30 minutes four times a week, add only 10 to 15 minutes the next week, then 20 minutes the next, and so on. Running more often should be your goal before increasing mileage, as this helps to build the habit of regular running (which makes it easier mentally) and gives your metabolism a boost every day. This may mean shortening your route temporarily for example, you might go from three half-hour sessions to five 20-minute sessions. After that, try adding

Above: At first, just add short loops on to your regular runs to increase your mileage gradually.

5 minutes to your run every week until you are running 40 to 45 minutes, five or six times per week.

Running for longer and more often can initially prove difficult to fit in, and you may struggle with motivation as inevitably you forgo half an hour in bed, or lunch with a friend to run. Find strategies to trick yourself into running: run as part of your commute or, on weekends, add running to regular activities such as visiting relatives or buying a morning newspaper. Add an extra 5-minute loop at the start of your regular route (rather than at the end when you will be more tempted to stop from tiredness). Allow yourself

Above: Running farther makes your body more efficient and powerful, so you can run faster.

to slow down slightly and enjoy the scenery, so that running is a relaxing time to look forward to rather than something to cram in.

Building distance

As well as running more often and for slightly longer each time, you should plan one long run per week, aiming to build up to between 90 minutes and 2 hours. This long run will teach your body to be more efficient at using fat for fuel, which means your body fat levels will drop and you will be able to run farther comfortably, without 'hitting the wall' – running out of carbohydrates to fuel your muscles, resulting in sudden tiredness and jelly legs.

When building up your long runs, as with regular training sessions, think in terms of time rather than distance to begin with. That way you will soon discover your natural pace, which will help you work out how far you are running. Remember the 10 per cent rule – don't build up your long run on the same weeks that you increase your other runs.

The idea of running for 16–19km (10–12 miles) at a time can be quite daunting, so try running three or four loops near your home or base so that you feel safe and are able to stop if you need to. On the other

hand, if you feel you might be too tempted to stop early, an out and back route should encourage you to keep going to reach home quicker. Start your long run early in the day so it doesn't interfere with your other plans, and take a sports drink so that you don't run out of energy or become dehydrated.

Below: Keep your pace easy on your longest run of the week and then take it easy the day after.

Rules for long runs
- Increase your total weekly mileage by no more than 10 per cent each week
- Don't try to run faster at the same time – build your foundation first
- Drink and eat more as your body uses more fuel
- Record your mileage and make sure you replace your shoes after about 800km (500 miles)
- Keep your pace easy, so you are able to chat or sing as you run
- When you introduce a long run, make sure you take it easy (and short) the days before and after

Learning Good Form

Becoming a runner is not just about getting into good habits. It's also about losing bad habits, and that includes many of the little quirks that make your running style unique – because those 'quirks' could prevent you from running to your best ability.

Running is as simple as putting one foot in front of the other. At least, that is the commonly held view. In fact, if you were to watch 100 runners, you would see 100 completely different ways of moving. There is no perfect running form, or even anything that could be truly described as normal. Instead individuals develop their own running style based on body shape, learned habits and, to an extent, the speed and distance they are running.

There is a limit to the extent to which you can change your running form, since most of your movements are made without conscious thought, but there is also a limit to how much you would want to change – after all, your body has developed a running style to deal with its own particular quirks, and even a style that looks unnatural and uncomfortable is not a problem unless it causes injuries. However, thinking about your form can help you run more efficiently.

Legs

Your leading knee should drive up high so that your thigh is parallel to the ground (or perhaps slightly higher). The lower part of the lead leg should stay tucked neatly under until your knee is high, then push down quickly to the floor. Your foot should not land too far ahead of you, but should be close to being underneath your body as you run,

Right: A self-conscious, shuffling gait is not uncommon, but straighten up and you'll find that your running becomes a lot easier.

Below: Use your upper body as well as your legs to help you move forward.

Above: Marathon runner Paula Radcliffe's style looks tense, with a famous 'nodding head', but it certainly works for her.

Above: Michael Johnson says that his strange, upright sprinting style made him the successful athlete that he is.

and you should be able to claw the ground underneath you with this foot then push off strongly into the next stride.

Pelvis
Your pelvis should be in a neutral position; that is, neither tilting forward nor sticking out backward. It should remain fairly still during running, without moving up and down or

twisting from side to side. Lack of stability in the pelvis is the root of many running injuries, as muscles around the pelvis and in the legs can easily be overworked when trying to keep your hips still.

Torso
The middle of your body, the torso, should always be strong and static as you run. Your abdominal muscles

should naturally tense up to stabilize your body, but try not to squeeze these muscles. There should be no twisting from the waist.

Arms and shoulders
The action of your upper body, and in particular of your arms and shoulders, has a surprisingly high impact on your overall running efficiency. Your shoulders should always be relaxed, positioned down and back so that your chest is open and you can breathe easily. Your elbows should be bent to about 90 degrees, and your arms should swing back and forth (rather than across your body) in time with the movement of your legs; this can help keep your leg speed and rhythm up.

Head and neck
Your neck should be long and relaxed, and you should be facing forward, looking straight ahead. Your face should also be relaxed; scowling, grimacing or grinding your jaw may seem inevitable during a hard run, but any movement, however small, wastes energy and has a knock-on effect, making your neck and shoulders tense, too.

Quick form fixers	
Problem	**Solution**
Poor knee drive	Get in to the habit of driving your knee by adding sets of four or five 100m sprints into your runs; running faster naturally encourages you to pick your legs up, and the habit will filter into your slower running.
Slouching and hunched shoulders	If you catch yourself slouching, try taking as deep a breath as you can, and imagine you have just seen the finish line of a race. This should encourage you to straighten up and open your chest.
Lazy arms	Run with very light weights in your hands (not more than about 500g/1¼lb each) or around your wrists. Carrying weights will make you more conscious of your arm action and help you to build momentum.

Simple Speedwork

There are many different ways to train your body faster, and all of them involve pushing yourself out of your natural comfort zone. But don't let that put you off – speedwork is time-efficient, satisfying and even enjoyable.

Introducing speedwork to your training can be a daunting prospect. Traditional speed sessions look, on paper, complicated and technical and you may think that running very fast is the sole preserve of experienced athletes. But introducing speedwork, which is any session that involves running faster than you have been, after just a few months of running is straightforward and has huge benefits.

Just one faster run per week will gradually extend your comfort zone, so that your relaxed running pace becomes faster naturally. It improves your cardiovascular fitness, so your heart rate stays lower for longer and recovers more quickly; it recruits fast-twitch muscle fibres, which you will need if you plan to race in future; and it burns more calories overall than slower runs. Speedwork is also enjoyable, adding an element of variety to your training.

Below: The track may be intimidating at first, but it's a forgiving surface which makes speed sessions easier.

Technical terms

There is really nothing complicated about speedwork in its purest forms, so try not to be put off by technical-sounding terms often seen in running schedules:

Reps: simply means 'repetitions' or 'repeats' and refers to the faster-paced parts of your speed session (for example, 4 x 400m reps indicates running 400m fast, four times).

Recoveries: in the context of a speed session, a 'recovery' is a period of easy jogging, walking or sometimes stopping altogether, in between faster reps.

Strides: a technique of fast but relaxed running, often used to inject some speed in to longer, easier runs.

Intervals: the term interval training actually covers all speedwork (and is used in other sports, too). It simply means interspersing intervals of hard and easy effort, though often in running it is used to refer to longer periods of fast running (that is, reps more than one minute long).

Fartlek: a Swedish word meaning 'speedplay', this is an unstructured form of speedwork.

Speedwork rules

For all its benefits, speedwork places extra stress on your body, so take care when you start out by following a few simple rules. Firstly, add speed slowly. Just as you need to increase mileage gradually to avoid injury, so you need to introduce speedwork gently. Start with just one session per week, and try not to sprint all-out; you will need practice to find out how to pace your faster runs.

Secondly, as you build more speedwork into your training, it is important that you make sure that you plan easy runs in between hard sessions. Your body needs time to recover to make fitness gains, so fit in a rest day or cross-training between long or fast runs.

Below: Speed sessions, especially on the track, add focus to your training and help you pace yourself.

Above: You don't need a track to run fast, but it is best to choose a softer surface to run on – smooth, flat lawns are a good alternative, and give more space to train in a group.

Above: Workouts with faster friends build your own speed and prevent speedwork becoming a chore.

You will also need to pay extra attention to your running style. You may find yourself striding out longer than usual, but it is more efficient to concentrate on increasing your leg speed, so you take more steps rather than longer steps. The more you push your body during a run, whether you are running farther or faster, the more your running style will count.

Making changes

Running tracks can be intimidating, but remember that hard runs need soft surfaces. Shin splints and joint pain are very common in runners who have just introduced or increased their speedwork sessions. The faster you run, the greater the impact will be on your body, so to counteract this, do faster sessions on grass or soft trails (or on a track if you can face it).

As well as changing venues, you may need to adjust your eating pattern on speedwork days. Pushing yourself harder can make you feel nauseous, so leave more time between your pre-run meal and the training

session. You have probably been avoiding caffeine before long runs to avoid dehydration, but research shows that a shot of caffeine before a fast session can help you run faster and may help to burn fat.

Finally, even if you usually prefer to run alone, speed sessions are much easier to do with other people, if only because you might need an extra push to get through the session. Training with faster friends can be a great motivator.

Below: It's a good idea to hire your local track with a group of friends for regular mixed ability sessions.

First Fast Runs

Speedwork takes many forms and for the fastest athletes it's finely tuned and technically perfect. For a beginner, though, your first fast workouts should concentrate more on variety and enjoyment so that you can push yourself without punishing yourself.

Although training faster will improve your overall speed, it would be a mistake to simply go out on your usual run and try to speed up from the outset – you'll almost certainly run too fast and won't be able to finish the session. Instead you need to practise running at different speeds for different lengths of time, from short, very fast sprints to longer sustained intervals of 10 minutes or more. It will take time to learn the different paces you'll need for speedwork but approach it as a bit of fun and you should become used to the way it feels to run faster. You don't need a track, a coach or set of complicated set of instructions

Below: Make use of the landscape for fartlek runs, changing pace as your surroundings change.

to speed up. Try these easy ways to speed up one of your regular runs, remembering to run easy for the first 10 minutes of every session.

Fartlek

From the Swedish word meaning 'speedplay', fartlek is the most enjoyable and easiest form of speedwork. It may sound difficult, but it just means including a few faster bursts into your run at random points; you could try using lampposts or street signs as start and finish points; changing speed when you change running surface; or, if you run with music, running faster during a particular song.

Left: Most runners enjoy the fast, relaxed feeling of a strides session, with short, intense bursts of speed.

Right: Spiral sessions in your local park help you learn to run at varying paces.

Race yourself

Just as you can build up running using a walk/run strategy, you can build up periods of faster running using slow then fast intervals. Pick a short route that usually takes 30 minutes to complete, and introduce five faster spurts of 200 to 300m (or 2 minutes). Gradually increase the length of the faster intervals and reduce the length of the slower sections, aiming to take five minutes off the whole route time over a period of a few months.

Strides

This involves using short, fast bursts used to pick up your overall pace and improve your form. During the last 10 minutes of a regular run, speed up for a 20-second burst, keeping your running action smooth and relaxed; you should feel as though you are floating. Slow down for

Below: Many people new to running find that their form naturally improves when they start to run faster.

40 seconds, then repeat six to eight times. Increase the number of strides on your run as you become stronger.

Musical sprints

If you are unable to vary the terrain of your run easily, try varying the soundtrack. Use an MP3 player to create an interval session by making yourself a playlist with songs of different tempos, and run in time to the music. Alternatively, run fast during the chorus of songs and slower during the verse. Make things more interesting by asking a friend to make the playlist for you, so you don't know what is coming up (or run with a radio, which should have the same effect).

Spiral session

Go to a large park that you know well, and run four or five loops starting with a large, outer loop and gradually decrease the distance. For the first, longest loop, which should take you about 10 minutes, stay at an easy jog. For each successive smaller loop, speed up slightly, until you finish with a 1- or 2-minute, very fast circuit. After your fastest loop, run the circuits back out in reverse order, finishing with an easy 10 minutes.

Team efforts

You might usually prefer to run alone, but arranging to do harder sessions with a group of friends means you are less likely to duck out and do another easy run. Team sessions offer you more variety and help to keep your mind off your aching muscles, too. Here are a few to start with.

Hares and hounds: slower runners in the group head out first and choose the route; after an agreed time (say 3 minutes), the faster runners head out to try to catch them.

Mixed intervals: play cat and mouse with a friend by running the same route with different intervals: after a warm-up, one partner could run 2 minutes fast, 2 slow, 2 fast while the other continues to run easy; then the first runner has a 5-minute slow recovery while the second runs a continuous fast 5.

Team fartlek: head out with a group of friends and, after your warm-up, take it in turns to shout out the start and finish of fast periods, so the rest of the group don't know what is coming.

Hill Running

When planning running routes, most people choose to avoid hills. This seems to make sense – after all, running is about moving quickly, not trudging up steep slopes and stumbling down the other side. However, hill running has many benefits.

How you run hill sessions depends on your goal, but there are some benefits that are common to all hill running. The most important is that it builds your overall strength; research has shown that the muscles in your legs are forced to work harder for each step when running uphill, so they become more powerful, which translates to faster running and better endurance on flat surfaces. It is not just good for your legs; your upper body will become stronger as you need to use your arms to drive yourself up the hill, and your core strength and balance are improved by holding yourself steady on uneven downhill sections. Hills can be used as a threshold session, since your heart rate invariably rises on the climbs, and the mental strength you learn from repeatedly running a tough climb will

Below: Choose hills that level out at the bottom, giving you space to recover.

Above: Conquering tough climbs makes you stronger – and rewards you with great views at the top.

serve you well when you return to the road. Few race routes are completely flat, so learning to run up and down hills will always give you an edge over competitors if you choose to race.

How to run hills

First, choose your hill carefully. Look for a hill with about a 10 per cent gradient, ideally off-road as this will be more challenging for your muscles, but less damaging in terms of impact. You need at least 400m (¼ mile) of hill, with a fairly flat area at the bottom for recovery running. If you can, find a hill in a park or open countryside, so that you have good views to take your mind off the hard sessions.

Prepare yourself mentally before running a hill session. Running uphill can be demoralizing since you slow right down and struggle to find a

rhythm, so remind yourself of the goals behind your session, whether that is getting fitter, racing or just the satisfaction of a hard run (see box). Decide whether it will help you more to focus on the task in hand or look for distractions.

Form is important when running hills to avoid injury and becoming tired. Lean in to the hill slightly as you run up, but do not hunch over. Keep your back strong and pump your arms back and forth. Run on the front of your feet and keep your strides short. Look ahead of you rather than up toward the summit, otherwise you will strain your neck and could lose your footing. Try to

Hill sessions

Endurance (for fitness and long-distance running). Run uphill for 2 minutes, jog down and immediately start your next run up. Your effort should feel continuous even though you are not sprinting up the hill. Start with a 10-minute block, increasing each session by 2 minutes every week.

Threshold hills (for 5K and 10K running). Run uphill for 45 seconds to 1 minute, fast enough that you can utter only one or two words. Jog easily back down and repeat 10 to 12 times.

Power hills (for sprinting and middle-distance running, or to add speed in the final few weeks before a race). Find a steeper hill and power your way up for 30 seconds; jog or walk back down slowly, then repeat. Make this session harder by using soft ground – try it on sand dunes. Do 10 to 15 repetitions, rest for 5 minutes, then another 10 repetitions if you can.

Above: As you climb hills make sure you keep your form strong and powerful to maximize the benefits.

keep your effort even when running uphill, even if that means slowing down. If you do have to walk, be purposeful and strong rather than trudging up.

Running downhill is, for many people, even more daunting than trying to run uphill. The trick is to be confident and allow gravity to carry you down, using quick, light steps and holding your arms out to the sides for balance. Keep your core muscles engaged to keep your balance and try to avoid leaning backward – you are more likely to injure yourself if you are constantly trying to put the brakes on. Watch the ground ahead of you and plan your route down as you go.

Below: Running down hills can be scary as you lose control, but it helps you to work on your balance.

Threshold Training

Pain in the muscles after a hard run is caused by the breakdown of a substance called lactic acid, which is produced when you train. Deliberately training at or just below this 'burning legs' level is known as threshold, or tempo training.

When you have worked hard on a run your legs burn afterward, and the elevator looks more appealing than staggering up the stairs. The reason for this discomfort is the build-up of hydrogen ions in your muscles, which raise the level of acidity of your muscles.

Although threshold training is probably the most difficult kind of running, both in terms of learning how to do it correctly and in terms of physical and mental endurance, it is well worth including in your schedule once a week. At the most basic level it helps to improve your ability to run at a sustained, fast

Below: Threshold training sessions are perfect preparation for the pain of running fast races.

pace. It encourages you to run with good form, which carries through into the rest of your running, and teaches your body how to use fuel and oxygen more efficiently. Training at this level raises your lactate threshold, so you can run harder for longer. However, the real value of threshold training is seen when you race. During any race of more than a 1.5–3km (1–2 miles) you will be running at your lactate threshold for long periods of time, and learning to cope at this level is crucial to staying strong to the finish line.

How to run at your lactate threshold

Judging your threshold pace is almost as difficult as running at it. Lactate threshold can be measured using analysis

Threshold pace – quick tips
• Try to do threshold sessions with a runner who is much faster than you and experienced at judging pace. Having someone act as a pacer will keep you running fast in the tough final stages of your session.
• Run threshold sessions over the same two or three familiar routes, since this will help you gauge your pace and your improvement over time.
• Threshold running takes as much mental strength as physical strength, but unlike longer, slower runs, distraction techniques will not be helpful. Practise concentrating on your pace, breathing and form, no matter how painful it feels.

Above: Training with a faster runner will keep you at threshold pace when you're ready to stop.

of your blood (taken during exercise) or analysis of the gases you breathe out during exercise; this determines the heart rate at which you reach your threshold. However, these methods are expensive and, for the everyday runner, unnecessary.

In real terms it is better to think about running as fast as you can for a prolonged interval – say 20 minutes.

Lactic acid explained

This is a by-product of your energy producing system. When you run steadily, your body uses the aerobic system, in which oxygen is used with carbohydrates to produce energy. When you run harder, you cannot breathe in enough oxygen to continue this process, so your muscles switch to anaerobic energy production. The different system for breaking down carbohydrates results in the production of lactic acid. In fact, lactic acid is not what causes the burning, heavy-legs sensation. When you train hard, lactic acid breaks down in to lactate and hydrogen ions, and it is the ions that cause the problem.

Even this can be difficult to judge, as you should not feel as though you are running fast to begin with; the trick is to find a faster than usual running pace that you are able to sustain all the way through your threshold interval, but which leaves you feeling as though you could not have run any farther at that pace. A good guide is the talk test: after a minute or two of running at threshold pace, you should only be able to utter one or two words at a time. If you are alone, use the breathing test: if you usually take two steps for each breath, when you are at your threshold pace you will breathe harder, with two steps for the inhale and one sharp breath to exhale. You can use a heart-rate monitor if you have one: for most active people, the lactate threshold is reached at around 80 to 85 per cent of their maximum heart rate (estimate your maximum heart rate by subtracting your age from 220), so aim to stay at or just below that. However, the best way to ensure you are running at the right pace is to practice.

Different approaches

There are two ways to approach threshold training. First, you can run long intervals with short recoveries, for example you might run a distance of about 1.5km (1 mile) – or for 5 to 10 minutes – three or four times at threshold pace, with just 1 minute recovery between each interval. Secondly, you can run continuous threshold loops, building up each week, starting with 10 to 15 minutes and gradually building up to 30 to 40 minutes at threshold pace.

Below: Learn to tune into your own body and focus on the sensations of sustained fast running.

Running Surfaces

Conditions underfoot can make a huge difference to your running and generally speaking, the faster the surface, the more damage it will do in the long term. Choosing the right surface for the right sessions will help you to stay clear of injury.

The great thing about running is that you can do it wherever you are. If wherever you are happens to be in a city centre, however, you will soon find that your legs and joints take a pounding as you bash out thousands of steps on concrete. Here is a quick guide to some of the most common running surfaces, and which sessions they suit best.

Concrete

For many people, this is the surface they run on most often, as it is what you will frequently found outside your front door or office. However, the crushed rock that forms the basis of concrete paths makes it an incredibly solid surface to run on, with the added benefit of being faster than other surfaces. It is also usually a fairly smooth, even surface. However, this hardness also produces a bigger shock through your

Below: Synthetic tracks are a joy to run on and are perfect for measuring your speed intervals.

joints, and regular running on concrete can lead to impact injuries such as shin splints. If the pavement is poorly maintained you also run the risk of falling or twisting an ankle.
Best for: short, easy, convenient sessions that cannot be done elsewhere.

Asphalt

The vast majority of roads are made from asphalt and, as a result, most road races will use this surface too. It has slightly more 'give' than concrete, and usually provides a smooth, fast, even ground for running. However, like concrete, it offers little cushioning and should not be the base for most of your miles. Running in traffic also poses obvious risks, while drains and potholes could catch you unawares and cause accidents.
Best for: race practice or short runs.

Track

Although they can be intimidating for beginners, tracks are great fun to run on. They are usually made from synthetic materials to give a softer landing and some bounce, and because they are so flat and even, your running should feel much easier. They also provide the simplest way of measuring your run. The downside to track running is that the repeated bends can put a strain on your knees and ankles (alleviate this by changing direction often) and that it can become boring running in circles.
Best for: speed training and races.

Trail

Man-made woodchip trails, or natural forest trails, provide great running surfaces. As well as being soft underfoot and usually quite even, they are often in relaxing, traffic-free settings such as parks or woodlands. On the downside they can be badly affected by extreme weather – treacherously muddy when it

Above: Running on grass gives your legs a welcome break from harsh concrete surfaces.

rains, or baked hard when it is sunny – and sometimes hide hazards, such as tree roots or potholes.
Best for: long runs.

Grass

Short, well-kept grass is a pleasure to run on and has the best balance of soft cushioning and firm ground for fast running. Unfortunately some of the best grass for running may be in forbidden areas, such as golf courses or maintained parks, but even hopping on to grass verges for short sections of your normal routes will give your legs a break. The soft ground also makes your muscles work harder so you will be stronger when you race on the road. On the downside, like trails, grass can be slippy when wet and the surface is sometimes uneven.
Best for: longer speed sessions, long runs.

Alternative surfaces

Sometimes a trip away or desire for a change of scene will find you running on more unusual surfaces.

Sand: provides a great workout for your legs; wet sand is a good soft surface for longer runs if you can find enough of it. Running on the beach can place a strain on your Achilles tendon and calf, as your heel sinks down into the sand every time your foot hits the ground.

Moorland: a soft, springy and forgiving surface, this is great for longer off-road runs. Can be a trip hazard.

Rocky trails: if you are lucky enough to live near mountains, you might encounter scree and rock trails. These are very good for working on your balance and co-ordination, but you will need special trail shoes to protect your feet from bruising on the hard, sharp rock.

Treadmills: when the weather is bad, treadmills are a great alternative to running outdoors, and their soft, flat, even surface is good for runners returning from injury. However, they don't really replicate running outdoors, so should not be a base for all training.

Below: Soft, smooth treadmills are perfect for returning to running after a period off due to injury.

Above: Off-road running can be glorious, but you'll need to watch your footing, especially on rough terrain.

Below: Training on sand is hard work – so many runners use it as a way to strengthen their legs.

Essential Strength Training

Lifting weights may not seem like an obvious way to train to run, but elite runners over all distances perform some resistance training most days. For a recreational runner, two sessions a week are enough to benefit your running, as well as overall fitness.

Strength training helps to prevent loss of muscle mass and bone strength as you age, speeds up your metabolism slightly, increases your muscle-to-fat ratio (so your body fat reading will be lower), improves your explosive strength so that you can run faster, and improves your endurance. Although many recreational runners worry that weight training will add bulk to their body that might make distance running more difficult, anecdotal evidence suggests that the farther you intend to run, the greater benefit you will reap from strength training.

To begin with, it is simpler to use the resistance machines in your gym to weight train, since these help you to isolate the correct muscles. Most fitness centres insist on you having an induction when you join, and although resistance machines are easy to use, it's worth having a demonstration from an instructor to ensure you get the technique right. They should also be able to advise you on how to fit weight training into your running week: usually you'd do weights on an easy run day, perhaps using the treadmill for your run session to give your legs a break from the road.

You can perform the following exercises in any order, but it is best not to work the same muscles twice in a row. If you do two sessions a week, you should soon start to see an improvement in your running and your general fitness. Keep your movements slow and controlled, without allowing momentum to help carry the weight (the weight should never crash down at the end of a set). During sets, do not allow the weight to come to rest completely. At first, you will need to use trial and error to work out how much you can lift; you should just be able to complete the final repetition with good technique. Increase the weights every 3–4 weeks (or whenever it starts to feel easy) to continue gaining strength. Do two sets of 10 to 12 repetitions for each exercise.

Lat pull-down

Works: Lats (upper and middle back), biceps, shoulders

1 *Stand up and firmly grasp the bar with both hands with a wide grip, with your fingers wrapped right around the bar. Slowly sit down on the seat, pulling the weight down as you sit down but still keeping both of your arms straight.*

2 *For the exercise itself, press your shoulder blades together, tense your abdominals, and pull the bar down in front of you until it is at chest height (be careful not to arch your back during the movement). Immediately raise it back up, staying in control of the weight.*

Leg press

Works: Calves, gluteals, quads, hamstrings

Adjust the seat so that your knees are just below right angles in the starting position. Tense your abdominals, and slowly push up until your legs are straight, without locking your knees, then without pausing, lower back down.

Leg extension

Works: Quads

Your knees should be free to move and the pad sitting on the lowest part of your shin. Raise the weight slowly until your legs are straight, then lower down.

Leg curl

Works: Hamstrings

1 Sit straight up in the seat. Both of your knees need to be slightly in front of the edge of the seat for this exercise, so the upper pad rests on them. Make sure that the lower pad, which hooks behind your ankles, is positioned just above your Achilles tendon.

2 Starting with both of your legs straight out in front of you, slowly lower your legs, pushing against the lower pad with your ankles, to lift the weight, until your knees are at right angles, then immediately bring them back up again to the starting position.

Wood chop

Works: Obliques, back, arms, shoulders

With the cable on your left, twist from the waist to grasp the handle, low down on your left-hand side, with your arms straight. With your abdominals tense, pull the handle up across your body to finish above your head on your right-hand side. Lower slowly down. Repeat on both sides.

Chest press

Works: Pectoral muscles, shoulders, triceps

Hold the hand grips then squeeze your shoulder blades together and tense your abdominals, and push the grips out until your arms are straight, then bring them back in to the centre without pausing. To work your triceps harder, hold the narrower, vertical grips.

Hip adductors

Works: Muscles on the inside of the thighs

Start with your legs in a wide V-shape and adjust the space between the pads to a comfortable starting position (without any feeling of stretch). Tense your abdominals and slowly bring your knees together, then smoothly open them out again.

Hip abductors

Works: Muscles on the outside of the thigh and hip

For this exercise, start with your legs together, with your feet on the rests. Make sure both knees are centred in the pads. Tense your abdominals and slowly push the pads out to a comfortable width, then slowly bring them back in.

Strength Training with Free Weights

Resistance machines are great for making sure you work muscles correctly and use a good technique, but as you gain strength and confidence it is worth swapping at least one session for strength training with free weights.

Using free weights for strength training is more time efficient than using resistance machines as you can work more than one muscle group at a time. You will also need to use your deep abdominal and back muscles throughout so your core strength and balance will improve, too. At first it is best to do these exercises with a fitness instructor or a more experienced friend, as technique is all-important: get it wrong and at best, you will not be making the most of your workout; at worst, you will become injured.

For your first few free-weights sessions, be conservative about how much you lift. If you use weights that are too heavy, you may strain your muscles. You will soon be able to tell whether the weight is challenging enough. Do two sets of 10 to 12 repetitions for each exercise and when you have become stronger, go through the sequence twice.

1 Barbell squat

Works: Glutes, quads, calves

1 Start with the barbell across your shoulders, with your back straight and legs hip-width apart. Bend your knees and slowly lower yourself into the squat, until your thighs are parallel with the floor.

2 Your knees should not go farther forward than your toes; keep your back straight, abdominals tense and stick your bottom out, so your motion is down and back. Then push your heels into the floor and push slowly back up.

2 Standing row

Works: Lats, shoulders, triceps

1 Stand with your feet hip-width apart, holding a barbell with your arms just wider than shoulder-width apart and palms facing away from you.

2 Lean forward slightly from the hips, bending your knees, keeping your back straight and allowing the weight to drop straight down.

3 Bend your elbows and bring the barbell up to your stomach, before lowering back down. Complete the set without resting or straightening up.

3 Weighted lunge

Works: Quads, glutes, hamstrings, hip adductors

With your legs hip-width apart, step forward and bend your knees to lower yourself toward the floor, so that both knees are at a right angle. Your front knee should not go farther forward than your toes. Push down through your front leg and come back to your starting position, before repeating on the other side.

Technique tips

With all free-weights exercises, make sure that you remember to:
• Tense your core muscles before starting and hold them steady throughout – this will help you balance and protect your back during the lift, as well as strengthening your core
• Breathe in before you start, and out as you feel the resistance (during the hardest part of the exercise)
• Try watching yourself in a mirror as you perform the exercises to check that your technique is right
• Keep a record of how much you are lifting for each exercise, so that you know when it is time to increase your weights
• Keep your movements controlled and steady, don't jerk or use momentum to lift weights

4 Bench press

Works: Pectoral muscles, shoulders

1 *Lie on a weights bench with a barbell or two dumbbells held level with your chest, with your arms bent.*

2 *Push the weight up slowly until your arms are straight, then lower until the weight is a few inches above your chest.*

5 Weighted calf raise

Works: Calves

1 *Stand on a low step, holding dumbbells in front of you close to your body. Slowly raise yourself onto the balls of your feet, taking care to remain steady.*

2 *Then slowly lower yourself almost back to the ground before repeating (you should not touch the ground between repetitions).*

6 Side lunge

Works: Adductors, quads, glutes

1 *Holding dumbbells, stand with your feet hip-width apart. Take a step to the side, with your leading foot pointing slightly outward.*

2 *Lower yourself until your lead thigh is almost parallel to the floor before pushing back up. Repeat the exercise on the other side.*

Core Strength Training

In recent years the traditional stomach crunch has been replaced by core strength exercises, but working on your deep abdominal muscles is about more than having a flat stomach. Core strength training is thought to protect against injury by stabilizing the spine and pelvis.

By building a stable core, you will give yourself a strong base for efficient running movements, so that in theory, you will be able to run faster and for longer. If you can, go to core stability classes – or Pilates, which uses the same concept – to begin with, since effective use of these exercises is all about proper technique. This can be hard to achieve for many people since core strength is rarely developed. Try and complete the following sequence two or three times per week.

Abdominal muscles

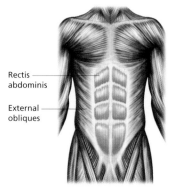

Rectis abdominis

External obliques

Transverse abdominis: The flat sheath of muscle that wraps around your torso lies beneath the other abdominal muscles.
Internal obliques: Run diagonally from the ribs to the hips between the external obliques and the transverse abdominis.
External obliques: Run across the internal obliques, in the opposite direction. Together the obliques give your waist shape and help to control twisting and sideways movements of your torso.
Rectis abdominis: The 'six-pack' muscle running down the front of your stomach, which is worked in traditional crunches.

1 Pelvic tilt

This is a good exercise for simply becoming aware of how to engage your core muscles. Lie on your back with your knees bent and feet flat on the floor. Place one or both hands under the small of your back. Keeping your breathing even, tense your abdominal muscles and pull your back toward the floor so that you are pressing down on your hands. Hold for a count of five, then release. Repeat 10 times.

2 Heel touches

Using the same starting position as above, engage your abdominal muscles and pull your back into the floor (to begin with, keep one hand under your back to make sure you are keeping the right muscles engaged throughout). Raise both legs off the floor with your knees bent at right angles, so that your shins are parallel to the floor. Very slowly lower one leg, keeping the knee bent, until the heel just touches the floor, then raise it and repeat with the other leg. Repeat 10 times with each leg.

3 Bridge

Lie on your back as before. Raise your hips so your body forms a straight line from shoulder to knee, and leave your arms straight on the floor. When you are stable, slowly raise one leg so that it is straight, in line with your body. Hold for a count of five, then lower back down, and repeat with the other leg. Repeat 10 times with each leg.

5 Plank

Lie on your front with your legs straight and toes tucked under, and your arms shoulder-width apart, resting on your forearms. Push up through your arms and toes, so that your body forms a straight line; be sure to tense your abdominals so that your back is supported. Aim to hold for 20 seconds at first, building up to 1 minute.

Technique tips
• Be careful not to suck in or hold your breath; keep your breathing easy and relaxed
• Keep your movements very slow and controlled, with your core muscles engaged throughout
• If you have any back pain or any of the exercises feel very easy, your technique is not quite right – have it checked
• Practise engaging your core throughout the day, when you are doing different activities, whether running, weight training, or even just sitting at your desk

4 Superman

Start on your hands and knees. Engage your abdominal muscles and slowly raise and straighten your right leg, at the same time raising your left arm, so that both raised limbs are level with your back. Hold for a count of five, then lower and repeat with the opposite arm and leg. Repeat the exercise 10 times on each side.

6 Side plank

1 Lie on your side with your legs straight, propped up on one forearm. Push up so that your body forms a straight line, resting on your forearm and the edge of your lowest foot.

2 Your top arm can either stay straight against your side, or to make the exercise harder, raise it straight up in the air. Hold for 30 seconds to start, building up to 1 minute.

Cross-training in the Gym

There is no doubt that the best way for you to achieve a better run is to run more. However, cross-training in the gym is an excellent way to continue building your fitness base without the impact and stresses of running.

You can use cross-training to work your running muscles or to build strength in areas that running does not. It is also a great way to burn fat and lose weight without adding extra miles. Cross-training in the gym is good for those days when the weather is so bad you lose the will to run.

If you have added weight training to your training programme, try 30 to 40 minutes of cardiovascular workouts before or afterward.

If you do decide to make cross-training a regular part of your weekly schedule, however, bear in mind that many of the guidelines that apply to building up running also apply to increasing cross-training. So, don't cross-train on rest days, or your body will have no time to recover from and adapt to your training. Build in cross-training gradually, starting with 20 to 30 minutes on an easy day or when you're planning a weights session. And listen to your body, especially when you're using the same muscles as you do when running; though cross-training is easier on your body than running, it is still possible to do too much, too soon and become injured.

Rowing machine

1 *The best all-over exercise in the gym, as well as one of the most intense calorie burners, this is a great way to warm up and cool down before a weights session. Good technique is vital: start with your arms straight, grasping the bar, push back with your legs, keeping your back strong and straight and leaning back as you go.*

2 *When your legs are fully extended, pull the bar smoothly into your upper abdomen, keeping your back strong and straight. Try racing yourself over a distance of 1,000 or 1,500m (1,060 or 1,640 yards) aiming to get faster each time you try it (this should take you about 5 to 10 minutes to complete).*

Navigating the console

Consoles across the different pieces of gym equipment are usually very similar and, in fact, will probably be identical if the different machines are all made by the same brand.

Quick start: most people press this to just hop on and start; you can adjust your speed and resistance to a comfortable level afterward.

Manual: press this setting and you will usually have to enter details like your age, weight, time or distance required, and resistance level or speed. Do this if you have a specific workout in mind.

Pre-set programmes: most gym machines have six to ten pre-set programmes including 'hill' and speed intervals, a good idea if you want a hard workout but are unsure how to achieve it.

Heart-rate pads: be aware that the reading from these pads may not always be very accurate. If you have your own heart-rate monitor, you should use that instead. The display usually shows a value for speed, cadence (rhythm) or rpm; ask the gym staff what the ideal values are for these and try to stick within those ranges during your steady workouts.

Treadmill

Although not strictly cross-training, even regular road runners can benefit from sessions on the treadmill. Treadmills are especially good for precise speedwork. Try a pyramid session, increasing your speed every 3 to 5 minutes peaking with a minute of all-out running, then decreasing. Use the treadmill to get the feel of running at different speeds, and use the gym's mirrors to check your form.

Elliptical trainer

After the treadmill, this is the machine that most closely replicates the action of running. It is easy to slouch on the elliptical trainer, so watch your form. Try interval sessions to build fitness: you can do this by increasing the resistance level for periods of 2 to 5 minutes, or by increasing your speed. Get a whole-body workout by alternating using your legs to power the machine with pushing through your arms and upper body.

Stationary bicycle

Adjust the seat before you start, so that your legs are fully extended at the lowest point of cycle. Use the bike for a fat-burning workout: try three or four 5-minute intervals of sprints, cycling fast for 8 seconds and easy for 12 seconds. Alternatively, use it to build endurance using 'brick' sessions: cycle steadily for 45 minutes to an hour, then jump straight on to the treadmill for 15 to 30 minutes.

Skip these machines

Step machine: *Many people believe using this will reduce fat around the hips and thighs, but it is not as effective a calorie burner as other machines.*

Arm crank ergometer: *Again, this does not burn many calories as it only uses the upper body, and does not provide any useful strength gains for runners.*

Ergonomic bike: *Given a choice, go for a traditional stationary bike, which will work you harder and use your running muscles more effectively.*

Cross-training Outside the Gym

Even lifelong couch potatoes find that their interest in other sports increases once they've built confidence through running. Cross-training can give you a more balanced approach to your running and, at the same time, strength and fitness that will make you a better runner.

Developing your fitness does not mean restricting yourself to the gym – once you have built your fitness through running you will be able to enjoy any other sport (sometimes with a little practice). These are some of the best non-gym additions to your running programme – try a session of cross-training on a rest or easy running day.

Cycling

Use your bike to replicate hard running sessions such as hills and speed intervals – you should find that hard cycling on a rest day leaves you with enough energy to run the next day. There is no need to buy a special road bike, but it is worth swapping the standard pedals for racing pedals and bike shoes. These allow you to clip your feet on to the pedals (you can release easily when you stop) so that you can pull as well as push the pedals for a smoother action and better workout for your legs. As on the stationary bike, aim for

Below: Cycling is a great way to get outdoors and increase your leg strength without the impact of running.

a cadence of 80 to 90rpm no matter what the terrain, which will mean learning to use the gears (switch down a gear if you are unable keep the cadence steady).

Inline skating

Skating is a fun way to strengthen your legs, build fitness and burn calories, though if you are new to it then having a few lessons is a good idea. Skating uses all the major muscle groups in your legs, and because you have to keep your balance, you will also work your upper body and core muscles, too. When you first start, try to relax and lean slightly forward, with your legs slightly bent and elbows at a 45 degree angle to centre your weight over the skates. Use diagonal strides to move smoothly forward (with your leading foot pointing slightly outward) for a more efficient, faster skate.

Swimming

Although not an obvious training tool for runners, swimming helps to build strength in your core, back and upper body, which will improve your

endurance and form while running. Swimming is only useful if you have good technique, so it is worth taking a class or two to improve. Learn to breathe on both sides (bilateral breathing) as this gives you a more balanced stroke; aim for long, strong strokes rather than fast strokes, as this will speed you up. Work on kicking from the hip and keeping your legs fairly straight, and your body horizontal. Once you have mastered the basics you can start to incorporate fast intervals and longer-distance swims to improve your fitness.

Aqua running

Running in a swimming pool looks slightly odd but is the perfect way to build running strength while giving your body a break from the impact of hitting a hard surface. You will need a special aqua running belt to aid buoyancy and keep your back straight in the water, and you can buy special shoes for extra resistance. It can be

Below: Experienced skaters make it look easy, but take a few lessons to get the most from your wheels.

difficult to gauge your effort while aqua running – it often feels too easy compared with road running – so try wearing a water resistant heart-rate monitor for a clear idea of how hard you are working.

Circuit training

If weight training in the gym leaves you cold, try outdoor circuit training classes. Ideally this will encompass a routine (or circuit) of six to ten exercises, doing each exercise for a short interval or set number of reps and moving quickly on to the next. This might include press-ups, crunches, pull-ups (using a climbing frame in a park), step-ups, shuttle runs, squats and lunges. Because circuits are completed quickly and with short

Above: Get your technique right and regular swimming will give you improved strength and co-ordination.

rests, you are working on your aerobic fitness and strength at the same time. You can also include some plyometric (jumping) exercises to improve your running speed.

Walking

For most of us, walking is involved in the early stages of our running lives, so you'll already know how beneficial it can be to building running fitness. However, once you're able to run continuously, walking can have a place in your training in its own right, especially if you choose more strenuous forms. Hill walking is a

Above: It may look strange, but aqua running is often used by elite athletes to train through injury.

good way to strengthen your running muscles with lower impact than running, helping you to avoid injury. It's also a good way to explore new running routes. You could try Nordic walking, using poles to exercise your upper body at the same time. It is best to have some instruction in this as you'll need to get the technique right to feel the benefit. If you do choose to add long walks to your routine, just be conscious of how much time you spend on your feet – you don't want to become too tired to run – and, as in running, make sure you wear supportive footwear.

Game over

Many people run to help them enjoy other sports, but if running has become your main focus then take care when choosing other sessions. Any sports that involve quick changes of direction and side-to-side movements will put you at greater risk of injury. These include football and all racquet sports, such as tennis or squash. When you swim, avoid doing too much breaststroke, as the kicking

action can injure your knees and hips. As running is a high-impact sport, and it is this impact that causes many running injuries, choose low-impact cross-training over other high-impact activities, such as dancing or aerobics.

Right: The sudden changes in direction involved in a game of football can put runners at risk of injury.

NUTRITION FOR RUNNING AND WEIGHT-LOSS

For many people, starting to run is just the first step in a move toward a healthier lifestyle. Whatever your reason for running, good nutrition enables you to perform well, make the most of your sessions and avoid injury and fatigue. Traditional diets do not fit with the special requirements of runners, so even if weight-loss is one of your goals, you will need to think carefully before cutting down what you eat and drink.

Above: Runners should think of food as fuel for their training.
Left: Running helps you lose weight, and losing weight helps you run.

Runners' Golden Food Rules

Becoming a runner means changing your attitude to food. Yes, you will be able to eat a bit more of what you fancy, but at the same time, eating a healthy diet is more important than ever to improve both your performance and your enjoyment in running.

There is nothing complicated about eating well – just follow these basic nutritional guidelines.

Never run on empty

Skipping meals is a bad habit for anyone, but for active people it can ruin an exercise session. Even if you run first thing in the morning, you should aim to eat a light snack an hour or two before you run. Good options include a banana and a small pot of yogurt, a handful of raisins, or if you find it impossible to stomach solids before running, try a sports drink.

Eat little and often

Using this strategy will keep your energy levels constant throughout the day, avoiding the surges and lethargy-inducing dips caused by eating large, heavy meals. By planning healthy snacks or light meals every two or three hours, you will be less tempted to give in to cravings for unhealthy foods, or skip a run because you are so hungry you choose to eat instead.

Below: Take healthy snacks, such as fruit, to give you an energy boost when you go out on long runs.

Eat the right carbohydrates

You will probably have heard that eating platefuls of carbohydrates (often abbreviated to carbs) is vital to fuel all exercise. While it is certainly true that the carbohydrates in your diet should give you most of your energy – around 60 per cent of the total calories you consume – all carbohydrates are not equal in terms of how quickly they are metabolized in the body. It is therefore important to plan

Above: As a runner you'll need to eat more so don't be tempted to skip meals.

exactly which carbohydrates you eat around your training sessions, making sure to use slow-release carbohydrates most of the time, with faster fixes for just before and after your training sessions.

(For a more detailed guide to the role that carbohydrates play in your diet, see Know Your Carbohydrates.)

What are antioxidants?

Antioxidants are nutrients that help to combat the effects of free radicals – the molecules in the body that are linked to ageing, muscle soreness, heart disease and cancer. Intense exercise produces more free radicals in the body (as does smoking, ultraviolet light and pollution), so runners need to consume more antioxidants in their diets to counteract this effect. Antioxidants include vitamins A, C and E, carotenes (found in fruit and vegetables), the minerals selenium, copper, manganese and zinc (found in whole grains, cereals and meat), and flavanoids (found in tea, red wine, garlic and onions, and fruit and vegetables).

Below: Including a wide range of fruit and vegetables in your diet gives you plenty of antioxidants.

Inject some colour

As a runner, it is particularly important to make sure you have enough vitamins and minerals. The best way to do this is to accurately measure your food and work out how much of each nutrient you are eating – but no-one wants to plan their meals with a calculator. A simple route to getting enough vitamins, including essential antioxidants (see box), is to make sure you eat a variety of different-coloured fruit and vegetables.

Eat some fat

Forget the idea that all fat is your enemy. Between 15 per cent and 30 per cent of your daily calories should come from 'good' fats – that is, polyunsaturated and monounsaturated fats as found in foods like vegetable oils, eggs, nuts and avocados. These fats can help lower levels of 'bad' LDL (low density lipoprotein) cholesterol, keeping your heart and arteries healthy. They are also an excellent source of fat-soluble vitamins (A, D and E) and omega-3 fatty acids, which have been shown to improve athletic performance as well as keeping the heart healthy.

You should try to avoid foods containing too much 'bad' fat. Saturated fat, which is found in meat and full-fat dairy products, can raise your levels of LDL cholesterol, while trans fats (hydrogenated fats found in some ready-made products such as bread, cakes and margarine) are worse still.

Include protein at every meal

The more active you become, the more protein you will need. Your body uses it to repair tissue damage and to build muscle, and it can also be used as fuel for exercise. Protein also helps fill you up, so you are less likely to crave unhealthy snacks. Make sure you include some protein in every meal: sprinkle seeds on your breakfast cereal, snack on handfuls of nuts, and have some lean meat, fish or eggs in your lunch and main evening meal.

Below: Not all fats are bad; for example, eggs are a great source of fat-soluble vitamins.

Above: Change the way you think about food – view it as fuel for your running, not 'excess calories'.

Do not diet

Most adults have been on a diet at some point in their lives. However, you will be a healthier, better runner if you can break out of the dieting mindset. Think about what you eat as fuel for your body's activities, and don't feel guilty about having the odd treat – your running can help you to burn it off. Look at building healthier eating and exercise habits long term, and you will be far more successful at keeping your weight down than you ever were with dieting.

Below: As well as healthy fats, nuts contain plenty of protein, so a handful makes a filling snack.

Runners' Golden Hydration Rules

One of the first pieces of advice given to novice runners is to drink more. But as most of us find, drinking gallons of water every time we run is neither practical nor effective. Here's how to solve your drink problems.

You have probably been told that you should always have a bottle of water on you at all times and should be sipping regularly when you exercise to avoid dehydration, which will not only damage your health but impede your performance. To an extent, this is sound advice. Getting hydration right is essential for comfortable, safe running.

The often-quoted fact that even a tiny drop in hydration – just one or two per cent of your body weight – leads to a much greater drop in performance is also true. However, drinking as much as you can, as often as you can is not necessarily the answer. During an hour of running

Below: You should be especially careful to monitor your hydration levels when training in hot conditions.

How much to drink

You will need to use trial and error to a certain extent to find a comfortable and beneficial amount of fluid for your training, but here are some good general hydration rules to follow:
• Drink 500ml (about 1 pint) of fluid during the two hours directly before your run
• Aim to drink 2–3 litres (3½–6 pints) each day (depending on your size and exercise level)
• Drink little and often rather than large volumes at once
• For every kilogram (2¼lb) of body weight which is lost during a run, drink approximately 1.5 litres (2½ pints) of water
• On short runs (up to one hour) there is no need to drink during exercise

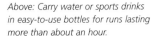

Above: Carry water or sports drinks in easy-to-use bottles for runs lasting more than about an hour.

you might lose up to 2 litres (3½ pints) of fluid, but your body is incapable of replacing that amount over the same time period.

Monitoring hydration

Instead of thinking about hydration in terms of filling up with liquid before and after a run, think about staying well hydrated generally. It is easy to monitor your hydration using one of these simple methods:

Weigh yourself (naked). Do this before and straight after a run. Every kilogram lost equates to one litre of fluid.

Monitor the colour of your urine. It should be very pale yellow (almost clear) most of the time. If it is very dark, you are dehydrated.

Above: Regular practice makes it easier to judge what and when you should drink during races.

Pay attention to your thirst. The old wisdom of drinking before you are thirsty is overly cautious, but it is certainly true that as soon as you feel thirsty your body is telling you to take in some fluid.

Although some level of dehydration is inevitable after a long run or race, it should not severely hamper your session. In fact, studies have shown that elite athletes regularly perform at modest levels of dehydration, and may even benefit from being slightly lighter as a result of carrying less water. However, it is important to be aware of the symptoms of severe dehydration, particularly if you are running in very hot or humid conditions, as in extreme cases this can be fatal. Signs to watch out for include: severe thirst, headache, lack of sweating, and confusion.

Drinking too much

While dehydration is still one of the biggest problems facing runners, particularly over longer distances, drinking too much water can be just as dangerous. Your body needs a certain level of sodium to function properly,

and filling up with plain water without losing it through sweat or urine can lead to a condition called hyponatremia, which means lack of sodium but is often known as water poisoning or over-hydration. This condition is increasingly common in larger mass races, where runners are slower and more likely to be overly conscientious about taking on water. The slower you run, the less fluid you lose through sweat, and the more opportunity there is to take a drink. Taking ibuprofen (an anti-inflammatory drug often used for joint and muscle pain) or aspirin will increase a runner's risk of developing hyponatremia. The symptoms are very similar to dehydration: headaches,

Above: Special sports drinks contain electrolytes which replace those that are lost through sweat.

nausea and confusion usually develop, along with bloating. Many runners are rightly very reluctant to reduce the volume of fluid they drink, as it can be difficult to judge how little is too little, so the simplest way to avoid hyponatremia is to drink sports drinks instead of water. These drinks contain electrolytes which replace those lost through sweat and they maintain your sodium levels. They also have the added benefit of containing carbohydrates, which will improve your running performance and fight off fatigue.

Good and bad drinks

Generally speaking, any fluid can be used to stay hydrated, but some are more beneficial than others, and some have side effects.

Good

Plain water: for runs up to one hour's duration, if required.

Sports drinks: for long runs over one hour.

Diluted fruit juice: for long runs.

Coffee or cola: just before hard or fast sessions, to increase alertness and speed.

Bad

Fizzy drinks: the gas in carbonated drinks makes them hard to take on the run, so many runners can't take on enough liquid to stay hydrated.

Thick drinks: some smoothies and shakes contain food that needs to be digested, so are absorbed slowly into the body.

Alcoholic drinks: any drink which contains more than 4 per cent alcohol speeds up the body's urine production, causing dehydration.

Eating for Weight-loss

If you're trying to lose excess weight, running will give you a head start, but if your progress is slow you may need to look to your diet for the answers. Strike a balance between cutting calories for weight-loss and eating enough to run well.

There is no secret to losing weight. Though many of us spend years searching for quick, easy ways to shed a few pounds, we know the answer is actually very simple. We just need to burn more calories than we are eating. Research has shown that most people underestimate the number of calories they eat, and then overestimate the number they burn, and runners are worse than the average person, eating more than twice as many calories in a single meal than they think. And while running will help you to lose weight, the opposite is also true: losing weight (by controlling your diet) will help you to run.

In order to work out what you should be eating, you need to have some idea how many calories you burn in a day. It is impossible for the average person to work this out precisely, but you can make an estimate. To work out the calories your body uses to function, first convert your weight into pounds (to convert from kilograms to pounds, multiply by 2.2), then multiply that number by 10. Then add half this number again to account for day-to-day activities such as walking around the office and housework. On top of this you should add approximately 100kcal (420kJ) for every 1.5km (1 mile) you run, and take into account other activities you do, such as cross-training or cycling to work.

Cut the calories
Roughly speaking, you need to cut out 500kcal (2,100kJ) per day to lose one pound of fat in a week (don't aim to lose more weight than this – you will be losing water and muscle

Right: Becoming more aware of what and how much you're eating is key to reaching a healthy weight.

rather than fat and your running performance will suffer). You can do this by cutting down your calorie intake by 500kcal or by burning an extra 500kcal through exercise. It's more practical to do both; add 25 minutes to your run (or add in extra activity such as a half-hour walk at lunchtime, or cycle to the gym) and cut out one 'treat' (for example, a caffè latte, chocolate bar or glass of wine are all worth around 200–250kcal, or 840–1,050kJ).

In the long term there's no need to become obsessive about how much you're eating, but to get used to eating the right portion sizes it's

Quick tips

These easy strategies are proven to help you eat less:
- Eat slowly
- Eat meals at a dining table, with no distractions (for example, television, newspaper)
- Have soup or salad before your meal, to help you fill up
- Say no to any unplanned snacks offered to you
- Always try to think about the reasons why you might be eating; perhaps you are bored, stressed or tired rather than actually hungry

Right: Try to eat your main meals at the dining table rather than on the couch – it could help you eat less.

best to monitor your food intake for a few weeks. Keeping an accurate food diary is an excellent way to do this. Start by writing down your current diet for a week, being completely honest, weighing everything you eat, and remembering to include 'accidental' snacks, such as accepting a few chips from a friend's plate or eating your children's leftovers. At the end of the week, use a calorie counter to work out just how many calories and grams of fat you normally eat. The chances are this will give you enough of a shock to cut down.

You can also try writing down how you feel when you eat. You will naturally feel more hungry the more you run – and you do need to eat more – but the trick is to learn to recognize true hunger. Many people snack when they are bored or feeling down, and while running should help to counteract these feelings, it will help to train yourself to disconnect eating from emotions.

Precise eating

After this, you can use your food diary to plan as well as to record what you eat. At the start of the week,

Below: Make sure you plan your snacks as well as your main meals to avoid getting hungry on the run.

devise a meal plan for each day, fitting it around your training sessions so that you always have enough energy to run and enough time to digest food before you go out. Shop for all the ingredients and try not to deviate from your shopping list. Knowing what you will eat every day means you're less likely to go for a quick, less healthy option. If you can, keep the food diary even after you've lost weight, as scientific research has shown that people who successfully manage their weight over several years record what they eat.

Once you know what a healthy portion of food looks like, you shouldn't have to weigh your food. You can use your hands as a general guide to portion sizes. Two handfuls is roughly one portion of breakfast cereal; two to three handfuls is a good serving of pasta, rice or salad; one handful is roughly one portion of fruit or vegetables. Servings of meat or fish should be roughly the same size as your palm. Measure fatty foods using your thumbs: one thumb is a 30g serving of cheese; two is 15g or one tablespoon of margarine or peanut butter.

On a plate

When you are planning a meal, you should mentally divide your plate up as follows:
• One-third should be carbohydrates (for example, pasta, rice, potato)
• One-third should be vegetables or fruit
• Of the remaining third: half should be lean protein. One-third (that is, one-ninth of the plate) should be healthy fats
• Refined sugary foods, cakes, sweets and 'bad' fats should make up only a tiny sliver of your plate.

Below: Follow these guidelines when preparing meals for a healthy, balanced diet.

Fat-burning Foods

Reducing excess body fat is a constant battle for all runners. When you run, your muscles have to literally carry your body fat around; and though some fat is used for fuel, most of it is useless for running purposes.

Luckily the very act of running, like any exercise, burns more calories, reducing the amount stored as fat, and eventually body fat decreases. Diet also plays a crucial role in reducing your body fat, but losing fat is not just about eating less fatty food (although this helps). Adding certain foods to your diet can actually speed up your metabolism (the rate at which your body burns calories) and, while eating them is unlikely to transform your body overnight, when combined with a weight-loss diet and exercise programme, they might give you an edge.

Lean protein

Foods containing a lot of protein are difficult for your body to digest. By increasing your intake of lean proteins, such as chicken, turkey, soya products, beans, peas and lentils, you will use up more calories breaking your meal down. Higher protein intake increases your thermic metabolism (see box). It also makes you feel fuller for longer, so you are less likely to snack on foods that result in extra calories and extra fat storage.

As a runner you should be eating more protein than the average person anyway as your body needs it to repair minor damage to muscles caused by hard training sessions. It can also be used for fuel when your carbohydrate stores are running low.

Chilli

Adding fresh chilli peppers to your food is a good idea if you want to burn more calories. Chillies have been found to contain a substance called capsaicin, which speeds up your metabolism. Spicy food is not just good for keeping your weight down, though. Some

Above: Very spicy food is not to everyone's taste, but hot chillies can help speed up your metabolism.

evidence suggests it can help fight off infections, which is useful if you run a lot, as hard training can weaken your immune system. The hotter the chilli, the greater the effect – but take care when eating before a run, as chilli can also upset your digestion.

Tea and coffee

Research suggests that taking caffeine before exercise may help your body to use fat as fuel. Caffeine also reduces your perception of effort, so training

Left: Foods which are high in protein and low in fat, such as beans, peas and lentils use a lot of energy in digestion.

Your metabolism

Your body burns calories (or kilojoules) in these three different ways:

Basal metabolism: the basic energy required for your body to function at rest.

Activity: the calories you use in all activities from sport to typing.

Thermic metabolism: the energy you use up digesting food.

harder seems easier and you use more energy; the added advantage is that you should perform better, too. Choose your caffeinated drink wisely: milky caffè lattes and cappuccinos can contain up to 200kcal (840kJ) – so are unlikely to help you lose weight – and, drunk just before a workout, can upset your digestion. Green tea, while low in caffeine, has also been shown to speed up your metabolism.

Calcium

You're probably aware that calcium is essential for good bone health – so crucial for preventing running-related stress fractures, and for women, it combines with regular running to decrease your risk of osteoporosis. But making sure you get enough calcium can also help your weight. Taking in around 1,200mg of calcium per day (just a couple of glasses of milk) from low-fat sources can speed up your basal metabolism. This effect has been shown to translate into weight-loss: a study of dieters in the USA found that people who ate three 150ml (¼ pint) servings of low-fat yogurt lost more weight than those who didn't eat yogurt.

Fibre

Many runner-friendly foods are naturally high in fibre: slow-release energy sources such as fruit and vegetables and wholegrain cereals, dark seeded breads and dried fruits. Eating foods that contain a lot of fibre slows down your digestion. As your body takes longer to process the food, it expends more calories doing so. Again, fibre is also good for making you feel full, so you are less likely to overeat, but eating too much before a run could result in digestion problems.

Salad

Items with high water and fibre contents, such as celery, lettuce and some dark green raw vegetables, can help you burn fat because your body will use more digesting them than it gains from metabolizing the energy contained in them. The high water content also means they can help fill you up if you're trying to adjust your portion sizes.

Above: Eat the dry, light meat in poultry (not the skin) and you'll burn fat and feel fuller for longer.

Above: Calcium-containing foods such as milk and low-fat yogurt build strong bones and help you lose weight.

Fat-burning workouts

Weight training: It is not true that you can convert fat into muscle, but weight training does increase your muscle mass, so that your ratio of muscle to fat is higher. Intensive weight training is a good calorie burner, and as your muscle volume increases, you will burn more calories, even at rest.

Below: By increasing your muscle mass with regular weight training you'll run better and burn more calories.

Low intensity training: Your body will always use carbohydrates as its first choice of fuel, so the quicker you run, the less fat you burn as fuel. Add a couple of long, slow runs per week and a higher percentage of the energy needed will come from fat, while the low intensity will have little or no impact on your other training.

Above: Short, sharp sprint sessions will burn those extra calories, but be careful not to overdo it.

Sprint intervals: Research has shown that lots of short, fast bursts of activity speed up your metabolism by releasing adrenaline into your bloodstream. Intense exercise also uses up far more calories than low-intensity sessions. You won't be able to do as much of this type of activity, however, as it stresses your body.

Know your Carbohydrates

From a non-runner's point of view, it probably seems that runners live on huge platefuls of pasta and endless bowls of porridge. For runners, carbohydrates take on an important role, providing the most efficient fuel for your working muscles.

Around 60 per cent of the calories you consume should come from carbohydrates. However, how you obtain that 60 per cent is crucial – when you consider that sugar is a form of carbohydrate, it is clear that some carbohydrates are healthier choices than others, and some will benefit your running more than others.

Eating pasta is a good place to start – hence the stereotype – but even the type of pasta you choose is important. As a general rule, unrefined, wholegrain carbohydrates are a better choice than highly processed carbohydrates, so eating wholegrain bread, pasta and brown rice is better than eating white bread or pasta. Colour is a good guide – the darker the better – but be careful that the food really is wholegrain rather than just less refined; for example, choose bread that is wholegrain rather than 'brown'.

Wholegrain foods are more beneficial for a number of reasons. They contain many useful nutrients that are lost during refining processes, such as B vitamins, fibre, iron, magnesium and selenium. Wholegrain

carbohydrates also provide slow-release energy, which helps prevent the peaks and troughs in blood sugar that can be detrimental to your training.

However, it is here that carbohydrate choice becomes quite complicated. As a general rule, slow-release energy from unrefined carbohydrates is better, but there are some exceptions. For example, if you want to top up your energy stores during a long run, you will need quick-release carbohydrates that are easy to digest rather than wholegrain foods.

Glycaemic index and glycaemic load

The concept of the glycaemic index (GI) of foods is useful for working out which carbohydrates to choose, and what to eat with them. The GI of foods is a measure of how quickly eating that food raises your blood sugar levels (and therefore how quickly it is digested and available for use as glucose during exercise). Foods are rated on a scale from 0 to 100 – the higher the number, the quicker the rise in blood sugar level from eating the food (see box for the

The glycaemic index: some examples		
	Food	**GI**
High GI	Glucose	100
(70 or higher)	Baked potato	84
	Rice cakes	78
	Wholemeal (whole-wheat) bread	71
	White bread	70
Moderate GI	Couscous	65
(56–69)	White rice	64
	Sweet potato	61
	Porridge	58
	Sultanas (golden raisins)	56
Low GI	Brown rice	55
(55 or lower)	Honey	55
	Banana	52
	Rye bread	50
	Strawberries	40
	Apples	38
	Low-fat plain yogurt	36
	Skimmed milk	32
	Lentils	26
	Peanuts	14

Below: Starting the day with a serving of wholegrain breakfast cereal or porridge gives you energy for running.

Below: Slow-release energy comes from low-GI foods such as apple, so this makes an ideal snack.

GI rating of some common foods). However, since few foods are eaten completely in isolation, it is also important to consider the combined GI of foods that you eat – for example, sweetened breakfast cereal has a high GI, but combine it with yogurt and the overall GI rating becomes lower, since the yogurt takes longer to digest and produces slower-release energy.

Eating low-GI foods is generally advised both for weight-loss and for running performance, since low-GI foods keep you fuller for longer and give you a more sustained burst of energy. However, the system is flawed in that it does not take into account the amount you eat of a given food, and this can lead to people avoiding useful, healthy foods because they have a high GI rating.

Another system called glycaemic load (GL) has been developed as a practical solution to this. The GL value of a food is worked out by multiplying its GI by the amount of carbohydrates in grams per portion, then dividing this number by 100. Again, eating low GL foods is better, and following a low-GL diet is generally less restrictive than following a low GI plan.

Carbohydrates and health

Eating the right carbohydrates at the right time is not just a question of keeping your weight down and running well. Carbohydrates are broken down into sugars and affect your blood sugar levels, so can affect your overall health. A typical Western diet heavy in refined carbohydrates has been linked to insulin resistance: where the body becomes insensitive to its own insulin, so blood sugar levels stay high for longer. This is part of what is sometimes called 'metabolic syndrome', a collection of symptoms including obesity, high blood pressure, and high cholesterol, which are thought to contribute to the development of serious conditions such as Type II diabetes and heart disease. Running is one way to lower your risk of developing these symptoms, but it's clear that diet plays a valuable role too – not least in helping you to get the most out of running so that it becomes part of your life in the long term.

Carbohydrates and running

As we've learned, different sources of carbohydrate are useful at different points in your training or racing day. Eating low GI foods just before or during an intense run (including most races) can result in nausea, indigestion and diarrhoea as your body struggles to digest the food at the same time as powering your working muscles. A typical race-day menu might involve a low GI breakfast eaten three to four hours before the race, followed by a moderate GI snack an hour or two beforehand (such as a banana or energy

bar), and quick-release carbs such as energy gels or energy drinks immediately before and during the race. Research has shown that eating low-GI carbs a few hours before exercise, and consuming 30g–60g quick-release carbs per hour during exercise, helps people to exercise for longer. It will take time to find out how your body responds to different carbohydrate sources during races and training but the key to a good run is making sure your body is well fuelled before and during the event. Don't leave it till the last few miles of a race to take on a gel or drink – studies have shown that it takes at least 30 minutes to absorb even quick-release carbs.

Right: Get into the habit of taking on energy drinks during training sessions.

Above: Bananas are popular with runners because they are a natural, portable form of low-GI energy.

Pre-run Training Snacks

It is tempting to reward yourself for running by filling up on chocolate bars or chips, but what you eat before and after training can make a real difference to your performance and recovery. These snacks can all be made in less than ten minutes.

Think about planning your diet and you probably focus on the largest meal of your day. This is not a mistake – after all, your main meals account for most of your daily calorie intake and are your best chance to take in essential nutrients. However, a good diet can easily be undone by poor snacking and choices of light meals. The simple solution is to prepare your own easy snacks both to fuel your running and to help your body recover afterward.

Aim to eat two to three hours before running if you can, choosing slow-release carbohydrates to avoid peaks and troughs in energy as you run. Your body can only hold enough carbohydrate to fuel two to three hours of running, so during a long session (over one hour) you might want to take in some energy as you go, in which case special sports drinks and gels available from sports stores, may be the best choice.

Below: Drink diluted fruit juice before a run – it will be easier for your body to digest than solid food.

Banana and peanut toastie

1 small banana
1 slice wholemeal (whole-wheat) bread
15ml/1 tbsp smooth peanut butter

Mash the banana in a small bowl with a fork. Lightly toast the bread, then spread with peanut butter, adding the mashed banana on top. Fold in half to serve.

Nutritional information per portion:
Energy 392kcal/1646kJ; Protein 12g;
Carbohydrate 56g; Fat 13g.

Breakfast pot

2 plain (unsalted) rice cakes
100g/4oz fresh raspberries
50g/2oz pomegranate (flesh and seeds)
150ml/¼ pint/²⁄₃ cup low-fat fruit yogurt
15ml/1 tbsp clear honey

Break the rice cakes into pieces and place in a small bowl. Mix in the fruit and yogurt. Drizzle the honey on top.

Nutritional information per portion:
Energy 318kcal/1335k; Protein 9g;
Carbohydrate 70g; Fat 1.8g.

Digestive problems

Many people find it difficult to eat before running, particularly early in the morning. If your food sits in your stomach, at best you will suffer from a stitch or heavy legs, at worst you may feel sick or have diarrhoea. However, it is best to eat something before training, so try to eat a little before running. The more liquid a food, the easier it is to digest, so start with sports drinks or diluted fruit juice, then try soft fruit, such as a ripe banana. As you become used to running on that, try more solid foods. Two hours between eating and running is usually plenty of time for your pre-training snack or drink to leave your stomach.

Energizing banana citrus shake

15ml/1 tbsp lemon juice
100ml/3½fl oz/scant ½ cup
* fresh orange juice*
1 banana, mashed
150ml/¼ pint/⅔ cup low-fat
* natural (plain) yogurt*
100ml/3½fl oz/scant ½ cup
* skimmed milk*
5ml/1 tsp clear honey
5ml/1 tsp finely grated fresh root
* ginger or 10ml/2 tsp ground ginger*

Place all the ingredients together in
a smoothie maker or blender, then
process on a low setting until the
mixture is smooth. Adjust the amount
of milk in the smoothie to change the
consistency. Serve immediately, or
keep chilled in the refrigerator for
up to 24 hours.

Nutritional information per portion:
Energy 296kcal/1243kJ; Protein 13g;
Carbohydrate 60g; Fat 2g.

COOK'S TIP

Investing in a juice extractor is
worthwhile if you want to be sure that
your fruit juice is fresh and pure. To
make orange juice, peel the fruit and
cut into large chunks before using the
juice extractor to juice.

Porridge with fruit and nuts

35g/1¼oz rolled oats
15ml/1 tbsp ground almonds
25g/1oz raisins, plus extra for topping
5ml/1 tsp cinnamon
100ml/3½fl oz/scant ½ cup skimmed
* milk, mixed with 100ml/3½fl oz/*
* scant ½ cup water*
15ml/1 tbsp clear honey
15ml/1 tbsp pistachio nuts, chopped

Place the rolled oats, ground almonds,
raisins, cinnamon, skimmed milk and
water in a large heavy pan over a low
heat and cook for about five minutes.
When the porridge is cooked, and
the milk has all been absorbed into the
oats, stir in the honey and leave to
stand for a minute. Sprinkle the nuts
and raisins on top of the porridge and
serve immediately.

Nutritional information per portion:
Energy 400kcal/1680kJ; Protein 13g;
Carbohydrate 59g; Fat 13g.

VARIATIONS

Add different toppings to your morning
porridge for variety. Try the following
combinations: chopped dried apricots
with pumpkin seeds, mixed berries and
natural (plain) yogurt, or sunflower
seeds, dates and sliced banana.

Quick tomato soup

5ml/1 tsp olive oil
1 small onion
1 clove garlic, crushed
400g/14oz can chopped tomatoes
400g/14oz can chickpeas, drained
* and rinsed*
15ml/1 tbsp tomato purée (paste)
10ml/2 tsp mixed dried herbs
5ml/1 tsp chilli powder (optional)

Finely chop the onion. Heat the olive
oil in a large, heavy pan over a
medium heat. Fry the chopped onion
in the olive oil for about two minutes.
Add the crushed garlic, chopped
tomatoes, chickpeas, tomato purée,
mixed dried herbs and chilli powder,
if using, to the pan.
   Stir the ingredients together
thoroughly and simmer over a low
heat for about five minutes, or until
the soup is heated through thoroughly.
Serve immediately. You can also
make a larger quantity of soup by
doubling the ingredient amounts,
then freeze individual portions for up
to one month. This recipe makes
approximately two servings.

Nutritional information per portion:
Energy 253kcal/1062kJ; Protein 13g;
Carbohydrate 33g; Fat 9g.

Post-run Training Snacks

It is important to take on some food or drink as soon as possible after running. A combination of carbohydrate and protein is best to restock your muscle glycogen and help your muscles repair any damage done by hard training.

After training is a good time to eat fast-acting carbohydrates, so if you are a fan of white bread or sugary foods, this is a good opportunity to indulge, though as always you should be mindful of eating empty calories. Your immunity is lowered by fast or long running so whatever your post-training treat, you should try to include plenty of antioxidant vitamins in the hours and days after a hard session.

Eat as soon as you can after finishing your run. You may find that you don't feel like eating, particularly if it is a hot day or you have trained harder than usual, in which case try to drink some fruit juice or a glass of milk. Eat some solid food once you feel better. Think of your post-run refuelling strategy as your pre-run snacks in reverse: start with something small and easy to digest, then an hour or so later have a light snack, then when you are hungry again go for a heavier meal.

Below: Drinking milk after training is a good way of ensuring you get your protein if you don't feel like eating.

Antioxidant boosting smoothie

1 small banana
80g/3oz mixed berries, such as
*   raspberries, strawberries, blueberries*
*   or blackberries (fresh or frozen)*
250ml/8fl oz/1 cup skimmed milk
1–2 drops vanilla extract

Peel and roughly chop the banana. Put the chopped banana into a blender or smoothie maker and then add the fresh or frozen mixed berries, milk and vanilla extract.

Blend all the ingredients together until the mixture is a smooth consistency. For extra protein, add a scoop or two of protein shake mix. Serve immediately in a tall glass, or chill in the refrigerator for up to 24 hours.

Nutritional information per portion: Energy 204kcal/856 kJ; Protein 10g; Carbohydrate 42g; Fat 0.6g.

Below: Fruit juices and smoothies are a good way to take in antioxidant vitamins and are very easy to digest.

Miso soup

1 sachet miso soup or 15ml/1 tbsp
*   miso paste*
400ml/14fl oz/1²⁄₃ cups boiling water
100g/3³⁄₄oz/scant ¹⁄₂ cup beansprouts
100g/3³⁄₄oz firm tofu, cubed
100g/3³⁄₄oz spring greens (collards),
*   roughly chopped*

Mix the miso and water together in a pan. Add the beansprouts, tofu and spring greens. Heat for 5 minutes.

Nutritional information per portion: Energy 238kcal/ 1000kJ; Protein 20g; Carbohydrate 20g; Fat 9g.

Quick protein fix

Eating enough protein is essential to enable your body to make a quick and full recovery from hard training sessions, but it can sometimes be a struggle to fulfil your daily requirements. A simple fix to this problem is to add protein shakes to your diet.

These come in powder form and are usually based around whey protein, providing about 15g (¹⁄₂oz) per serving. They often contain different vitamins and minerals as well as 200–300kcal (840–1,260kJ) of energy. If you don't like the taste of the shakes, you can always add a scoop or two of the powder to other foods such as porridge, desserts or fruit smoothies.

Above: Avocados have a high carbohydrate content and are full of the 'good' fats that your body needs.

Guacamole pasta

40g/1½oz wholemeal (whole-wheat) pasta
1 small avocado approx 50g/2oz
150g/5oz/⅔ cup low-fat natural (plain) yogurt
1 clove garlic, peeled and crushed
5ml/1 tsp lemon juice
1.5ml/¼ tsp chilli powder
2 tomatoes, chopped
15ml/1 tbsp pumpkin seeds

Fill a large pan with water and bring to the boil. Cook the wholemeal pasta for about six minutes (or according to the packet instructions) in the boiling water. Meanwhile, mash the avocado in a large bowl using a fork. Add the natural yogurt, crushed garlic, lemon juice, chilli powder and chopped tomatoes. Mix together well. Strain the pasta, put into a bowl and stir in the avocado mixture. Sprinkle the pumpkin seeds on top to serve.

Nutritional information per portion:
Energy 380kcal/1596kJ; Protein 17g;
Carbohydrate 41g; Fat 17g.

Sandwich fillings
A fresh sandwich makes the perfect recovery food after a lunchtime run.

HUMMUS AND VEGETABLE
50g/2oz hummus
1 carrot, grated
50g/2oz chopped red (bell) pepper
15ml/1 tbsp fresh coriander (cilantro)

Nutritional information per portion:
Energy 138kcal/580kJ; Protein 5g;
Carbohydrate 15g; Fat 7g.

CHICKEN SALSA
100g/3¾oz roast chicken breast, sliced
30ml/2 tbsp salsa
1 handful spinach leaves

Nutritional information per portion:
Energy 231kcal/970kJ; Protein 28g;
Carbohydrate 3g; Fat 5g.

EGG AND PESTO
1 hard-boiled egg, sliced
15ml/1 tbsp red pesto
1 handful rocket (arugula)

Nutritional information per portion:
Energy: 200kcal/840kJ; Protein 13g;
Carbohydrate 1.5g; Fat 15g.

PRAWN AND SPINACH
5ml/1 tsp curry powder
Small pot of natural (plain) yogurt
100g/3¾oz prawns (shrimp), cooked
1 handful spinach leaves

Mix the curry powder and yogurt together in a small bowl. Add the prawns and spinach and mix.

Nutritional information per portion:
Energy 204kcal/856kJ; Protein 32g;
Carbohydrate 12g; Fat 3g.

Nutritional values for bread
When calculating nutritional values for sandwiches, remember to add the nutritional values of the bread you choose (values per slice):

	Energy	**Protein**	**Carbs**	**Fat**
Seeded Wholemeal	234kcal/983kJ	9g	32g	8g
(whole-wheat)	172kcal/722kJ	7g	33g	2g
Rye	153kcal/642kJ	6g	32g	1g
White	160kcal/672kJ	6g	32g	1g
Plain bagel (1)	216kcal/907kJ	7.7g	42.8g	1.6g
Multigrain wrap	185kcal/777kJ	5.1g	32.2g	4g

Below: Rye bread contains the least calories so is a good choice if one of your running aims is losing weight.

Below: White bread is full of fast-acting carbohydrates so is best eaten after training, if possible.

HEALTH AND INJURY

Runners tend to be more aware of their body than other people. This is a good thing, since it is rare to spend a lifetime running regularly without encountering injury. The good news is that running injuries can usually be cured within a few weeks, and most can be avoided altogether. This chapter will guide you through the symptoms and treatments of some common running injuries, and show you how best to run throughout your life, no matter what age or life stage you have reached.

Above: Sports massage is a common treatment for running injuries – but it's not always this relaxing!
Left: Steady, sensible training increases are key to avoiding serious injury problems.

Common Injuries

Running has a reputation for causing more injuries than other sports. While this is not really fair, it is true that the repeated impact of thousands of steps places strains on your lower body. Here are some of the most common problems, their causes and how to deal with them.

Plantar fasciitis

The plantar fascia is a thick band of tissue under your foot running from front to back. Plantar fasciitis occurs when the tissue becomes inflamed, causing a dull pain under your foot. The pain may be worse on waking and, at first, feels better once you start walking or running, as the foot warms up.

Causes: High, stiff arches in your feet or low, flat arches can put a strain on the plantar fascia. A tight Achilles tendon or calf also puts more pressure through the foot, as does overpronating (your feet rolling too far inward on impact). Your shoes might also be the culprit: worn out shoes or too firm soles are another cause.

Treatment: This may require weeks of rest, during which stretching of the fascia itself is recommended: you can do this by rolling a golf ball under your foot, from big toe to little toe. Stretching your calf and Achilles may help. It is also worth seeing a podiatrist to check you are wearing the right shoes.

Instant relief: Freeze water in a paper cup, then peel off the cup and roll your foot over the ice. If you need a quick fix, use a cold drink can.

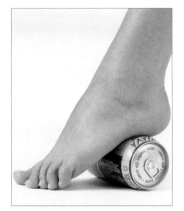

Above: Rolling the sole of your foot over something firm and cool alleviates plantar fasciitis pain.

Ankle sprain

A sprained ankle is the overstretching (or, in severe cases, breaking) of the ligaments around your ankle, usually on the outside.

Causes: This injury is always sudden, generally caused by stepping on a sharp camber or obstacle. Weakness in the ankle and fatigue are also factors, as you will be less able to correct your ankle position.

Treatment: RICE is always the best treatment (see box). You will usually need to take six to eight weeks off running. Once the initial swelling has died down, you can start balance exercises to rebuild strength and balance in your ankle.

Instant relief: Painkillers are effective – and often necessary – with this injury. Anti-inflammatory drugs may be taken to reduce swelling.

Achilles and calf pain

The Achilles tendon runs from your heel up to your calf muscle. Tightness in the Achilles often leads to problems in the calf, and vice versa. Achilles pain is usually sharp and felt just above the heel, while a calf strain is felt farther up.

Causes: Weak or inflexible calves cause both Achilles and calf problems. Running on hills and soft ground aggravates the problem. Speedwork

Achilles and calf pain

Right: Tight calves and tight Achilles tendons (under the calf muscles) often go together.

Plantar fasciitis

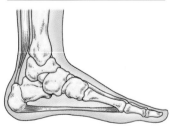

Above: The pain comes from inflammation of the plantar fascia, which runs under the foot.

Ankle sprain

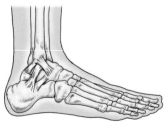

Above: The delicate, complex ligaments around the ankle become stretched in an ankle sprain.

Right: Calf pain can often be a result of tightness in the Achilles tendon at the back of the heel.

RICE

This is the first treatment for any acute injury that could become inflamed. It stands for rest, ice, compression and elevation. Stop running straight away, ice the injured area for 10 to 20 minutes, apply a compression bandage (ideally, have a sports professional apply the bandage so that it is not too tight), and if possible, raise the injured area above your heart.

Below: It is important to elevate and apply an ice pack to an ankle injury.

can contribute as it tightens up the calf muscles. Overpronation can sometimes be a factor.

Treatment: Stretching and strengthening of the calves should help. Try heel raises on a step, raising yourself up using your good leg and lowering with your weight through the injured leg. You may be able to run through a mild calf strain, but Achilles injuries usually require rest.

Instant relief: Wear shoes with a slight heel, or place heel lifts (no greater than 1cm/½in high) in your shoes to take the pressure off. (However, regularly wearing high heels can be a contributing factor to the injury.)

Shin splints

The term shin splints refers to any pain felt down the shins. Although worse during running, pain may be felt when walking.

Causes: Inflammation in the muscles, tendons or around the bones in your shins. Sometimes shin pain is caused by compartment syndrome, an inflammation of the thin fascia over the compartments of the muscles in your shins. Shin pain is often a result of sudden increases in mileage and running on hard surfaces. Worn out shoes and overpronation are also factors, and the pain may be linked to tight or weak calves.

Treatment: Stretching the calves and shins helps, as does deep tissue massage carried out by a physiotherapist. Self massage can help: place one thumb on top of the other on the inside of your shin, press hard and run up to the knee, repeating this right across the shin. It may be worth visiting a podiatrist to analyse your gait and recommend the correct shoes, or orthoses (special insoles to correct your gait). If you have severe compartment syndrome, surgery can be used to make a small incision in the fascia and release the pressure.

Instant relief: Simply kneeling with your feet flat on the floor (top down) provides some relief, and ice is very effective.

Shin splints

Left: Shin pain is very common in runners. It is often caused by inflammation around the bones in the shin.

Runner's knee

Otherwise known as patellafemoral pain syndrome, runner's knee is a sharp pain directly underneath the kneecap. As well as making running painful, it can be difficult for sufferers to use stairs or sit for long periods with their knees bent.

Causes: This condition was once thought to be the result of worn-down cartilage in the knee, but is now believed to be the result of the kneecap tracking to one side. This movement could be due to the wrong shoes (either too cushioned, allowing the kneecap to move too much, or not providing enough support for overpronation), weak quadriceps (particularly on the inside of the leg), tight hamstrings, or high-arched feet.

Treatment: Correcting the problems in the runner's gait that cause the kneecap to move is the best form of treatment. This could involve stretching the quads and hamstrings, or seeing a podiatrist for advice on shoes or orthoses. Performing slow, single-leg half squats (so you don't fully bend the knee) can help the kneecap to track properly.

Instant relief: Rest and ice, keeping the leg as straight as possible.

Runner's knee

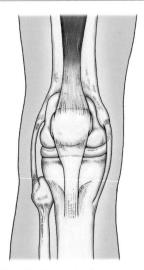

Above: The sharp pain of runner's knee is thought to be caused by the kneecap tracking to one side.

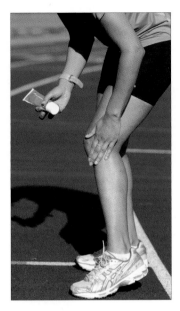

Above: Applying a freeze gel to the knee provides temporary relief, but don't ignore symptoms.

Other knee problems:

Anterior cruciate ligament (ACL) injury The ACL crosses underneath the kneecap, helping to keep the bones in the lower leg in place. It is most commonly damaged through twisting or sports involving a lot of lateral movement, such as football or hockey. This injury is too painful to run through and usually requires surgery.

Baker's cyst An inflammation of the bursa (fluid-filled sac) between the bone and muscle at the back of the knee, which becomes painful (the swelling is clearly visible). Anti-inflammatory drugs and RICE usually cure it in time.

Meniscal injuries There are two menisci (thin, fibrous cartilages) on the surfaces of the knee, one on the inside and one on the outside. The meniscus on the inside is more commonly damaged, and can be torn through twisting or bending the knee. Small tears may repair on their own but often keyhole surgery is required to remove the damaged part of the meniscus (recovery is very quick after surgery).

Above: Support bandages can help keep the knee in place and ease the pain of some injuries.

Iliotibial Band Syndrome (ITBS)

This condition has a very distinctive kind of pain, a dull ache on the outside of the knee, which can occur about ten minutes into a run. If you run through it, eventually any bending of the knee becomes very painful, especially walking downhill or down stairs. The ITB is a thick band of tissue running from the hip to just below the knee, and the pain is caused when the ITB becomes tight and rubs across the bones at the side of the knee with every step.

Causes: Running too far on a cambered surface or downhill can bring on this problem, though it may also come on through sharp increases in mileage. Overpronation and wearing the wrong running shoes can be factors. Lack of flexibility in the gluteus muscles and hamstrings can also cause the ITB to tighten.

Treatment: A notoriously difficult problem to cure, ITBS can be treated simply if caught early. Complete rest for a few days as soon as the symptoms appear can make a difference, after which stretching and deep tissue massage (performed by a physiotherapist) are the usual treatments. You can stretch the ITB by standing up straight with your legs crossed over (the painful leg should be behind the 'good' leg), then leaning sideways in the same direction as your back leg.

Instant relief: Straightening the leg and icing it as soon as symptoms appear should provide some relief and help recovery. It is best not to attempt to run through any symptoms of ITBS.

Hamstring injuries

A large tear in the hamstring usually happens mid-run and will be painful enough to stop you running. It may bruise and swell. Even a minor overuse strain in the hamstring can be very painful as the muscle is so large and so involved in running.

Causes: The hamstring helps propel you forward at speed, so sprinting and jumping are common causes of sudden tears. Introducing speedwork

and hillwork too quickly, or changing running surface or shoes are also common culprits.

Treatment: Massage can help with strains, though a severe muscle tear will take several weeks of rest to heal. Improving general flexibility right through your legs and hips should help the injury to clear up and stop it recurring.

Instant relief: For a tear, ice will provide pain relief, while if you are planning to run through a strain, try wearing compression kit to keep the muscle warm and flexible.

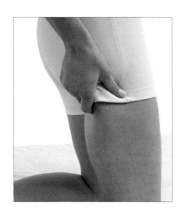

Below: Injuries to the hamstring muscle often occur quite suddenly in the middle of fast sessions.

Above: Regular massage, including self-massage, can help you to recover from muscular injuries.

Hamstring injuries

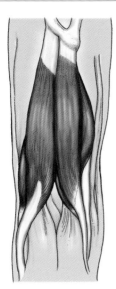

Above: The large hamstring muscle helps propel you forward and tears are very painful.

Pulls and tears

When people are injured, you may hear them talking about pulling, straining or tearing a muscle. These injuries are all in fact muscle tears, but a pull or strain is usually the result of minor tears that will heal in a week or two, while a more severe muscle tear results in loss of function in the muscle (you cannot run through the pain), swelling, and sometimes bruising. It may take several weeks to heal an injury like this.

Right: Pain in the lower back is often a symptom of a problem elsewhere, such as around the pelvis.

Piriformis syndrome

The piriformis is a muscle deep in the buttock that helps rotate the leg outward and stabilizes the hip. If it becomes tight, you will feel a pain deep in the buttock when running, and if you try to run through it you might also have tightening and pain down the back and inside of your thigh, or in your lower back.

Causes: The piriformis usually becomes tight when it is forced to do the work of other, larger muscles, so weak gluteal muscles, abductors and core abdominal muscles can all contribute. Increasing speedwork or mileage too quickly are also factors, and lack of general flexibility makes the problem worse.

Treatment: Once the piriformis is tight enough to be painful, it usually requires deep tissue massage to release the muscle. Strengthening the core, glutes, hip abductors and adductors should help, and stretching all the major muscle groups is also essential.

The piriformis itself is hard to stretch, but try lying on your back with both knees bent; rotate the leg of the affected buttock outward and bring the ankle up to rest on the opposite knee in a figure 4 position, then reach around and grasp the back of your other leg, pulling both legs in toward your chest.

Instant relief: Give yourself an easy massage by lying down on the ground with a tennis ball under your buttock. Slowly roll the ball underneath you, putting as much of your weight as possible on the affected hip.

Osteoarthritis (hip)

This is much more common in older runners than younger ones. Osteoarthritis is a degenerative condition which produces a dull ache and stiffness in the hip joint and may reduce your range of movement.

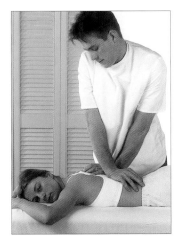

Above: Osteopaths can help make sure that your spine is aligned correctly, preventing injury.

Causes: Age and genetic factors are often behind osteoarthritis, and while running may aggravate it, it has not been shown to increase your likelihood of developing the condition (contrary to popular belief).

Treatment: Regular stretching should help to keep the joint mobile, and you should switch to soft but even running surfaces to reduce the impact through the joint. Glucosamine supplements

Pelvis

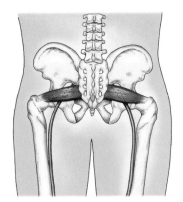

Above: The pelvis is a complex structure and problems with its alignment cause pain both above and below it.

can help. In severe cases, hip replacement surgery may be necessary.
Instant relief: Anti-inflammatory drugs should ease the pain.

Back pain

Most people will feel back pain at some point in their lives and, for runners, this tends to be in the lower back. Problems in the lower back may be hard to self-diagnose as you could feel the pain lower down – for example sciatic pain can be felt right down your leg.
Causes: If your back pain is chronic (rather than the result of a sudden, twisting or bending movement), then it could be the result of a number of problems. Weak abdominal muscles, resulting in poor posture, are a common cause. Gait problems, including leg length discrepancy, can lead to back pain. Problems in your gluteus or piriformis muscles can also be felt in the lower back.
Treatment: Though you may be able to run through mild back pain, you should look for the cause and correct it as soon as possible to avoid further problems. Strengthening your core and back muscles should help. You should have a gait analysis to rule out biomechanical problems,

> ### A holistic approach
> No matter how precisely you can pinpoint the painful area, no part of your body works in isolation. Running injuries, unless caused by a specific accident (such as an ankle sprain), are usually the result of chronic problems in more than one area of the body. Instability or weakness in your core can lead to a misaligned pelvis, which in turn stresses the muscles in your legs when you run.
>
> If you have a recurring injury, or one which refuses to go away, visit a physiotherapist to work out the cause of your problems so you can correct it in the long term.

and it is worth visiting an osteopath to make sure that your spine is correctly aligned.
Instant relief: Alternating hot (using a hot water bottle) and cold (using ice) should help to relieve the pain temporarily. At night, try sleeping on your side with a pillow between your knees.

Below: Simple, regular stretches can help to alleviate back pain and prevent problems worsening.

Avoiding Injury

There is nothing more frustrating for a runner than being incapacitated by an injury. That frustration is usually heightened by the knowledge that the problem could have been prevented, or at least its impact lessened.

Running injuries are almost always the result of a number of controllable factors. Here are some of the most common causes of injury and how to avoid them becoming a problem.

Too much, too soon

The list of sports injuries that can be caused by this basic error is almost comprehensive. In between sessions, your body becomes stronger by adapting to the stresses you place on it during training. By piling on miles or intensity, your body has little opportunity to adapt, and damage occurs. Never increase your mileage by more than 10 per cent a week. Don't increase more than one element at a time, be it speed, distance, or cross-training, and take into account other increases in activity, such as a new cycle commute to work, or even just an increased workload in the office.

Below: Stretching should be a relaxing part of your training, so use the time to reflect on your workout.

Above: Take regular breaks from training to avoid overtraining, which can lead to a decline in performance.

Overtraining syndrome

If you are training hard but not seeing a noticeable improvement, or carrying a chronic, low-level injury, you could be suffering from overtraining syndrome, which is brought on by long periods of intensive training. Symptoms can include extreme fatigue, depression, persistent colds and a decline in running performance. Fix the problem by taking a complete break from running for two weeks, which you can spend reviewing your goals.

Yoga and Pilates

It may not necessarily be the first thing that springs to mind as a runner, but taking a few classes in yoga and Pilates is a very good way to improve your core strength, flexibility and body awareness, all of which can help you to avoid injury. It is always better to attend classes rather than attempt exercises on your own, as doing them incorrectly is at best useless and at worst potentially harmful. Before starting a new class, ensure it is at the right level for your experience, and in the case of yoga, that it is the right type: you should try to avoid overly strenuous forms such as power yoga or bikram yoga (where the room is kept very hot).

Right: Even learning the very basics of yoga and Pilates can help you be more in touch with your body.

Above: The best athletes make stretching an essential part of their post-run routine to avoid injury.

Regular rest is important to help your body recover from training. Never train hard two days in a row. Schedule one rest day per week and have an easy training week every six to eight weeks.

Poor shoes

If you don't replace your shoes regularly, you can't expect them to provide enough cushioning and support for the thousands of footfalls that they will endure. They can be costly, but avoiding the expense of new shoes usually results in the much greater expense of sports injury treatment. As a general rule you should replace shoes every 800km (500 miles) or six months, but this will vary on different factors like your shoes, gait, weight and running surface. You should check your shoes for wear and tear at least once a month. If possible, buy two pairs of running shoes and alternate wearing them, so each pair has a chance to decompress and dry out after every use.

Poor conditioning

Becoming a better runner is not just about running. The more you run, the more obvious your weak points will become, which is why good overall conditioning is essential. Start every run with a 10-minute warm-up jog, and spend 10 to 15 minutes afterward stretching all your major muscle groups. As you build up your training, you should also include strengthening work such as hill running or weight training, so that your body is stable and balanced when you take to the roads. Lack of flexibility combined with muscle imbalances (for example, if your quads are stronger than your hamstrings) is a recipe for injury.

Do not ignore biomechanical faults either, as these become exaggerated when you run. Give yourself a quick check standing straight in front of a mirror: you should be able to see, for example, whether one shoulder sits higher than the other, or if your hips are level. Do a single leg squat slowly and see whether your knee points forward all the way down. If you spot anything potentially troublesome, see a podiatrist or physiotherapist for a full assessment.

Running environment

Where and with whom you run can be a major factor in avoiding injury. If you run on very hard surfaces such as pavement or asphalt, you are at risk from impact injuries. On the other hand, if you always run on sand, you risk straining your Achilles tendon. Running the same route all the time is problematic, as you will be running on the same camber and potentially stressing one side of your body.

Below: Rest and relaxation are just as important for your development as hard training sessions.

Injury Specialists

It is difficult to know who to turn to when you become injured through running. There are a range of health professionals who can help with sports injuries in different ways, but the most important thing is to find someone you trust and who cares about your sport.

Though running is undoubtedly good for your overall health, you'd be extremely lucky to go through a lifetime of the sport without becoming injured at some point. Unfortunately treating these injuries can be expensive, especially if you don't get the right diagnosis – and that depends on you finding the right health professional in the first place. Whichever route you take, if you have a persistent pain that doesn't respond to rest quickly, don't just hope it will go away. See one of these people who can speed your recovery and, perhaps more importantly, help you to find ways of preventing a relapse.

Your family doctor

As with any health problem, your family doctor is a useful first port of call for running-related trouble. Though he is unlikely to solve the problem himself, your doctor will be able to make a first diagnosis and refer you to a specialist for further treatment. For acute injuries, a doctor may be best placed to help, as he will be able to assess how serious the damage is and order X-rays or scans; he can even refer you to a surgeon if necessary.

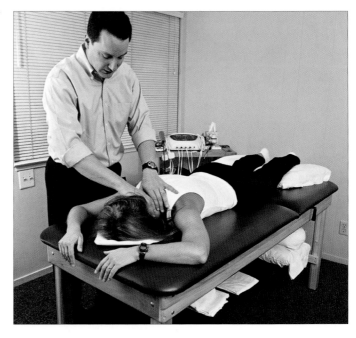

Physiotherapist

If you have a long-term or relatively minor injury, your doctor will often refer you to a physiotherapist, and

Above: Sports physiotherapists are trained to use different treatments for a range of injuries.

many runners go straight to the physio once an injury has set in. A physiotherapist can diagnose and treat almost all sports injuries, and will look at the injury in the context of your whole body, often examining your overall posture and gait to determine underlying causes. Physiotherapists usually treat injuries using massage, and by prescribing stretching and strengthening exercises. They are often trained in a wide range of disciplines including deep tissue massage, acupuncture, strapping and using ultrasound to break down scar tissue. Some physiotherapists will also refer you for for further examination in the form of scans and X-rays.

Finding Dr Right

Most sports-injury specialists operate privately, so check that they are fully qualified; most disciplines have regulatory boards so start with these organizations to find a trustworthy professional. Before you book an appointment, check that the person you have chosen has interest and experience in sports injuries. Don't be embarrassed to ask about their qualifications. If you know other runners, ask them for recommendations.

Right: Do not be embarrassed to ask your doctor about their qualifications.

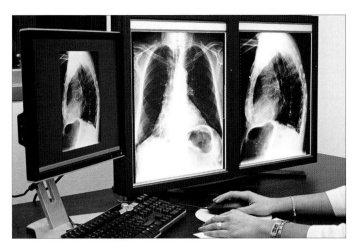

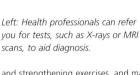

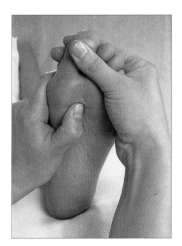

Left: Health professionals can refer you for tests, such as X-rays or MRI scans, to aid diagnosis.

and strengthening exercises, and may be trained in acupuncture and strapping (to support your muscles).

Sports masseur

While not usually able to help with serious injuries, sports masseurs can offer pain relief and can help with muscular problems by loosening stiff muscles. It is a good idea to see a sports masseur if you have a muscle strain, especially in larger muscles such as the gluteals or hamstrings. Regular visits to a sports masseur, even before injury occurs, may help with flexibility and with recovery from training.

Podiatrist

Also known as chiropodists, podiatrists are thought of as foot specialists but will usually examine your gait from head to toe to determine the root of a running injury. They will usually watch you walk up and down or on a treadmill, and will perform a static examination to look for potential problems. They can refer you for X-rays and further tests. They also prescribe orthoses, special insoles to correct your gait, and can advise you on shoes. Again, it may be worth seeing a podiatrist before becoming injured to prevent problems before they occur.

Chiropractor

Sometimes known as 'back doctors', chiropractors focus on the back, particularly the spine, and will 'clunk' your back and neck back into the correct position. However, they also work on joints all over the body, so can treat a wide range of sports injuries, in particular lower back pain, ITB syndrome and hip problems.

Like physiotherapists, some chiropractors use ultrasound, and some use electromagnetic pulse therapy to encourage healing.

Below: Podiatrists will often perform static examinations of your feet to look for problems.

Osteopath

An osteopath may also 'clunk' your bones but the treatments they offer usually involve working on the muscles and tendons around your joints to balance your body. Osteopaths take a holistic approach to injury treatment, so they will examine you for weaknesses all over the body and may advise you on nutrition and cross-training. It may be useful to see an osteopath early in your running career, even if you are injury free, to determine any weak spots. Osteopaths may prescribe stretching

Below: Some runners swear by regular sports massage as an effective means of injury prevention.

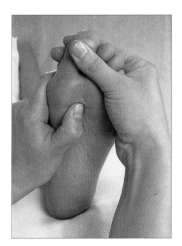

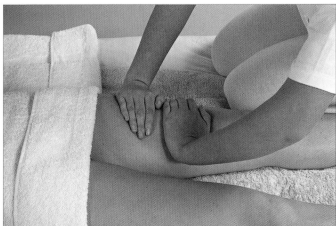

Alternative Injury Treatments

Sports injuries can often be very difficult to diagnose and even harder to treat, so it is no surprise that runners are often open-minded about the methods of treatment that they will try. Some may be sceptical, but the results speak for themselves.

Many of the methods of healing used on running injuries are on the fringes of conventional medicine, but for every one of these treatments there are thousands of runners willing to swear by its effectiveness.

Acupuncture
More and more health professionals are choosing to add acupuncture to their range of skills as it becomes more accepted in all areas of medicine. In traditional acupuncture, which comes from ancient Chinese medicine, very fine needles are inserted just beneath the skin at different points along meridian channels – the theory being that chi (energy) should run freely down the channels, and when they become blocked this is what causes physical problems.

Whether or not you believe in Chinese medicine, several studies have shown that acupuncture can help with pain relief, and with specific running injuries.

Below: A session of acupuncture could help to release muscle tightness, easing sports injuries.

In one piece of research, acupuncture was successfully used to treat plantar fasciitis, with needles placed along the arch of the foot and on different muscle trigger points on the calf. It is thought that acupuncture works on sports injuries both by reducing any tightness in the muscles and by prompting the brain to release painkilling chemicals.

Reiki
Another treatment based on an ancient Eastern philosophy, Reiki is a Japanese word meaning 'universal life energy'. Practitioners of Reiki are able to channel this life energy to promote both physical and mental wellbeing. In a Reiki session, they will place their hands on or over the problem area, with the idea being that by channelling the life energy they will help the body to heal itself. Reiki is used for a wide range of physical, mental and spiritual problems, and once you have been trained in Reiki, you can use it on yourself as well as on other people.

Right: The meridian channels used in acupuncture. Energy (chi) should be allowed to flow freely around the body.

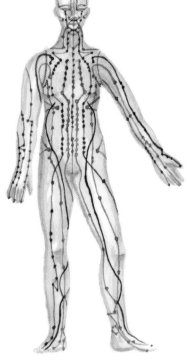

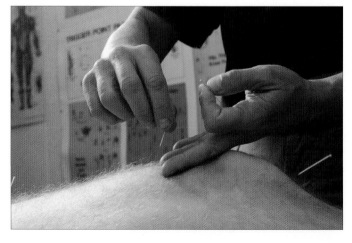

Electromagnetic pulsed field therapy (EMPT)
Like acupuncture, EMPT is employed by health professionals to treat sports injuries. As the name suggests, during treatment, electromagnetic pulses from a small machine are passed through the injured area (applied through a wrap around the affected limb). EMPT is said to work by realigning the ions in the cells of the damaged area; it also improves circulation and therefore oxygen delivery, helping speed the healing process. Regular users say it can reduce pain, swelling and muscle tightness to relieve injuries. Again, it is possible to use this treatment on yourself, as the machines are available either to buy or hire.

Simple self-help

Runners are used to being active and in control of their bodies, so injuries are always frustrating, especially when treatments involve so much trial and error. However, keeping a positive outlook can really help with your recovery, so keep these strategies in mind during any lay-off:

• Remember that the vast majority of runners recover fully from their injuries, and many are even better runners after the break

• Do something positive to help your recovery each day, whether it is a stretch, massage or icing your injury

• Do some activity every day: walking and swimming are usually safe for injured runners

• See your time off as a chance to meet up with non-running friends and have fun

• Set yourself goals in other areas of your life, so you don't feel bad about missing any running targets

Below: Staying positive by meeting up with friends helps you recover from injury faster.

Hypnotherapy

For many people, the idea of being hypnotized still conjures up images of someone swinging a watch in front of your face. However modern hypnotherapy is more a method of programming your brain through visualizations and affirmations. This may help with sports performance but can also be useful for the treatment of injuries. Research has shown that athletes hold on to the memory of pain from an injury long after the physical

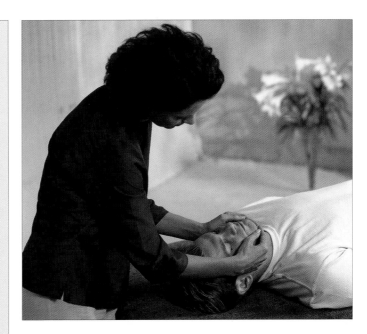

damage has disappeared. Hypnotherapy can use visualization of a positive outcome to overcome stress or anxiety about the injury, which may be at the root of residual pain.

SCENAR therapy

This treatment was originally developed in the former USSR to treat injury and illness on its space programme. Later it was used by the Soviet Olympic team, and is still used by many sports-people to treat injuries. SCENAR involves the stimulation of nerves using electrical currents via a small, handheld machine, operated by a health professional who will have trained specifically to use the equipment. The SCENAR (Self-Controlled Energo Neuro Adaptive Regulation) machine is used first to test nervous response and identify problem areas, and then to treat them. The theory behind it is that it 'reminds' the body of the original injury, stimulating the healing response – though the newer the injury, the quicker and more effective it is said

Right: You can use self-hypnosis and visualization to help your own recovery.

Above: Reiki practitioners are able to channel the body's life energy to help banish aches and pains.

to be. Where it is effective, just two or three treatments are enough to resolve the injury.

Reflexology

Though it is thought to have origins dating back thousands of years, reflexology as it is practised today was popularized in the early 20th century. The therapist applies pressure to different zones on the feet (and sometimes hands) which are said to correspond to other parts of the body. Its use for treating sports injuries is mainly for pain relief, and it should be used in conjunction with other forms of treatment.

Running for Life

Running is a flexible sport. Not only can you adapt it to your changing circumstances, but it can help with challenging life stages. To make the most of what running can offer you at these times, be creative with the way you train.

It's easy to see why elite athletes run so well: all they have to do is train and recover, and they have teams of experts on hand to help with any changes that take place over time, such as having children, getting injured or just growing older. For the rest of us, exercise has to fit in around changing lifestyles, family and career. When your life alters the way you train, you may need to adjust your goals and expectations for running accordingly, but in return, running will help you cope with stressful changes, both physical and emotional.

When life becomes busy, running is often the first thing you drop. But staying physically fit helps you cope with pressure, changes and stress and running is known to benefit your mental wellbeing too. Make time for even a short run no matter what else is going on in your life,

Below: Having a baby does not have to mean the end of your running career – with the right kit you can run together.

and you'll feel stronger, calmer and better able to tackle some of these difficult periods.

Pregnancy

The days of doctors advising pregnant women to take things easy are long gone. Pregnancy is not the time to start running from scratch, but if you already run then you can carry on as long as your body will let you. Running can help alleviate many of the common, unpleasant symptoms of pregnancy, including mood swings, excessive weight gain and poor sleep. Staying fit through your pregnancy will also leave you stronger for labour when the time comes.

If you plan to run throughout pregnancy, you should tell your doctor or midwife from the outset – they will be able to advise you on how best to adapt your training. Drop intense training such as long runs and speedwork, and have a session with a personal trainer to adapt your strength and flexibility work. During the last half of

Above: It's safe to run at low intensity throughout your pregnancy.

pregnancy, your body produces a substance called relaxin, which makes your joints more flexible – this enables your pelvis to stretch during birth, but also leaves you susceptible to injury.

Pregnant runners' quick tips
- Try to keep your heart rate low (below 140 bpm) and your body temperature down
- Wear two sports bras for extra support and comfort
- Don't try to start or increase running during pregnancy
- After giving birth, don't try abdominal exercises until your rectus abdominis muscle has closed up again (it will separate down the middle of your stomach during pregnancy)
- Practise pelvic floor exercises regularly – stress incontinence is very common after giving birth and may be worsened by running

After giving birth, if there are no complications you can start low-intensity training within days if you feel comfortable. Wait until you can run pain free, and start at a low intensity. Don't try to jump back in to your pre-pregnancy training and don't try to lose weight too quickly – if you are breastfeeding, you will need the extra calories to produce milk. Once you begin training again you may be pleasantly surprised: pregnancy gives your cardiovascular system extra training, your pain threshold is higher and many women find they are more confident. As a result, you may find yourself a quicker runner.

Work stress

While runners who have successful work lives are often also very successful sportspeople, it is easy to underestimate the impact a busy career has on your ability to run well. Of course, lack of time is the main problem, but work stress also impacts on your general health through the release of hormones, lowering your immunity and making you feel too tired to run well.

Although running is an excellent way to cope with busy periods at work, you may need to revise the way you train. If you know you are facing a hectic few weeks, avoid

---

Veterans' quick tips
• Run on softer surfaces, which are easier on your joints
• Stay motivated by switching distances, so that you are not chasing 20-year-old best times
• If you take part in races, view your results in the context of your age category. Check your times against the World Association of Veteran Athletes (WAVA) age-grading tables
• In training, focus more on flexibility as this will naturally decline, and will affect your speed
• Allow yourself more time to recover from hard runs

setting ambitious running goals that will just put you under more pressure. Instead, dedicate short blocks of time (30–45 minutes) on set days of the week for running, leave your watch (and phone!) at home and just enjoy the break. Set these appointments in stone as you would an important work meeting; you may not feel you have the time to run, but remember that it will most likely lead to a more productive day, as well as an easier return to more structured training when your busy spell is over.

Ageing

Slowing down is of course an inevitable part of growing older and you will find that running becomes harder from your mid-30s onward. However, as long as you are prepared to change the way you train and race, you can still enjoy running and, if anything, the benefits can be even greater as you age.

Regular exercise will help you to fend off many age-related problems including high blood pressure, weight gain, loss of mobility and muscle tone, loss of bone density, and slowed metabolism. Runners also lose their VO2 max (the rate at which the body can use oxygen) around 50 per cent slower than non-runners – which means that you will stay fitter for longer.

Above: Keep running as you grow older and you could avoid many age-related health problems.

However, no amount of training will enable you to completely out-run the ageing process. All of the processes listed above will still continue to take place, albeit at a much slower rate than if you were not running or doing any exercise at all. The consequence of ageing is that you will run slower for the same amount of effort, and accepting this fact is key to continuing to enjoy running. You may also find that you need more recovery time between hard runs, and that you are much more susceptible to injury. To avoid this, run less often and introduce some cross-training to reduce the impact on your body.

On the days that you do run, you will need to work hard to maintain your fitness, so aim for about three or four good quality sessions per week. Include at least one session of short, sharp speedwork to help maintain mobility in your joints, and be more diligent than ever about stretching out your muscles after you run. Weight training is also more important, as it helps to counteract loss of muscle mass and keeps your bones strong. Try to aim for about two sessions of weight training per week.

High flyers' quick tips
• Save time and stress by making your run part of your commute, taking you away from the hassles of road rage and public transport failures
• Watch that your diet doesn't start to fall apart when you are working long hours. Take raw vegetables and fruit to snack on and make sure you don't miss meals
• Think about changing your goals – for example, instead of going for a personal best at a marathon, aim to pace a first-timer
• Make sure that you do not scrimp on your sleep, as it will impair your recovery from running as well as your ability to work efficiently

Children's Running

Almost as soon as a child can walk, he or she starts trying to run. With childhood obesity rates increasing, it is more important than ever to encourage children to engage in physical activity, and you may even find you have a champion in the making!

By the time they reach school age, many children have lost a lot of their initial energy, but if you show an interest in keeping your child active you can make the most of his natural urge to run around. That doesn't mean your child should be doing speed drills every morning, but by encouraging energetic play you can instill a lifelong love of exercise for the sake of it – and perhaps nurture a talent for formal athletics later in life. Here's how to involve your child in your sport from preschool to early adulthood. Remember, of course, that children have their own special needs, and that eventually they may not share your passion for running.

Preschool children
From when they learn to walk until the age of five, children should not do any structured running at all. They are still developing quickly, and have undeveloped vision, gait and co-ordination, so it is better to encourage active play rather than running. Luckily this comes naturally to most preschool children; all you need to do is provide a safe, ideally outdoor, environment for them to play in.

Above: As a child's age reaches double figures, she can train to run a mile at a time, but should not train too hard.

Below: Preschool children should be encouraged to play actively rather than run seriously.

Age 6 to 11
Children should have developed a more controlled running motion by this age, but their natural tendency is still to run in short, fast bursts. They may have trouble running efficiently, as their limbs are out of proportion to their muscle mass. Incorporate running into physical games, and include ball skills to improve co-ordination. Think in terms of time spent on activity (aim for 20 to 30 minutes, three to five times per week) rather than distance covered.

As children near the end of middle school, their growth may begin to accelerate. This can lead to growing pains, and active children may suffer from a condition called Osgood-Schlatter syndrome. This causes sharp pain just underneath the kneecap, and is a result of strain being placed

---

Keeping cool

Children are more prone to overheating (and to cooling too quickly) than adults. They are not as efficient at sweating, and have a greater skin surface to body weight ratio, which means they pick up and lose heat very quickly. Ensure they train in lots of thin layers that can be removed or put back on quickly, and don't allow children to train during the hottest part of the day. It is also important to ensure that they drink plenty of fluids, as many children will forget to do so themselves.

on the soft growth plate at the end of the leg bone just below the knee. The condition disappears once the child is fully grown but should not be ignored or run through. In fact, it is not advisable for children to try to run through any pain since they may be causing damage that may last into adulthood. Providing the child has no problems, they can start to run over longer distances (up to a mile) to learn endurance.

Age 12 to 16
As children grow into teenagers their training can become more focused. This is a good age to start competing over short distances (up to 5K), and is often when running talent becomes more obvious. Physically they may still have problems caused by their rapid development. Teenagers' limbs grow so quickly that they can seem clumsy, as the brain struggles to keep up, resulting in poor spatial awareness. It is a good idea to teach young runners good form at this age. Teenage girls need to become used to training through their menstrual cycle and with increased

Right: From age 12 upward, more structured training sessions can be introduced if the child wishes.

body fat, which will slow them down. At the same time it is important that they do not become concerned with keeping their body fat at a low level, as this will interrupt menstruation (as well as potentially leading to longer term body-image problems). For both sexes, bones are still developing and stress fractures are a risk; counter this by training on soft surfaces wherever possible.

In their mid to late teens, most children can cope with training sessions almost as intense as adults. However, it is still a good idea to maintain interest in other sports both to provide respite from the impact of running and to help the young athletes explore which activities they enjoy most.

Age 16 to 18
Most children are almost fully grown by this age and are able to cope with high mileage training. However, races should still be kept short and

varied – up to 10K on cross-country courses, tracks and roads. As endurance does not develop until the mid to late 20s, it makes sense to concentrate on faster events at this stage.

Fussy eaters

Active children need to eat more than those who exercise less, but resist the temptation to calorie count for your child (they should definitely not become preoccupied with food). Instead try to pay attention to their appetite and energy levels, which should indicate whether they are eating enough. Don't allow your children to eat extra junk food to make up for training. Instead, ensure they have extra protein in their diet (research suggests 1.1 to 1.2g per kg body weight per day is the right amount for active children) for growth and repair, as well as extra calcium for growing bones and plenty of different vitamins to help them metabolize food.

Right: Young children enjoy being active, so find open, safe environments for them to run around in.

STARTING EVENTS

The word 'race' may bring you out in a cold sweat,
but competing adds a new level to your sport, no matter
where you finish. Your training will have a new focus,
and you will find motivation in trying to achieve more
from each run. The excitement, camaraderie and sense
of personal triumph of your first race will stay with you
forever. In this chapter you will find out how to race and
why you should do it, and there are examples of the
best beginner-friendly races running has to offer.

*Above: Once you start taking part in larger events you will soon see that running really
is for anyone and everyone.*
Left: The New York City Marathon, the original 'people's race', is a great event for first-timers.

Why Run an Event?

Although the idea of pinning on a race number and pitting yourself against others may seem daunting at first, once you have run in a race you will never look back. Taking part in organized events is a great way to make contact with the wider running community.

Left: Enter a race with a big field, and you'll see that running is a very inclusive sport.

If you are feeling nervous about filling in your first race entry, take a look at some of the great reasons to race:

More motivation
Running your first complete, non-stop mile gives you an incredible high. After a few months, however, covering the same route over and over again, that mile starts to feel like a chore. Entering a race gives you renewed focus and a reason to vary your training – in fact it might be when you start to think about training, rather than simply going for a quick jog.

Fitter and faster
Seeing the date of your race marked on the calendar will spur you on to think about running to a structured plan for the first time (you will find examples for the most popular distances in this chapter). This target alone is enough to transform your fitness, as the satisfaction of ticking off each session makes you push yourself harder and run faster than you thought possible. You will rediscover that 'first mile' feeling in no time.

Confidence
Many new runners don't even think of themselves as runners. They tell friends and family that they are just jogging or plodding around the block. As soon as you reach the start line of your first race, however, you will definitely know that you are a runner. If your training has gone to plan, you will exceed your own expectations as the atmosphere of the race and adrenaline rush boost your

performance. You will have achieved something millions of people never have the courage to experience.

Self-discovery
Every run tells you that you are a determined, disciplined person, but in a race you might shock yourself with your own strengths. Your ability to dig deep and push on, whether you are sprinting for the end of a 5K or pulling yourself through the 18th mile of a marathon, is something you will always be able to call on in difficult situations.

Community
Running can sometimes be a lonely sport. In fact many beginners choose to run alone, worrying that they will feel too embarrassed if they run with others or that they won't be

Below: Racing makes you push yourself to your limits and helps you learn about yourself.

Above: Having a race to focus on helps you train harder and become fitter than ever.

able to keep up. Take a look around you at the start of any race – especially those with big fields – and you will see that the running community really does embrace people of all ages, shapes and sizes. Racing is a great way to meet other runners in your area, to chat about trainers, niggling aches and routes for the first time with people who understand, and to experience the support and camaraderie of other runners. It is also a good opportunity to involve your friends and family in your new interest; bring them along to cheer you on and perhaps it may even inspire them to join you next time.

Rewards

Research has shown that people who compete for intrinsic rewards (for example, to build their confidence or achieve an ambition) do much better than those who compete for extrinsic rewards (perhaps to please their friends). However, you can use these external rewards to help spur you on by ensuring they mean a lot to you. Use races as a way of seeing places you have always wanted to explore, or to raise money for a charity close to your heart; race for a medal to make up for missing out at school sports days.

Below: The more people there are taking place in a race, the less likely you are to finish in last place!

Beat the excuses

'I'm not competitive' Racing is not necessarily about competing against other runners, but about pushing yourself harder. Even the most mild-mannered jogger finds it hard to resist a sprint for the finish!

'Racing is too stressful' Take care of the logistics, and you can think of racing as just a chance to run in new surroundings with a few hundred like-minded companions. Relax!

'I can't afford to race' Big events run by professional organizers can be costly, but choose a smaller, local charity event and you are sure to get value for money. Keep an eye on your local paper or library noticeboard for events.

'I'm scared I'll finish last'
It is surprisingly difficult to finish in last place, especially in bigger races. Rest assured that even if you are last over the line, you will still have achieved more than most people just by completing a race – and there will still be plenty of cheering spectators waiting at the finish line to help you celebrate.

Choosing your Event

The image of thousands of people having a carnival in the London or New York City Marathon is enough to get thousands more people running. When considering your first race, a marathon may seem the obvious choice, but it is worth starting small and working your way up.

There are several factors to consider when choosing your first event. The big public events covered by the media have tens of thousands of finishers, and these are often good choices for first-time racers. Lots of runners (and media coverage) means there will be lots of supporters along the route, and the course is usually accessible to spectators so your friends and family can be there. As a participant you are far less likely to be left alone at any stage of the route as the field never truly spreads out. Facilities and organization are almost guaranteed to be

Below: If you want to use a race to raise money for charity, a well-known event might work best.

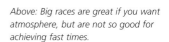

Above: Big races are great if you want atmosphere, but are not so good for achieving fast times.

good in a big race, and the day feels more like an event than a race. This is not to say that smaller races should be avoided. Ask around local running clubs to find good, beginner-friendly races. If you are anxious about coming last, check last year's final finisher time and ask the organizer if there is a cut-off point. It is a good idea to find a race in a park or town centre where there are always crowds to cheer you on; rural races are beautiful but can be lonely.

Finding inspiration

It is also important to consider your motives for running the race. You may have been inspired to race by the sight of club runners tearing through your local 10K, but if a fast time is not your goal then look around

Most popular race distances					
Event	Distance	Build-up	Minimum training (beginners)	Time to complete	Frequency and season
5K	5km (3 miles)	6–12 weeks	3 walk/run sessions per week; one session at least 40 mins duration	25–40 mins	Traditionally a summer event; 5K weekly series run all year round
10K	10km (6.2 miles)	2–4 months	3 sessions per week; one session at least 1 hour long	40 mins to 1hr15	Take place most weeks of the year; more common in summer
Half-marathon	21km (13 miles)	4–6 months	3–4 sessions per week, running up to 90 mins at once	1hr35 to 3hrs	Often combined with big marathons; or one month before big marathons
Marathon	42km (26.2 miles)	1 year	3–5 sessions per week; long runs up to 3 hours plus one faster session	3hrs30 to 6+ hours	Take place all year round, but with spring and autumn peaks

Above: Smaller races can be good build-up events for your main target race.

at other events. On the other hand, if you know you want to run fast, then a fun run with 2,000 joggers is not the best place to bag a personal best. If you would like to raise money for charity, find an event your friends and family will have heard of – they will be more inclined to support you. Think about what you would like to get from the day: do you want a medal for your efforts? Would you like to meet other runners over cake or a beer afterward? Do you want an event your whole family can take part in? Race organizers will be able to provide all the information about what is on offer.

Race distances

It is sensible for beginners to start their racing career with a short race, but many people do dive in with a half-marathon or even a marathon. The most popular race distances are listed in the table.

Below: Research your chosen race so you know what the terrain and crowd will be like.

Know your field

Make sure you know what kind of event you are turning up to.

Road races: the most popular races are run on roads or tarmac, and these are usually the easiest races for beginners.

Track races: usually much faster than road races and may not always be open to the general public; it is important that you check before you go. Traditionally take place during the summer.

Cross-country races: avoiding footpaths, cross-country races traditionally take place during the winter months and are muddy, hilly and very tough. The start is often very fast, which can sometimes be intimidating for beginners.

Trail races: more laid-back than cross-country, these races are a great way to get back to nature and explore forests, nature reserves and parks on soft, forgiving ground. Not good for fast times.

Fell races: a specialist category for brave runners. Fell racers run up and down fells or mountains. The distance is often shorter than a road race but the terrain is far more difficult.

Great Beginnings

There are thousands of races on offer when you are ready for your first event. These are some of the biggest, brightest and friendliest, with great crowds, fun costumes and runners of all shapes and sizes taking part.

Race for the Cure, nationwide, USA; Race for Life, nationwide, UK
Distance: 5K
Date: May–July
Finish times: Not recorded; from 20 minutes to more than 1 hour

It is impossible to overstate the effect that these events have had on the whole running community, as well as in terms of charity fundraising. The charity Susan G. Komen for the Cure was set up in 1982 by Nancy G. Brinker, who promised her dying sister Susan Komen that she would fight to end breast cancer. The first Race for the Cure took place in Dallas, Texas, the following year, with just 800 runners. Now it is the biggest fundraising series in the world, with well over one million people running in the events every year. The charity's flagship event, the National Race for the Cure in Washington DC, is the world's biggest

5K run: more than 15,000 people took part in 2015.

Although a much younger event, Cancer Research UK's Race for Life series has had as big an impact on women in the UK. Since the first event in 1994, more than two million women have taken part, with around 750,000 in 2007 alone taking part in nearly 300 events. In 2006, it set a new Guinness World Record for the biggest simultaneous stretch with 115,000 women performing identical stretches at 24 Race for Life events.

These events have inspired millions of women to take up running, in a welcoming environment. You can walk, race, or walk and run the 5K distance, and for most women involved, it is the first step toward a happy lifetime of running. If traditional 'serious' races intimidate you, try one of these.
ww5.komen.org;
raceforlife.cancerresearchuk.org

Above: The Race for the Cure series includes the world's biggest 5K, in Washington DC.

Above: The UK's Race for Life raises money for cancer research charities.

Great Santa Race, Las Vegas, USA; Santa Dash, Liverpool, UK

Distance: 5K

Date: December

Finish times: Not recorded; approx 18 minutes to 1 hour

The best way to ensure you don't take your first event too seriously is to dress up, but you are unlikely to stand out from the crowd at these 5K races. Competitors must wear the Santa suit provided, though you can customize it if you prefer. There are dozens of Santa runs around the world, but the Great Santa Race in Las Vegas and the Santa Dash in Liverpool are the biggest and enjoy a friendly rivalry, each aiming to set a record for the most Santas in one place. In 2013, Las Vegas retained the world record with over 11,000 Santas taking part, but competition is hotting up, with new races in Italy and Australia joining the race.

Both the Las Vegas and Liverpool events are great for first timers: the city-centre routes pass famous landmarks (admittedly very different), from the bright lights of Vegas to the historic waterfront

and architecture of Liverpool. These events enjoy plenty of crowd support, and of course, the Christmas spirit imbues a party atmosphere. Both are run to benefit local charities.

Las Vegas: opportunityvillage.enmotive.com
Liverpool: www.runliverpool.org.uk

Above: The Liverpool Santa Dash runs through the city centre and past its famous waterfront.

Below: Friendly competition between Santa races keeps thousands of Santas returning to Las Vegas each year.

Men's Health Forum Scotland 10K, Glasgow, UK

Date: June

Finish times: 32 minutes to 2 hours

Despite the huge success of women-only races, it has been thought that men would not be attracted to single-sex events in the same way, but the fast-growing popularity of this 10K shows this might not be true. The event is part of a countrywide programme of jogging for health in Scotland which, so far, has been hugely successful. Scotland's men are among the least healthy in Europe but that is set to change. The first MHFS 10K in 2006 had 500 runners; that increased to 2,000 the next year and the organizers hope for 5,000 in future events. The race does as much to challenge stereotypes about Glasgow as it does for the image of Scottish men, running through beautiful (and undulating) Bellahouston and Pollock parks. It is run on Father's Day every year, so crowds of proud family and friends line the route.
www.mhfs.org.uk

Below: The MHFS 10K aims to replicate the success of women-only events in encouraging new runners.

ING Bay to Breakers 12K, San Francisco, California, USA

Date: May

Finish times: 33 minutes 42 secs (record) to 4 hours

The world's biggest road race is also one of the oldest, having started in 1912 as the Cross City Race, a bid to raise morale in San Francisco following a devastating earthquake six years earlier. Today about 50,000 people take part every year, from international athletes to walkers, to costumed fun runners. There is even a separate 'centipedes' class:

Above: The Bay to Breakers race has some spectacular views, as well as some spectacular costumes.

groups of 13 runners who must have a set of feelers at the front and a stinger at the back. Runners also have to look out for the 'spawning salmon', who run from the finish to the start through the crowds. Bands line the route from the Embarcadero through Golden Gate Park to the ocean and although it is a hilly course, no one seems to mind.
www.ingbaytobreakers.com

BUPA Great North Run, Newcastle, UK

Date: September

Finish times: 59 minutes 37 secs to 4+ hours

The Great North Run is a product of Britain's first running boom, and began in 1981. The race's founder, the Olympic 10,000m runner Brendan Foster, was inspired by running the Round the Bays race in New Zealand two years earlier. From 12,000 runners in that first event, it has become the biggest half-marathon in the world with more than 35,000 finishers each year. The fast course attracts top athletes and first-time runners alike, and now sells out many months in advance. The course begins just outside the city centre, with back runners taking 20 minutes just to reach the start line, before heading through cheering crowds in Newcastle itself. Running over the famous Tyne Bridge about a mile into the run is a great moment. The locals are rightly proud of this event and turn out in their thousands to support it, usually offering drinks and snacks to runners from their homes in the last few miles of the race. The last mile along the seafront is thronged with cheering spectators to spur you on to a strong finish. www.greatrun.org

Below: The start of the 500 Festival Mini Marathon, which takes runners over the same course as the famous Indy 500.

Above: Athlete Kara Goucher of the USA wins the Great North Run in Newcastle, England, 2007.

OneAmerica 500 Festival Mini Marathon, Indianapolis Motor Speedway, USA

Date: May

Finish times: 1:02:53 to 3:30+

Ever dreamed of zooming round the famous Indianapolis Motor Speedway, home to the Indy 500? This family-friendly event can make that dream come true. The half-marathon started in 1977 and two years later officially became part of the 500 Festival. It's now America's biggest half, with about 35,000 runners. In 2008, for the first time in the event's history, the finish was a dead heat, with Kenyan runners Lamech Mokono and Valentine Orare crossing the line neck-and-neck. Farther back in the field, the atmosphere is relaxed and support is great, with pre- and post-race parties including live music and food. www.500festival.com

Virgin Money London Marathon, London, UK

Date: April

Finish times: 2:07 to several days

Inspired by the New York City Marathon, the London Marathon first took place in March 1981 with 6,255 finishers. Now it is one of the biggest – and most oversubscribed – running events in the world, with 125,000 applicants competing for some 45,000 places, of which around 38,000 finish the race. The course has changed several times over the years, and now starts in Greenwich, south-east London, running through some of the capital's most deprived areas during the first half, where thousands of Londoners line the street to cheer runners on (many from pubs along the roadside). The second half of the race shows the other side of the city, crossing over Tower Bridge, heading

Above: The Mall outside Buckingham Palace provides an inspiring home straight for the London Marathon.

out to the skyscrapers of Docklands, then running back along the Embankment, past the Houses of Parliament to the finish on the Mall outside Buckingham Palace. Like most big city marathons, the front end of the race sees fierce athletic competition and world records set, but the race is most famous for the thousands of 'fun runners' competing against themselves, running in fancy dress, and raising millions of pounds for charity. In any case you are unlikely to be last, as one man has dedicated his marathon efforts to just that: Lloyd Scott has run the marathon in a suit of armour, and dressed as Indiana Jones pulling a 136kg 'boulder'. In one attempt, during which he wore an antique diving suit, Scott took more than eight days to complete the course.
www.virginmoneylondonmarathon.com

Left: Crossing Tower Bridge over the River Thames tells runners they are almost at the halfway point.

TCS New York City Marathon, New York, USA

Date: November
Finish times: 2:09 to 10 hours

The original 'people's marathon' began in 1970 but really became a mass race four years later, when the course was redesigned to take in all five boroughs of New York City. Starting on Staten Island, runners cross the Verazzano Narrows Bridge and head on through Brooklyn and on to Manhattan, on a route that includes stunning views of the Empire State Building and the Chrysler Building. Throughout, the community spirit and support of all the diverse ethnic groups that make up the city's population show visitors what makes New York so special, and the finish in Central Park, with the cheers of thousands of spectators, stays with runners forever. In 2001, just weeks after the 9/11 terror attacks, the race was

Below: New York City Marathon runners enjoy crossing the famous Verazzano Narrows Bridge.

Above: American Tour de France cyclist Lance Armstrong (centre) joined the first-timers in 2006.

a poignant testament to the city's indomitable character. Like the London Marathon, the race is hugely oversubscribed, and more than 700,000 people have completed the race over the years. The front of the race has seen some dramatic finishes, including a sprint between the Kenyan Susan Chepkemei and the women's world record holder Paula Radcliffe in 2004, which marked Radcliffe's triumphant return to form after dropping out of the Olympic marathon in Athens that year. Run this race and you will be in the company of celebrity runners too: in 2006, the cyclist Lance Armstrong made his marathon debut here in a very respectable 2:59:36. It is a more challenging course than London, with the bridge crossings providing hills that can seem like mountains after miles of running, but being part of the event that introduced running to millions of people around the world makes the pain worthwhile.
www.tcsnycmarathon.org

5K Event: Walk/Run Schedule

Five kilometres is an unimaginable distance for most of us when we first start running. But you will be amazed how easy it is to reach this milestone with a simple, structured training plan that will gently push your fitness to a new level.

Time target: 30 to 40 minutes
Starting point: Four 30-minute walk/run sessions per week for at least six weeks

You may feel intimidated before competing in your first 5K event, imagining hundreds of lithe, Lycra-clad runners tearing around the course at top speed. The reality is that 5K is the most beginner-friendly distance, and thousands of people choose to walk all the way round, especially in the larger events such as Race for the Cure and Race for Life. Even for more experienced runners, there are advantages to retaining walk breaks through your first race. It is a good way to break up the distance, to pace yourself, stretch out your body and give your legs a rest from the impact of running. Taking walk breaks doesn't necessarily mean a slow time, either – you can run as fast as you feel comfortable in the run sections, and you may find you finish quicker overall since you are less likely to tire.

Sessions

Walk/run pyramids. Speed sessions are not just for fast or non-stop runners. Picking up your pace during the run segments of your session helps to keep things interesting as well as improving your fitness. Try running a pyramid session: after a 2-minute warm-up, complete five sets of 4 minutes run, 2 minutes walk. Run the second run segment slightly faster than the first, and the third as fast as you can maintain for 4 minutes; the fourth slower again, and the fifth back at your easy pace. End with a 5-minute cool-down walk.

Event practice. As you approach your 5K, find out as much as you can about the practicalities: whether there will be water on the course, what time of day it starts, and the precise route of the run. Then try to have a dress rehearsal, going over the route at your planned pace, practising drinking every 15 minutes, and working out the best time to eat beforehand. This will help you to relax on the day of the event.

Long walks. Regular, long walking sessions are the best way to practise your strong walking technique for the event. We take walking for granted but it can be incredibly tiring, which leads to a drop in posture and pace. Use your once-a-week long walk sessions to think about walking briskly and with good form – it may help to set an alarm on your watch every

Left: Stay upright and strong during your weekly long walk sessions to make the most of them.

5K event: walk/run schedule

	Session one	Session two	Session three	Session four
Week one	Walk 10 mins; run 2 mins/walk 2 mins x 5; Walk 5 mins	Cross-train, 30 mins	As session one	Walk 30 mins at a brisk pace
Week two	Walk 10 mins; run 2 mins/walk 2 mins x 5; walk 5 mins	Cross-train, 30 mins	Walk 10 mins; run 3 mins/walk 1 min x 5; walk 5 mins	Walk 35 mins at a brisk pace
Week three	Walk 10 mins; run 3 mins/walk 1 min x 5; walk 5 mins	Cross-train, 30 mins	Pyramid session with run 3 mins/walk 1 min x 5	Walk 40 mins at a brisk pace
Week four	Walk 10 mins; run 4 mins/walk 1 min x 5	Cross-train, 30 mins	Pyramid session with run 4 mins/walk 2 mins x 5	Walk 45 mins at a brisk pace
Week five	Walk 10 mins; run 5 mins/walk 1 min x 4	Rest	Pyramid session with run 4 mins/walk 1 min x 5	Walk 40 mins at a brisk pace
Week six	Walk 5 mins; Run 5 mins/walk 1 min x 4	Cross-train, 30 mins	Pyramid session with run 5 mins/walk 1 min x 4	Event practice (dress rehearsal with drinks, on course if possible)
Week seven	Walk 1 min/run 5 mins x 6	Cross-train, 30 mins	Pyramid session with run 5 mins/walk 1 min x 5	Walk 40 mins at a brisk pace
Week eight	Walk 1 min/run 5 mins x 6	Rest	Walk 1 min/run 5 mins x 3	5K race

10 minutes as a reminder to check your posture. Don't think of it as a walk but as a fat-burning and all-over conditioning session.

Race day

If you are entering a 5K with a big field, you will need to think about the people around you as you change pace, especially if you are with a large group, as some races can be very crowded. At the start of the race, mention to those around you that you are planning to run for five minutes then walk for one, and if you are part of a group, call out, 'Walk!' or 'Run!' as you switch pace, to warn the crowds around you. Try to step smoothly from walk to run so that you don't cause any hold-ups.

Right: On the day of your first race, although it may be difficult, try to stay relaxed and stick to your walk/run plan.

5K Event: Intermediate Schedule

Running or walk/running regularly should have given you confidence in your ability to build your own fitness. So why not put what you have learned to good use and test yourself with a more challenging intermediate routine.

Time target: 25 to 35 minutes
Starting point: Four 20-minute runs a week for at least six weeks

If you are already able to run 5km comfortably without stopping, then entering a 5K event is likely to be more about testing yourself and meeting other runners than it is about completing the distance. There should be no room for complacency, however. Although relatively short, this is one of the most difficult race distances to get right, as it can be very tempting to sprint from the start, thinking you don't have far to run. This schedule should help you to get round the course comfortably and to the best of your abilities.

Sessions
Long intervals. To run a successful 5K, you need to learn to run fast for long periods of time. The best way to do this is to add threshold runs to your schedule, but you can start by simply running some long, fast intervals. The first interval of each set should feel fast but comfortable, so that by the last interval you are tired but still able to run at the same speed. It takes practice to get these intervals right, so don't be scared of them – you can always adjust your pace.

Long runs. When you are competing in a 5K event and aiming to run all the way round, the distance itself should not hold any fear for you. To make

Above: Practise for race day while you're training, running on the same route if possible.

sure you reach the start line feeling confident, once a week you should run 5km or farther in training, so that when the day of your event finally arrives, the distance will seem like nothing.

Race day practice. If you can, find the route of your chosen event and jog round it beforehand. Otherwise, practise running as precise a 5K as you can, dressed in your race-day kit and eating and drinking as you plan to do on the big day. Since you are not taking any walk breaks, it is especially important to work out when to eat,

5K event: intermediate schedule

	Session one	Session two	Session three	Session four
Week one	Run 20 mins	Run 25 mins	Run 20 mins	Run 30 mins
Week two	Run 20 mins	Warm-up 5 mins; 2 x 5 mins fast, 2 mins slow; cool-down 5 mins	Cross-train 30 mins	Run 30 mins
Week three	Run 25 mins	Warm-up 5 mins; 2 x 5 mins fast, 2 mins slow; cool-down 5 mins	Cross-train 30 mins	Run 35 mins
Week four	Run 25 mins	Warm-up 5 mins; 3 x 5 mins fast, 2 mins slow; cool-down 5 mins	Cross-train 30 mins with harder intervals	Run 40 mins
Week five	Run 25 mins	Warm-up 5 mins; 2 x 8 mins fast, 3 mins slow; cool-down 5 mins	Cross-train 30 mins with harder intervals	Run 45 mins/ Race day practice
Week six	Run 25 mins	Warm-up 5 mins; 2 x 8 mins fast, 3 mins slow; cool-down 5 mins	Cross-train 30 mins with harder intervals	Run 50 mins/ Race day practice
Week seven	Run 25 mins	Warm-up 5 mins; 3 x 6 mins fast, 2 mins slow; cool-down 5 mins	Cross-train 30 mins with harder intervals	Run 45 mins
Week eight	Run 25 mins	Warm-up 5 mins; 15 mins faster pace; cool-down 5 mins	Rest	5K event

as your risk of indigestion and cramp are higher the faster you go. Practise taking caffeine before you run, too – it could prove a big help.

Cross-training. When you start running, cross-training can help to build fitness, but as you move on you can use non-running sessions to help build your speed and stamina. Try making your cross-training sessions harder by increasing the resistance for 5 or 10 minutes. Alternatively, use the time to try yoga or Pilates classes, which will increase your flexibility and strength, helping you to stay injury free up to race day.

Warm-ups and cool-downs. If you have just moved up from walk/run training, the warm-up and cool-down parts of your hard sessions are really important as you won't have the walk sections to cushion your body. Get carried away

Right: Completing long runs in your training will make sure you're comfortable over the whole 5K distance when it comes to the event.

running fast from a standstill, and you could end up unable to complete your intervals or, worse still, injured. The cool-down is very important to loosen up your muscles and help you recover from the

hard work you've just done. Your warm-up and cool-down jogs should be very easy; you should almost feel that you're running too slowly, and you should be able to hold a conversation easily.

10K Event: Walk/Run Schedule

Conquering a 10K is something you can really be proud of. It takes real dedication to teach your body to keep going for an hour or more, but building up that strength will be worth it. It's a great base for tackling longer events and a popular distance in its own right.

Time target: 1 hour to 1:15
Starting point: Four 30-minute walk/run sessions a week for at least eight weeks

Whether you choose to take part in a 10K event as your first race or as a step up from the shorter 5K, the longer distance can feel extremely daunting, especially when you see the faster runners zipping around the course in 35 minutes or even less.

For a recreational walk/run participant, a 10K race is likely to take at least an hour, so it becomes more of an endurance than a speed event. The key factor in your training for this type of event is to concentrate on building up your overall strength and fitness so that you can finish strongly and try to enjoy the race all the way round – soon those 10 kilometres (6 miles) won't seem like such a big deal after all.

Sessions

Hill walking. Just as hill running sessions are very beneficial for building up strength, walking up hills is also a good idea if you plan to spend a significant proportion of your 10K event walking. Hill walking will help to improve your overall strength, but its main purpose in your event preparation is to help you walk more powerfully, using your whole body, instead of slumping along between runs. As in hill running sessions, pump your arms to power up the hill. Try not to take long strides as they are less efficient and you

Above: Use your regular training sessions to find the walk/run ratio that will work best for you.

		10K event: walk/run schedule		
	Session one	**Session two**	**Session three**	**Session four**
Week one	4 mins run/ 2 mins walk x 5	4 mins run/2 mins walk x 2; 10 mins hill walking; 4 mins run/2 mins walk	4 mins run/2 mins walk x 4	Walk/run 35 mins
Week two	4 mins run/ 2 mins walk x 5	Walk/run fartlek, 20 mins	Cross-train, 30 mins	Walk/run 40 mins
Week three	5 mins run/ 1 min walk x 5	4 mins run/2 mins walk x 2; 10 mins hill walking; 4 mins run/2 mins walk	5 mins run/1 min walk x 5	Walk/run 45 mins
Week four	5 mins run/ 1 min walk x 6	Walk/run fartlek, 25 mins	Cross-train, 30 mins	Walk/run 50 mins
Week five	5 mins run/ 1 min walk x 6	5 mins run/1 min walk x 2; 15 mins hill walking; 5 mins run, 1 min walk	5 mins run/1 min walk x 5	Walk/run 1hr
Week six	5 mins run/ 1 min walk x 6	Walk/run fartlek 30 mins	Cross-train, 30 mins	Walk/run 1hr
Week seven	5 mins run/ 1 min walk x 7	5 mins run/1 min walk x 2; 20 mins hill walking; 5 mins run, 1 min walk	Cross-train, 35 mins	Walk/run 1hr15 mins
Week eight	5 mins run/ 1 min walk x 6	Walk/run fartlek, 30 mins	Cross-train, 30 mins	10K event

will tire easily. When you reach the top, jog down gently and walk back up again until you have completed the allotted time for your session.

Walk/run ratio. In this walk/run schedule, you will be working toward a walk/run split of 5 minutes running, 1 minute walking, but during your training try to experiment with different time splits to see which works best for you. If you are finding that you feel quite comfortable running continuously for more than 10 minutes at a time, it may be worth trying to run all the way round your event (in which case, you should follow the Intermediate Schedule for this distance).

Long walk/runs. Overcome your fear of the longer distance by trying to complete at least one longer walk/run each week – don't worry too much about the distance that you cover, but instead think about spending a long time on your feet. Use the time to practise your walk/run technique and to get into a good,

steady rhythm. One of the great advantages of a 10K event is that it is quite easy to pace because the distance is a nice, round number. So, if you can complete 1 kilometre with a 5-minute run/1-minute walk, you will finish the 10K race in an hour.

Walk/run fartlek. Your main aim in your first 10K event is to complete the distance, but some speedwork will still be very useful to you. Find a group of friends to train with, and take it in turns to call out, 'Run!' or 'Walk!' throughout your session. You can also vary the pace of your runs and insert short sprints between walk sections. These sessions will not only build your fitness, but will also help you cope during the race if you are unable to stick to your planned pace or walk/run splits because of the crowd.

Below: Fartlek training with friends can help you cope with unexpected changes of pace on race day.

Above: You can use regular long walk/run sessions to practise pacing for your 10K race.

10K Event: Intermediate Schedule

It's easy to see why 10K races are so popular: the distance is long enough to be a challenge and short enough to run fast, once you're an experienced runner. The even kilometre splits also make it easy to pace – as long as you get your training right.

Left: Training for a fast 10K involves your first really long runs, so take friends along to make it easier.

Speed sessions. A 10K race is far from being a sprint but it is still very important that you have a good solid base of speedwork in your legs before you reach the actual event. This intermediate 10K schedule includes some longer fast intervals that are closer to the speed you will want to reach in your event, and some faster strides to work on your overall speed and running style.

If you haven't included any speedwork in your training before, you should pay close attention to how your body feels after these sessions, and cut back on your sessions if you feel any recurrent pain in the same place – speedwork is great for building fitness, but it can also lead to serious injuries if your body is not properly prepared.

Below: Use your long-run sessions to explore new areas while you build up your endurance.

Time target: 45 minutes to 1 hour
Starting point: Four 30-minute runs a week, including one longer run 45+ minutes, for at least six weeks

When you have been running regularly for a few months, there is every chance that you could complete a 10K event without too much extra training. To understand why this race distance is so popular, you need to try racing it instead of simply running it. Like the shorter 5K, it is a difficult distance to get right, as you need to run at a sustained, barely-comfortable pace. The beauty of 10K, however, is that you have much more room to pace. Provided you don't set off too fast, you will be able to redeem your performance in the second half of the race.

Sessions
Long runs. You may think that it is unnecessary to run a distance farther than 10km in training for a 10K race, but doing so will in fact make you feel far more comfortable when you reach the start line. You want to finish the race feeling strong rather than exhausted and ready to collapse. Completing these longer training runs also builds your fitness base for after the race, so that you will be able to increase your race distance for future events.

Right: Mentally divide your 10K into two halves and try to run the second half slightly quicker.

Out-and-back sessions. As well as being one the most basic (and the most fun) forms of speedwork, out-and-back sessions are perfect practice for a 10K event. You should think of the race in two halves: the first 5K is almost a warm-up, where you gradually come up to speed, while the second half is an all-out race. There should not be a huge difference in time between your first and second halves, a 51:49 split is usually recommended.

Racing the second half of the race faster is known as a 'negative split' and is a commonly used tactic by many runners. It may not be the best approach for everyone, but for beginners it is the easiest and safest option.

10K event: intermediate schedule

	Session one	Session two	Session three	Session four	Session five
Week one	Run 30 mins	Warm-up 10 mins; 4 x 800m/ 3 mins fast with 400m/90 secs recovery; cool-down 10 mins	Rest/cross-train 30 mins	Run 30 mins	Run 45 mins/ 6.5–9.5km (4–6 miles)
Week two	Run 30 mins	Warm-up 10 mins; three sets of 8 x 100m strides with 100m easy and 3 mins jog between sets	Rest/cross-train 30 mins	Run 30 mins	Run 55 mins/ 8–11km (5–7 miles)
Week three	Run 30 mins	As week one	Cross-train 30 mins	30 mins out-and-back run	Run 1 hour/ 9.5–13km (6–8 miles)
Week four	Run 30 mins	As week two	Cross-train 30 mins	40 mins out-and-back run	Run 1hr10/ 11–14.5km (7–9 miles)
Week five	Run 30 mins	Warm-up 10 mins; 6 x 800m/3 mins fast with 90 secs recovery; 10 mins cool-down	Cross-train 30 mins	30 mins out-and-back run	Run 1hr20/ 13–16km (8–10 miles)
Week six	Run 30 mins	Warm-up 10 mins; 15 mins fast with 8 x 100m strides at random; 10 mins cool-down	Cross-train 30 mins	40 mins out-and-back run	Run 1hr20/ 13–16km (8–10 miles)
Week seven	Run 30 mins	As week five	Cross-train 30 mins	50 mins out-and-back run	Run 1 hour/ 9.5–13km (6–8 miles)
Week eight	Run 30 mins	As week six	Cross-train 30 mins	30 mins out-and-back run	10K event

Half-marathon: Walk/Run Schedule

For obvious reasons, a half-marathon is often used as a warm-up for the full distance, but it's also a good goal to aim for in itself. You'll need commitment and patience, but having achieved it you can really call yourself a long-distance runner.

Time target: 2:15 to 2:45 hours
Starting point: Five 30-minute walk/run sessions per week; should be able to walk/run for 1 hour

Some runners might find the description of a race as a 'fun run' slightly offensive. Unfortunately 5K and 10K races, especially those with many thousands of participants, are often billed as fun runs. If you find that a little off-putting, then the half-marathon is a very good distance at which to start your racing life. Even the most flippant of spectators would have to concede that 21km (13 miles) of running and walking is about more than fun: it is about months of hard training and,

on the day of the event itself, a lot of willpower and determination. That's not to say you won't enjoy it, and as a walk/runner, you will have the advantage over your faster fellow runners, as the walk breaks provide a natural way of pacing for the longer distance. You will always have something left at the end of a half-marathon using this approach.

Sessions

Being a back marker. In a shorter 5K or 10K race, although walk/runners may feel like they are miles behind the winner, the truth is that you will finish within half an hour of them. As you hit longer race distances, however, the gap widens, so that

in a half-marathon you might finish an hour or more behind the leader. Be more careful about choosing your race, and make sure there are no stringent cut-off times. If you can, go for a half-marathon that is part of a full marathon event. These are often one lap of a two-lap course, so that you are guaranteed company all the way round. You will also have a really good opportunity to mix with the front runners and see some top-class running. Don't let the idea of being among the back markers discourage you in any way – runners of all speeds are generally very supportive of each other, and you should find an atmosphere of mutual respect at most races.

	Half-marathon: walk/run schedule				
	Session one	**Session two**	**Session three**	**Session four**	**Session five**
Week one	Walk/run 30 mins	Walk/run 30 mins	Cross-train 40 mins	Walk/run 30 mins	Walk/run 1hr
Week two	Walk/run 30 mins	Walk/run pyramid	Cross-train 40 mins	Walk/run 30 mins	Walk/run 1hr10
Week three	Walk/run 30 mins	2 x walk/run; hill walk 15 mins; 2 x walk/run	Cross-train 50 mins	Walk/run 30 mins	Walk/run 1hr10
Week four	Walk/run 30 mins	Walk/run pyramid	Cross-train 1hr	Walk/run 30 mins	Walk/run 1hr20
Week five	Walk/run 30 mins	2 x walk/run; hill walk 20 mins; 2 x walk/run	Cross-train 1hr20	Walk/run 30 mins	Walk/run 1hr30
Week six	Walk/run 30 mins	Walk/run pyramid	Cross-train 1hr40	Walk/run 30 mins	Walk/run 1hr45
Week seven	Walk/run 30 mins	Walk/run pyramid with 2 extra-fast runs in middle	Cross-train 2hrs	Walk/run 30 mins	Walk/run 1hr45
Week eight	Walk/run 30 mins	2 x walk/run; 20 mins hill walk; 2 x walk/run	Cross-train 2hrs20	Walk/run 30 mins	Walk/run 1hr30
Week nine	Walk/run 30 mins	Walk/run pyramid with 1 extra-fast run in middle	Cross-train 2hrs	Walk/run 30 mins	Walk/run 1hr45
Week ten	Walk/run 30 mins	Walk/run pyramid	Rest	Walk/run pyramid	Half-marathon

Time off. While you might be able to get away with struggling through a 10K event on very little training, the half-marathon is more than double that distance and most definitely requires some endurance practice. For a walk/runner, completing very long distances in training can take up huge chunks of time and can be very hard on your legs and feet, so use the longer cross-training sessions in your schedule to build up your endurance base while giving yourself a break from running and walking.

Cycling is the best alternative, as you will still be able to get out into the countryside, and you will be working your legs hard. However, any activity you feel comfortable doing for 90 minutes or more will help. Try hopping around all of the different types of equipment in your gym to keep your cross-training sessions interesting.

Speed and strength. Use the walk/run pyramid session from the 5K schedule, but take each pace down a notch – even your easiest run pace. Your slowest run should feel almost

Below: You may find it useful to do some training on your own in case you find yourself alone during the race.

uncomfortably slow, and at your fastest you should still be able to talk in short sentences. In the later weeks of your training, repeat the middle, faster-run segments as directed in the plan, to challenge your fitness levels. Your schedule also includes hill-walking sessions to build up your strength in the lead-up to your race.

Your longest walk/run sessions. The half-marathon is a long distance that requires a much higher volume of training than you've been used to if you've only been running shorter events up to now. Your long walk/run session (session five on the table, opposite) will regularly take you over an hour of training in one go. The idea

Above: You may find yourself some way behind the leaders, but other runners are always supportive.

is to feel confident that you can complete 21km (13 miles) comfortably, so don't feel the need to push yourself too hard during these first long sessions. To begin with, plan routes that are made up of several short laps so that you can cut down if something goes wrong; ideally stay near your home at first so that you can pick up drinks or stop to use the toilet if you need to. As you become more confident with longer runs, you can go farther afield and use these training sessions to enjoy discovering new places and new scenery.

Half-marathon: Intermediate Schedule

Once you have gained some running experience and want to really push yourself, half-marathon training is a good place to start. This training plan is not too heavy-going and should get you ready to run a half-marathon time you can be proud of.

Time target: 1:45 to 2:15 hours
Starting point: Five runs a week including one speed session and one run of 1 hour

The biggest obstacle to running and enjoying a successful half-marathon is in its name. It is often regarded as a

build-up race for the full marathon distance, and many people fail to train properly for 21km (13 miles) and are subsequently disappointed with their results. The race is placed awkwardly in a marathon training plan, and the runner is unable to think of the race as a whole. Make

the race a goal in its own right, and you will find it a rewarding distance when you are ready to move up from 10K: it is long enough to really challenge you but short enough to run fairly fast without completely wearing yourself out.

Sessions

Pick and mix speed sessions.
Running intervals of varying pace and length is a great way to build up to a half-marathon. Although your aim is to run at as even a pace as possible, you will need the strength to surge past others as gaps appear in the field and to put in a good sprint finish at the end. Longer speed sessions are good for developing your overall pace. If you have avoided training on a track until now, give it a try – you may find it helps you to focus on the session in hand, without having to keep looking at a watch or listening out for an alarm.

Long, long runs. As with shorter 10K events, it is not necessary to run farther than the race distance in training for a half-marathon, but doing so will definitely help you. Your long runs will quickly head past the 90-minute mark, but try not to view this as a chore. Set out early on a weekend morning, relax, take it slowly and enjoy the fitness you have built up. It is also a good idea to use these runs as race practice, so try to do at least one run at the exact time of day that your race will start, and practise eating and drinking before and during the run.

Left: It can be lonely, but a few early-morning long runs will really pay off.

Half-marathon: intermediate schedule				
	Session one	**Session two**	**Session three**	**Session four**	**Session five**
Week one	Run 40 mins	Warm-up 10 mins; 4 x 800m fast, 400m slow; cool-down 10 mins	Cross-train 40 mins	Run 30 mins	Run 1hr/9.5–13km (6–8 miles)
Week two	Run 40 mins	Warm-up 10 mins; 1 x each 200m, 400m, 800m, 1,200m fast with 200m recoveries; cool-down 10 mins	Cross-train 40 mins	Run 30 mins	Run 1hr15/13–16km (8–10 miles)
Week three	Run 40 mins	Warm-up 10 mins; 20 mins faster with 5 x 200m sprints; cool-down 10 mins	Cross-train 40 mins	Run 30 mins	Run 1hr30/16–19km (10–12 miles)
Week four	Run 40 mins	Warm-up 10 mins; 6 x 800m fast with 400m recoveries; cool-down 10 mins	Cross-train 40 mins	Run 40 mins	Run 1hr30/16–19km (10–12) miles
Week five	Run 40 mins	Run 50 mins	Cross-train 50 mins	Run 40 mins	Run 2hrs/19–22.5km (12–14 miles)
Week six	Run 40 mins	Warm-up 10 mins; 1 x 200m, 400m, 800m, 1,200m, 600m, 300m; cool-down 10 mins	Cross-train 40 mins	Run 40 mins with 10 x 100m strides at random	Run 2hrs20/21–26km (13–16 miles)
Week seven	Run 30 mins	Warm-up 10 mins; 3 x 1,200m fast with 400m recoveries; cool-down 10 mins	Cross-train 40 mins	Run 40 mins	Run 2hrs30/ 19–22.5km (12–14 miles)
Week eight	Cross-train 30 mins	Warm-up 10 mins; 6 x 800m fast, 400m slow; cool-down 10 mins	Run 40 mins	Run 40 mins with 2 sets of 5 x 200m fast, 200m easy	Run 2hrs/ 19–22.5km (12–14 miles)
Week nine	Run 40 mins	50 mins fartlek	Run 40 mins	Cross-train 50 mins	Run 1hr30/16–19km (10–12 miles)
Week ten	Cross-train 30 mins	Run 30 mins with 5 x 100m strides at random	Run 30 mins	Rest	Half-marathon

Break it down. The half-marathon is an awkward distance and this often catches first-time competitors out. They will either approach it as a 10K and run far too fast early on, or worry about the long distance, run slowly and find that they could have run much faster.

The trick to pacing this event is to forget about running even splits. Rather than thinking of it as 21km (13 miles), break the distance down into two sections: a 16km (10-mile) easy run, with a 5km (3-mile) race at the end. When you are used to racing, or if you are very confident of your abilities, you can run fairly fast all the way through, but as a beginner it is much safer to run fairly comfortably for that first 16km (10 miles). Once you have reached that point, gradually increase your speed and feel yourself running smoothly and quickly toward the finish. As the distance is so much longer than 10K, some people find it easier to count down the miles than to count up.

Right: Even though race pace for a half-marathon is quite slow, fast speedwork will help you finish strongly.

Facing the Marathon

The respect and trepidation with which athletes approach the marathon is not surprising. No matter where you fall in the race pack, the 42km (26.2-mile) distance of a marathon will test you to the limits of your endurance, both mental and physical.

The marathon requires not just months of dedicated training, but sound planning and deep thought before you even commit to that training. Asking yourself 'What's my motivation?' is as important for a potential marathon runner as it is for an actor. Willpower is the driving force behind the months of hard training you will need to put in as well as the gruelling event itself. Whether you are racing for a charity

Below: Many thousands of runners successfully complete marathons – and you could be one of them.

close to your heart, a landmark birthday coming up, or just a bet with a friend, the marathon must mean a great deal to you if you are to succeed.

At the same time it is important that you choose a race that you really want to do. Rather than picking a local event that is 12 to 16 weeks away (the minimum amount of time you will need to train), find an event that you can become passionate about: perhaps in a beautiful place that you have always wanted to visit, or a famous race that you have seen on television and would like to try.

Quick checks

Ask yourself these quick questions:
• Am I running pain-free all of the time?
• Can I give up my Saturday nights out for two or three months?
• Will my family be happy to cope without me some evenings?
• Is my diet balanced and healthy?
• Will I be free from major work projects for the next three months?
If the answer to all of these questions is 'yes', then you are ready to start marathon training.

Right: If you are looking for that extra bit of motivation, choose an event in a place you have always wanted to visit.

Build your base

Before you start any of the marathon schedules in this book you will need to have attained a good base of fitness. If you are a total beginner, a marathon is not an ideal first race as, ideally, you need a year to steadily build up your strength and fitness. Choose a goal race only when you feel really fit and strong. Similarly, if you become injured, don't use a marathon goal to force yourself to run again, but wait until you have fully recovered. Your body needs this build-up time to develop the systems that will support you through the race.

The rest of your lifestyle may need tweaking to support your training. If you have been running for months but still harbour bad habits, such as a poor diet, smoking or a stressed-out work life, you should concentrate on ironing out these issues before you think about increasing your exercise load. If you are prone to recurring injuries, look at why these happen – perhaps you have skimped on buying good shoes, or you need to have a gait analysis. Unlike shorter races, the marathon will find out

your weak spots, so limit them as much as possible. While you are thinking about your lifestyle, decide whether you really have enough time to train for a marathon. There is a big difference between squeezing in five 30-minute runs a week, and the 7 to 10 hours (maximum) training per week required for your marathon schedules.

Find your motivation

It may seem obvious, but a love of running is crucial. Setting yourself a marathon target to force yourself to run more, perhaps because you want to lose weight or test yourself, won't work if you find the act of running boring or repetitive, or if you would rather stay in bed on a Sunday than go for a long run. If the marathon is not for you, that's fine – plenty of people enjoy long running lives doing shorter events or not racing at all. At the same time, if you have become addicted to running, you need to be prepared to broaden your horizons. Cross-training, whether through stretching routines, weightlifting or just enjoying other sports to recover from hard running sessions, is an essential ingredient in marathon training.

Finally, training for a marathon requires strict honesty. You may be able to fool yourself about how many miles

you have run in training, but 29km (18 miles) into the event you will be faced with the stark truth. Stick to your schedule as much as you possibly can, and if circumstances mean you miss sessions, be honest and revise your targets. You also need to be honest with yourself about what you can achieve. By the end of your training, you may well find that you can go farther than you had ever dreamed.

Below: Nothing beats the pride and satisfaction you will feel on running your first marathon.

Below: Review your lifestyle and diet before you start training to iron out any potential problems.

Marathon: Walk/Run Schedule

You may still feel like a beginner, and you may still prefer to take walk breaks while you train, but don't feel the marathon is beyond you. In fact, with the right training, you'll be in the perfect position to enjoy 'the big one'.

Time target: 4:30 to 6 hours
Starting point: Four sessions per week with one longer (1 hour) session, for at least six months

You may feel a little self-conscious about taking walk breaks during a race, but in a marathon you will find walk/runners often have the best experience. You can savour the atmosphere of the race, make new friends, and enjoy the sights and sounds on the course. However, the distance is a test no matter what your speed, so be aware that you may go through a rough patch toward the end of the race. Good, solid training can work wonders to reduce the

Below: As a walk/runner you'll have a better chance to soak up the atmosphere than the front runners.

impact of that low, and you can finish the race with a smile and a great sense of achievement.

The long walk/runs are the most important part of your schedule, as these sessions most closely resemble the marathon. You will never be out for longer than 3½ hours even though your race time might be 5 or 6 hours. This maximum is for practical reasons – it may be difficult to find time for a 5-hour session every weekend, and it will also avoid unnecessary damage to your body. Instead, intensive cross-training sessions will help supplement the long walk/runs.

You may feel pushed for time as your training increases, but don't neglect conditioning work. Your schedule includes hill-walking sessions but, if you can, fit in extra sessions of light strength work. It is a good idea

Above: You won't cover the full distance in training, but your long walk/runs are very important.

Walk/runners quick tips

• Practise carrying food and drink on your long walk/runs – find a small, comfortable day pack or waist pouch to carry food in
• Study the race route to find out where places like the toilets and water stations are beforehand
• Keep your feet comfortable with the right socks, shoe lacing and blister plasters in spots where you know your shoes rub
• Find out where the best spectator spots are, then ask your friends and family to come along and support you on race day
• If you are feeling strong during your last mile, you can skip the last walk break and sprint to the finish – it will feel fantastic!

Marathon: walk/run schedule

	Session one	Session two	Session three	Session four
Week one	Walk/run 30 mins	Walk/run 30 mins	Cross-train 30 mins	Walk/run 1hr
Week two	Walk/run 30 mins	Walk/run 30 mins with 10 mins hill walking	Cross-train 30 mins	Walk/run 1hr15
Week three	Walk/run 30 mins	Walk/run 30 mins with 10 mins hill walking	Cross-train 45 mins	Walk/run 1hr30
Week four	Walk/run 30 mins	Walk/run 35 mins with 15 mins hill walking	Cross-train 45 mins	Walk/run 1hr45
Week five	Walk/run 30 mins	Walk/run 35 mins with 15 mins hill walking	Cross-train 1hr	Walk/run 2hrs
Week six	Walk/run 30 mins	Walk/run 40 mins with 20 mins hill walking	Cross-train 1hr	Walk/run 2hrs15
Week seven	Walk/run 40 mins	Walk/run 40 mins with 20 mins hill walking	Cross-train 1hr	Walk/run 2hrs30
Week eight	Walk/run 40 mins	Walk/run 40 mins with 20 mins hill walking	Cross-train 1hr15	Walk/run 2hrs45
Week nine	Walk/run 40 mins	Walk/run 40 mins with 20 mins hill walking	Cross-train 1hr15	Walk/run 3hrs
Week ten	Walk/run 30 mins	Walk/run 30 mins	Cross-train 1hr	Walk/run 2hrs30
Week eleven	Walk/run 40 mins	Walk/run 40 mins with 20 mins hill walking	Cross-train 1hr15	Walk/run 3hrs
Week twelve	Walk/run 40 mins	Walk/run 45 mins with 25 mins hill walking	Cross-train 1hr15	Walk/run 3hrs30
Week thirteen	Walk/run 30 mins	Walk/run 30 mins with 10 mins hill walking	Cross-train 1hr	Walk/run 3hrs
Week fourteen	Walk/run 40 mins	Walk/run 40 mins with 20 mins hill walking	Cross-train 1hr	Walk/run 2hrs30
Week fifteen	Walk/run 40 mins	Walk/run 30 mins with 10 mins hill walking	Cross-train 45 mins	Walk/run 1hr30
Week sixteen	Walk/run 30 mins	Rest	Walk/run 30 mins	Marathon

to add some yoga or Pilates to improve your body awareness, so you naturally walk and run taller.

If you have been training by time rather than distance, find out how far you travel in each run and walk set using a running track. Find a run and walk pattern that fits evenly into a mile (approximately four laps of the track). This will help you pace yourself in the race, as well as to give you a finish-time estimate for the race.

After each intensive week, your training drops off slightly to allow your body time to recover and become stronger. At the end of the schedule you will notice that your training volume drops right off – this is known as tapering and enables your body to store much-needed energy for the main event.

Left: Using a small waist pouch like this one makes it easier to carry fuel while you run.

Right: Use intensive cross-training, such as cycling, to build up your fitness without impact.

Marathon: Intermediate Schedule

Running a marathon without walking is an ambition held by many beginners. If you can run for an hour at once then you're closer to achieving that dream than you might think. Your four-month training plan will build on that hour of endurance while increasing your speed.

Time target: 3:30 to 4:30 hours
Starting point: Five 30-minute runs per week including one speedwork; ability to run for 1 hour

Running a marathon in a time of less than 4:30 is not easy, but you will be in good company. In most marathons, the majority of runners finish between 3:30 and 4:30, so you will never be alone. This might feel like a disadvantage in the first half of the race, as the volume of runners holds you back, but in the tougher final stages the other people around you will keep you going. The marathon is all about the last 9.5–13km (6–8 miles) and avoiding the wall – the point 2 to 3 hours into the race

Below: In big-city events such as the Paris Marathon, you'll be in good company at 3:30–4:30 hours.

> ### Quick tips
> • As your training increases, place greater importance on sleep by adding 30 to 60 minutes per night
> • If you become injured or over-tired, drop your speed sessions for a week. If you take time off, don't try to make up for it later
> • On race day, if there are no official pacers, look for someone running a similar pace to you and use them as a marker to avoid starting too fast
> • Split the race in two in your head; for the first 25.5km (16 miles), distract yourself with the views and fellow runners, then bring your mind back to the race and focus on finishing

Right: If possible, train with someone you can race with too – you can help to pace each other.

where your muscles run out of fast fuel. Nutrition, pacing, mental strength and honest training will see you through this tough time.

Over the following 16-week plan, you will run 29km (18 miles) or more five times. While these long sessions will seem daunting at first, they will fill you with confidence for your race. Don't be tempted to push yourself beyond a distance of 35km

(22 miles) in training – you will simply wear your body down before the race itself. As a beginner you should keep long runs at talking pace. At least once, you should use one of your long runs as a race practice: run in 4 or 5-mile loops and set up a water station at your home so that you can practise taking on sports drinks. This will boost your marathon performance, help you to avoid hitting

the wall, and protect your immune system from being dampened by the marathon. There are three different types of faster session in your schedule: threshold running, interval sessions to build your overall speed and increase fitness, and strides to help improve your form. Start these sessions with a 10-minute warm-up jog and then end with a 10-minute cool-down.

	Session one	Session two	Session three	Session four	Session five
Week one	Run 30 mins	6 x 800m	Run 30 mins	Run 30 mins with 5 x 200m strides	9.5km (6 miles)
Week two	Run 30 mins	15 mins threshold	Run 30 mins	Run 40 mins	13km (8 miles)
Week three	Run 30 mins	8 x 800m	Run 30 mins	Run 30 mins with 5 x 200m strides	16km (10 miles)
Week four	Run 30 mins	15 mins threshold	Run 30 mins	Run 8 x 800m	19km (12 miles)
Week five	Run 40 mins	1 x 200m, 400m, 800m, 1,200m with 200m recoveries	Run 30 mins	Run 40 mins with two sets of 3 x 200m strides (200m in-between strides)	22.5km (14 miles)
Week six	Run 40 mins	20 mins threshold	Run 40 mins	Run 40 mins with two sets of 3 x 200m strides (200m recoveries)	25.5km (16 miles)
Week seven	Run 40 mins	8 x 800m	Run 40 mins	Run 40 mins with 8 x 200m strides	29km (18 miles)
Week eight	Run 40 mins	20 mins threshold	Run 40 mins	Run 8 x 800m	32km (20 miles)
Week nine	Run 40 mins	6 x 800m	Run 40 mins	Run 40 mins with 5 x 200m strides	25.5km (16 miles)
Week ten	Run 40 mins	10 x 800m	Run 40 mins	25 mins threshold	29km (18 miles)
Week eleven	Run 40 mins	2 x 200m, 400m, 800m, 1,200m with 200m recoveries	Run 30 mins	Run 40 mins with two sets of 5 x 200m strides (200m recoveries)	32km (20 miles)
Week twelve	Run 40 mins	8 x 800m	Run 30 mins	Run 40 mins with three sets of 5 x 200m strides (200m recoveries)	Half-marathon race/24km (15 miles)
Week thirteen	Run 30 mins	10 x 800m	Run 40 mins	Run 40 mins with two sets of 5 x 200m strides (200m recoveries)	35km (22 miles)
Week fourteen	Run 30 mins	6 x 800m	Run 40 mins	2 x 15 mins threshold with 10 mins recovery	26km (16 miles)
Week fifteen	Run 40 mins	8 x 800m	Run 40 mins	Run 40 mins with three sets of 5 x 200m strides (200m recoveries)	19km (12 miles)
Week sixteen	Run 30 mins	Rest	Run 30 mins	Rest	Marathon

Marathon: intermediate schedule

The Perfect Race Week

Training for your first race is hard work. So hard that you might forget about the race itself until the week before, when it suddenly dawns on you that all your effort is about to be put to the test. A little organization will go a long way in keeping you calm on race day.

Some runners find themselves becoming consumed with nerves and thinking about the 101 things that could go wrong – but they won't. Thousands of people successfully cross the finish line of a race every week, and you will almost certainly be one of them, but what you do – and don't do – in the week before your race can make a difference to your race experience.

Hopefully you will have trained hard for 6 to 16 weeks, so don't work too much in the last week. The effects of your training on your muscles and cardiovascular system will already have taken hold, and little you do at this stage will make any difference. On the other hand, a last over-zealous speed session could give

Below: Eating extra fruit and vegetables helps keep you healthy the week before your big race.

Above: Wind your training down to allow your body to recover in time for the big day.

you an injury, ruining your race chances. The longer your race, the more important it is to cut back (taper) your training this week.

Eat for success

Instead, pay a little extra attention to your diet and fluid intake during race week. This is not the time for a complete overhaul, so if you have made it through training on nothing but cake then so be it, but for most people it is a good idea to cut out junk food and make sure you have extra fruit and vegetables. If your race is longer than 10K, try carbohydrate loading: eat plenty of low-GI carbohydrates and increase your intake by 100 to 200kcal per

main meal. The idea behind this is that the extra carbohydrate will be stored in your muscles (as you will be training less hard than usual), ready for race day. Be careful to drink plenty of water, too, as hydration is cumulative: drinking gallons of water on the morning of your race will be of little use if you are dehydrated from the days before.

Be prepared

It may seem obvious, but ensure that the logistics of your race are sorted out, so you can relax. Double-check details such as directions to the start, what time you should arrive (usually at least an hour before the race start time) and whether you can park nearby. Make sure you have your

Below: Hydration is cumulative, so make sure that you drink more all week, not just on race day.

Above: Prepare yourself mentally for the race ahead, by trying to visualize a positive experience.

race number or know where to collect it from, and pack a bag for the race the night before. Try to persuade friends or family to come along with you, so they can help you remember everything and get there on time.

Once everything is in place, you will need to deal with your own final mental preparation – possibly the hardest element to get right at this stage. Allow yourself to think about the worst-case scenarios, but instead of dwelling on them, imagine how you might deal with them and bounce back. Spend 5 minutes every day visualizing yourself crossing the finish line strong, happy and in your target time, if you have one. If you have kept a training diary, look over it to remind yourself how well prepared you are. If you are still nervous on the morning of the race itself, simply think of it as a relaxed run with a few other people – and above all, try to enjoy yourself!

Below: Check that you have all your food, drink and equipment ready the night before your race.

Race week do's and don'ts

Do:
• Sleep well, especially during the two nights before the race
• Have a glass of wine every night if this is usual
• Relax and see friends to distract yourself from nerves
• Go for a few easy runs to keep your legs loose
• Have sex the night before the race if you want to – there is no evidence to suggest that it will affect your race performance on the day

Don't:
• Cram in last-minute miles or speed sessions, or try new sports
• Use the time off running to party every night
• Dwell on missed training sessions
• Buy new shoes for race day – stick with what you have trained in

---

JOINING THE ELITE

Covering the basic areas of training can produce
good results in your running. However, to
produce great results, you will need to learn from the
greats. This chapter will tell you more about the history
of athletics, both professional and amateur, and
introduces some of the athletes and coaches who have
shaped the way that runners train today. You will also
learn about some of the special sessions that the top
runners use to give themselves an edge.

Above: Amateur runners can win races if they learn from top athletes' methods.
Left: You have to train fast to race fast – as these runners have learned.

A Brief History of Athletics

Today, it is difficult to imagine the world of running without the Olympic Games, the pinnacle of achievement for the athletes taking part. Yet the Olympics and the tradition of athletics that has grown up around them are relatively modern.

Organized athletics is thought to date back to about 4000BC, when short running races were held in Egypt. The Olympic Games as we know them today began much later.

Early days

The first records of the Olympic Games are from 776BC. The Games were held in honour of the Greek god Zeus, and were held at the site of an important shrine to him at Olympia. To begin with, the Games consisted of running events, including a short sprint of around 190m (620ft), the length of the stadium. Up to 40,000 spectators would watch. Women were not allowed to compete, but ran in games in honour of Zeus's wife, Hera, where they would race over a similar distance to the men.

Although officially the Games were held for amateur athletes – the only prizes received were garlands –

Below: The first Olympic Games were held in ancient Greece, attracting international athletes.

those who won were revered in their home communities. Then, as today, the event attracted competitors from many different countries, but unlike the modern Games, they did not stop during wartime. A temporary truce would be called when the Games took place every four years, so that athletes could compete against each other. However, over time, the Olympics fell into decline, until eventually the Games were banned in AD393 by the Roman emperor Theodosius.

Organized games were held elsewhere in the world, but the development of athletics was far from linear. The separate strands of amateur and professional athletics have caused contention from the sport's beginnings right through to the present day, and early athletics meetings in Britain were often more about prizes than participation. In the Middle Ages, running, jumping and throwing events were held to win food, money or clothing, although competitions also took place for fun. Britain's own Olympick Games began in 1612 in the Cotswolds, the idea of a local man named Robert Dover. These Games, which include throwing and jumping events as well as sack-racing, shin-kicking and a 5-mile cross-country run, still take place every year.

In the 18th century, the sport became more popular than ever, though focus had shifted to winning money. Walking and running events – pedestrian races – were common in Britain and America. Gentlemen would pit their footmen against each other, placing huge bets. Over time this grew into an industry, with professional pedestrians training and racing full time; races or exhibitions charged entry fees to spectators in addition to making money from gambling.

Above: The Olympic flame is taken around the world before the start of the modern Games.

The rise of the amateur athlete

By the 19th century, running had started to become a mass-participation sport. Tracks were built at sports grounds all around Britain, the first at Lords cricket ground in 1837. Sports became part of school life at public schools and universities both in the UK and in the USA, and friendly competition between colleges became popular. In contrast to the purely commercial pedestrian events, this movement toward amateur sports sprang from a belief similar to that held by the ancient Greeks many years before – that participating in exercise was both morally and physically beneficial.

In Britain, Oxford and Cambridge universities would compete against each other regularly, and American universities followed suit, with the Intercollegiate Association of Amateur

Time-keeping

It wasn't until the end of the 19th century that stopwatches were accurate enough to keep trustworthy records. Today it is difficult to imagine the sport of elite running without a focus on time, which is now sometimes deemed more important than the race result itself – an event might be considered a poor race if none of the competitors ran especially fast. But until the 18th century, runners simply raced against each other. Then, horse-racing clocks were used, and finally in 1855, a stopwatch with a second hand was invented, which meant that running races could then be timed to the second.

Athletes of America formed in 1875, and its first championships held the next year. Meanwhile, amateur athletics clubs were formed in London

Below: In 2004 the Olympics returned to their home in Athens, where the first modern Games were held in 1896.

Right: Baron Pierre de Coubertin founded the International Olympic Committee in 1894.

and New York, and gradually throughout the two countries. Governing bodies were set up: the Amateur Athletic Association (AAA) in England in 1880 and the Amateur Athletic Union in the USA eight years later.

Gradually the two countries began to compete against each other in friendly meetings, and against other European countries. This growing participation in amateur sports at English and American universities inspired a young French aristocrat, Baron Pierre de Coubertin, to come up with the idea of reviving the Olympic Games. General interest in the Games was increasing thanks to excavations at the original site in Greece, and de Coubertin was able to found the International Olympic Committee in 1894. He hoped that the first modern Olympic Games would improve international relations, and he placed the emphasis

not on winning, but on taking part; an ethos which holds true at the Games today. The first Games were held in Athens in 1896 – with the new event of the marathon, as well as traditional sprints, throwing, jumping and an arts programme – and were a huge success.

The Modern Olympics

The first modern Games in Greece in 1896 were a huge success. Athletics, and running in particular, has grown hugely in popularity since then, but as well as great advances, the Games have had their share of problems.

Following the success of the first modern Olympic Games in 1896, the Games of the second Olympiad in 1900 provided a shock for the IOC. Much to the annoyance of the Greeks, the Games were moved to Paris. This time they had to compete for the public's attention against the World Fair, being held in the city at the same time, and where the Greek public had greeted the Olympics with enthusiasm, Parisians were less forthcoming. The programme of events was spread over four months, and with so much happening in Paris it was not entirely clear what was part of the Olympics and what was not. As a consequence the full results were not compiled until several years later.

Athletics grows in popularity
The popularity of amateur athletics continued to grow, however, with more clubs opening around the UK, Europe and the USA. After the 1912 Olympics, it was

Below: Female athletes take part in the track and field events at the Olympics for the first time in 1928.

felt that athletics needed a governing body. To fulfil this need, the International Amateur Athletics Federation or IAAF (which now stands for International Association of Athletics Federations) was set up, with 17 member nations.

Meanwhile the Olympic movement grew, although World War I put a stop to the 1916 Games. In fact, despite

Above: Jesse Owens gives an American-style salute on the winners' podium at the 1936 Olympics in Berlin.

de Coubertin's original concept of promoting peace and understanding through sport, the Olympics became a reflection of political tensions around the world, with a difficult history of boycotts, spiralling budgets and late-running building works – areas which still pose challenges to the Games today.

However, the Games also held up a mirror to some of the more positive changes taking place worldwide. In 1928, following a campaign by the women's governing body, the Federation Sportive Feminine Internationale (FSFI), women were allowed to compete in track and field events at the Olympics for the first time. Progress was set back when, during the women's 800m final, many of the competitors collapsed from exhaustion, and the distance was deemed too demanding for women. From then until the Rome Games in 1960, women were not allowed to race farther than 200m; the women's marathon was not introduced until 1984.

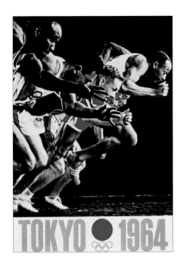

Above: An official poster for the 1964 Tokyo Games, which were the first to be televised worldwide.

Dark clouds over the Olympics
The rise of the Nazi party in Germany, followed by World War II, had profound effects on the Games. At the 1936 Games, held in Munich and presided over by Adolf Hitler, the now-legendary black American athlete Jesse Owens defied Nazi beliefs with his incredible successes: gold medals in the 100m, 200m, long jump and 4 x 100m relay. The war put a stop to the Games until 1948, when the event was held again in London. The Games were a success in spite of ongoing food rationing, makeshift facilities and the banning of some of the countries that had been involved in the war, including Japan and Germany.

A worldwide event
Technological advances have had a huge impact on the Games. Records became more accurate in 1932 with the introduction of the photo finish and automatic timing for the 100m sprint.

In 1960, the Rome Olympics saw the Ethiopian Abebe Bikila win the men's marathon barefoot, marking the beginning of African athletes' dominance

Right: Ethiopian Abebe Bikila runs the marathon barefoot in Rome in 1980, going on to win the gold medal.

of distance running. These Games were the first to be shown on television, and the 1964 event was the first to be shown worldwide. This helped to drive interest in athletics even more, and to further commercialize the sport, so that the original amateur ideal was hard to maintain. At the same time, advances in athletic performances generally meant that athletes had to go to more extreme lengths to stay at the top, so many trained full-time and needed to earn money from their sport. However, it was not until the early 1980s that the IAAF relaxed the rules on amateurism.

The 1970s and 80s saw some of the most troubled years in the Games' history. The 1972 Munich Olympics were overshadowed by tragedy, when a terrorist attack on the Israeli team killed 11 athletes as well as 5 of the terrorists and 1 policeman. The event continued after a memorial service, with competitors agreeing that the attack should not stop the Games. The 1980 Games in Moscow were also indirectly marred by violence: in response to the Soviet Union's invasion of Afghanistan, several countries boycotted the event. The UK team ran against the wishes of their government, but this produced one of the greatest British competitions in Olympic history. The 1,500m specialist Steve Ovett beat Sebastian Coe in his favoured event, the 800m. Coe had his revenge by winning the 1,500m.

Above: American Joan Benoit celebrates winning a gold medal in the first ever Olympic marathon for women in 1984.

The biggest challenge faced by the sport now is a problem with banned substances, a controversy that has raged since the Canadian sprinter Ben Johnson was famously stripped of his 100m gold medal at the 1988 Games in Seoul. Having survived so much, however, there is no doubt that the competition, which attracts more than 10,000 athletes in 300 events, will continue to push the limits of human speed, strength and endurance.

Training Methods of Great Runners

To the experienced athlete today, it may seem that there is nothing new to learn in athletics training. Throughout the 20th century, experience, science and instinct honed the different approaches to running, and the foundation was laid for modern training.

The great coaches who developed and popularized new training methods were, in their time, often considered to be eccentric and, like all good leaders, their larger-than-life personalities often earned them as much criticism as praise. However, there is no question that runners owe a debt to these groundbreaking men (and many more besides).

Percy Cerutty (1895–1975)
Through the 1950s and 60s, Cerutty coached dozens of top Australian middle-distance runners. He led Herb Elliott to Olympic gold over 1,500m in 1960, and from 1956 to 1962, helped him become perhaps the best 1,500m and mile runner in the world. Although at the time Cerutty's methods were considered unusual at best, his training philosophy is one that would be recognized by many of today's runners.

Below: Olympic gold-winning athlete Herb Elliott climbs a rope under the strict supervision of trainer Percy Cerutty.

Above: Franz Stampfl (left) advises the Oxford University athletics team, 1954.

Cerutty took a holistic approach to training, and developed his own philosophy, which he called 'Stotanism' – a mix of 'Spartan' and 'stoicism'. He taught his athletes to accept both defeat and triumph, pain and success without showing their emotions. This would have required considerable strength of character, as Cerutty was a believer in intense, high-quality training to yield results. Instead of circuits or intervals around a running track, his athletes made use of the landscape around them, and Cerutty was famous for encouraging them to run up and down sand dunes to build strength (a method still used by runners from sprint to marathon distance). He also taught them to appreciate healthy eating, and was a keen practitioner of yoga.

Franz Stampfl (1913–95)
Although he took a very different approach to Cerutty, Franz Stampfl had just as much success: it was Stampfl who coached the British runner Roger Bannister to the first sub-4-minute mile in 1954. He left his native Austria

for the UK in 1936 as an anti-fascist, and coached in Northern Ireland. On the outbreak of war, he was arrested and deported as an enemy alien. Stampfl was sent to Australia, but returned to the UK after the war. In 1955 he returned to Australia, where he coached a number of Olympic athletes including Ralph Doubell and Merv Lincoln.

Stampfl's scientific training methods came from his own experiences. He had been a skier in Austria, and on switching to track and field was shocked at how little training was done. He set about devising measured ways to teach the body to adapt to stress, most notably through intense interval sessions, during which careful notes were taken of time, distance, and the athlete's pulse. Stampfl's style was perhaps more dictatorial than Cerutty's, but the two shared a belief in the effectiveness of very hard training, and Stampfl would teach his athletes to train through pain.

Above: Peter Snell, coached by Arthur Lydiard, crosses the finish line first in the 800m at the 1960 Olympics.

Arthur Lydiard (1917–2004)

Although he struggled to find recognition for his methods during his career, Lydiard is often regarded as the father of modern coaching for middle- and long-distance runners. His programmes formed a blueprint for many of the training plans used by elite and recreational runners today.

Lydiard was a firm believer in 'base' training – that is, running long distances at relatively low speed to build a foundation of fitness. Even 800m or 1,500m runners, he argued, should run 100-mile weeks in the early stages of their training year. He also championed the idea of periodization, helping athletes to peak just before important competitions. However, his methods were considered extreme by some, and he clashed with the athletics establishment in his native New Zealand, and later in Mexico and Venezuela. Despite this there is no doubt that his ideas were successful: at the 1960 Olympics, his four New Zealand athletes (Peter Snell, Murray Halberg, Barry Magee and John Davies)

Right: Franz Stampfl coached Australian Ralph Doubell, winner of the 800m at the 1968 Olympics.

won six medals between them. While Lydiard's high-volume methods still attract criticism, his model of base training combined with hills and speedwork is still very much in evidence today.

John Smith (b. 1951)

In the past, it was believed that the best sprinters were born, not made, but the phenomenal speeds achieved by athletes in the last 25 years are as much a result of great coaches as great athletes. John Smith, a former international sprinter for the USA, has overseen numerous world and Olympic successes, including Maurice Greene's 1999 100m world record of 9.79 seconds. Working at the University of California and now through HSI (Hudson Smith International), Smith believes that great sprinting comes from relaxing, simplifying and breaking down the sprint. He breaks down the 100m sprint into five phases: reaction, drive phase (coming out of the blocks), transition (moving into full sprint), maximum velocity, and the finish or 'holding on' phase. Carefully moving through each phase, and spending as much time as possible in the maximum velocity phase, is crucial to the athlete's

Above: John Smith's coaching methods helped sprinter Maurice Greene to victory in the 100m in 1999.

success. As well as the physical aspects of sprinting, Smith teaches his athletes to stay humble when they win, and to stay confident when they lose. Smith's accessible methods and delivery continue to make him one of the best sprint coaches in the world.

Advanced Base Building: Twice-a-day Training

For endurance athletes at any level, building a base level of fitness is the first, crucial step to achieving full potential. For a runner, this means building up to running five or six days a week in the first instance.

If you want to make the jump from achieving average results to being a real contender in races, then you will need to increase your training volume. Some coaches place greater emphasis on base training than others, but all agree it is important. A coach might use the analogy of building a house: you have to build a strong, solid base before you can put the roof on, and the greater the height of the building, the wider and stronger the base must be. So, if you want to run fast over long distances (from the mile upward), you need a strong foundation of low-intensity training before you can add strength and speed elements.

Below: Train both in the morning and evening to spread out your running volume over the day.

The safest and most manageable way to increase training volume above the 75–105km (50–70 miles) per week mark – typical of recreational distance runners at a fairly high standard – is to switch to twice-a-day training. Increasing the volume in one session is both impractical in terms of fitting it into your working day, and dangerous in that it subjects your body to greater stress. Two runs a day allows your body time to recover in between.

The second run

Like all new elements of training, the second daily run must be added gradually to avoid injury and overtraining. First, it is important to be training once a day, every day. On your rest day, do a short recovery run

> **What base training does**
> • Trains your cardiovascular system and aerobic fitness
> • Builds capillaries in the muscles, so more oxygen reaches them
> • At low intensity, makes your body more efficient at using fat as fuel
> • Improves oxygen use in slow-twitch and type IIa fast-twitch muscle fibres (which don't contract as fast as type IIb fast-twitch fibres, and can use the aerobic energy system as slow-twitch fibres do), so they will work better for longer

instead of resting completely. If you feel this is excessive or you are prone to impact-related injuries such as shin splints, you could swap to a longer

Twice-a-day training: tips
• Leave 4 or 5 hours between runs to give your body time to recover
• Do not add a second run either very early or very late in the day, as this will compromise your sleep, which in turn compromises recovery
• If you are prone to impact injuries, or start to suffer them while training twice a day, consider making your second session a cross-training session
• Remember you need to make up for the extra mileage by adding the necessary extra calories to your diet

Right: Elite marathon runners, such as Kenyan former world-record holder Paul Tergat, train two or three times a day.

training cycle, for example having one day off in ten instead of one in seven. Then add a second run to two of your training days, ideally days where your main session is speedwork.

The second run should be an easy run of 30 to 35 minutes. The easy run tends to work better as the first session of the day, when it can serve as a recovery run for the previous evening's session, and a 'wake-up' run before the main speed session. Running faster is naturally easier later in the day as this fits better with the body's biorhythms: the muscles are stretched out and warm and the metabolism is working more efficiently. Most runners also find it mentally easier to do the gentler run early on.

Adding more runs
Once you have become used to running in the morning of your speedwork days, add another two runs, then another two, until you are running twice a day, six days a week. On your long run day, stay at one run until you plateau, as running twice on this day results in a daily mileage that can be difficult for your body to recover from the next day. If you do introduce a second run on this day, consider limiting your long run to 30km (20 miles) at the very most. Complete the long run early and use the easy run later as a recovery session.

Above: On your long run days, try to stick to one run to allow your body to recover fully.

Who trains twice a day?
As you would expect, all elite distance runners train at very high volumes. For marathon runners, this means an easy week of not less than 160km (100 miles). The world's fastest marathon runners, including Britain's Paula Radcliffe and Kenya's Paul Tergat, will train two or three times a day even on easy days.

Twice-a-day training is not for everyone. Before you make the huge commitment, ask yourself what you hope to get out of it. If the answer is to complete a 4-hour marathon, it may not be worth it; if on the other hand this is your chance to break through from good club level to your national team, or to break a club record, then training this way for three or four years can help you achieve your dream.

Killer Speed Sessions

Successful runners have a high pain threshold. In order to progress, runners have to be prepared to push themselves to their limits. This may sound intimidating, but as long as hard training is planned carefully, it is one of the most exciting parts of being a runner.

The recreational runner will often find themselves going through year after year of the same kind of training, but elite athletes know the real value of sessions that test their psychological strength as much as their physical ability. These 'killer' speed sessions, which should leave you feeling as though you have nothing left in the tank, work for several reasons. They prove one of the most repeated rules of running: that in order to run faster, you have to run faster.

Below: Very fast speed sessions are psychologically difficult, so do them in a group or with friends.

This applies no matter what distance you are training for. Really hard training sessions help your body to develop the physiological backup to support you in fast races: your oxygen and fuel delivery systems will work much more efficiently, your running economy will improve, and you will become mentally tougher. These sessions also teach you about pace judgement, and races will feel easier as a result.

The training sessions that follow are split into three different groups: short, sharp sessions; middle-distance and threshold sessions; and long sessions. All these sessions are valuable, and you can adjust the

distances or times involved depending on exactly what you are training for. Various studies have been carried out on the true value and effects of speed training, and overall they don't offer any conclusions about which type of session most improves speed and fitness. However, speak to any group of runners and you will find that hard sessions in any form will, performed regularly and correctly, lead to gains in speed. You may also be surprised by how quickly results happen – just eight to ten weeks of fast work, providing you have the requisite base fitness, can result in personal best times over a number of distances.

Above: Keep a positive approach to speed sessions: don't see them as a chore.

Short, sharp sessions (reps up to 400m)

Half and half. Warm up with 10 to 15 minutes of easy running, then speed up to approximately your mile race pace for 30 seconds. Slow down to a 'cruising' pace – fast but relaxed, as opposed to easy – for 30 seconds. Repeat until you can no longer maintain your fast pace for 30 seconds, then cool down with 5 minutes of easy running or walking.

The 200 test. Even if you are used to speedwork, you are probably cautious about the number of reps you perform at one time. Elite athletes and their coaches rarely share that approach, however, and might run up to 40 short repetitions in one session. Emulate this with a 200m test: warm up with 10 minutes of easy running, then on a track, run the 200m straights at 800m pace and jog easily round the bends. Start with two sets of four laps (eight 200m repetitions), building up to three sets of eight laps with 5-minute recoveries in between. End with two easy laps.

Short pyramid. This is a shorter, faster version of the standard pyramid session. Start with a 10-minute warm-up and some stretches. Run 100m, 120m, 140m, 160m, 180m, and 200m starting at a 400m pace for the 100m stretch and running each rep slightly slower, finishing with your 1-mile pace for the 200m repetition. Run a 200m recovery between each repetition. Then, run a 5-minute recovery jog, and repeat the distances, this time running each as fast and evenly as you can. End with a 5-minute cool-down.

Below: Some speed sessions, such as the 'half and half', don't require a track.

Middle-distance and threshold sessions

Variety show. Mix the length of your intervals to recreate the bursts and lulls of races, and to get your body used to running hard when you are already tired. Warm up with a 10 to 15 minute jog. Then run 4 x 200m fast, 200m easy; 2 x 1,000m at mile race pace with 5 minutes recovery in between;

then 1 x 200m, 400m, 200m, 800m, running the 200m and 400m at mile pace and the 800m repetition at 5K pace, and taking a 200m recovery between each. Cool down with a 5-minute jog.

5K 'personal best' session. Cheat your way to a new 5K personal best. Take your current 5K best time and

Left: Use your 5K personal best as the basis for a tough 5 x 1,000m interval session.

round it down to the nearest minute, then divide this time by five (so if your personal best time is 19:21, round it down to 19, divide by 5 = 3:48). After warming up, run 5 x 1,000m at this split time with 400m easy recoveries in between. When this session becomes easy, take another 30 seconds off your new '5K personal best' (so 6 seconds off each 1,000m repetition), or reduce the recoveries to 300m.

Race pace session. Warm up, then run a 5–4–3–2–1 session at your race paces. Start with 5 minutes at 10K pace, then 4 minutes at 5K pace, 3 minutes at 3K pace, 2 minutes at mile pace, and 1 minute at 800m pace. Have a 90-second recovery jog between each repetition. When you have finished the set, do a 5-minute recovery jog then repeat, building up to three sets in total as you become fitter.

Below: At the track, mix up different lengths and speeds of intervals to recreate a race environment.

Pacing

These sessions assume that you are familiar with your race paces over a full range of different distances. You will need to use your recent race times to complete these sessions properly. Since very few runners race over all distances regularly, you can test yourself over the different distances by racing against three or four friends, or just running time trials on your own. If you are not familiar with a particular distance, try it three or four times over a few weeks (unless it is a marathon), as you will need to get used to pacing yourself at that distance before you can run your best time. It is also a good idea to have someone else time you, as this will provide you with a more accurate result.

Above: Completing some long runs at your marathon race pace is difficult but worthwhile.

Long-distance sessions

Marathon race pace. It is generally advised to complete your long runs at a very easy pace, but some runners – including many elite athletes – do theirs at or close to marathon race pace. You should aim to race a marathon just below your lactate threshold; if you have had this measured you can use a heart-rate monitor to stay five beats per minute below your threshold. Otherwise, aim to run at 80 per cent of your maximum heart rate. To start with, run the first 6.5–8km (4–5 miles) slowly, gradually increasing the amount of time you run at marathon race pace.

Dream marathon pace. Pick a marathon goal time that is significantly faster than your current time. In the middle of your long run, try three 1-mile runs at this 'dream' pace – so if you would love to run a sub-3-hour marathon, run three 6:56-minute miles – with half a mile of recovery in between. This teaches you to run hard in the middle of a long run, and shows you how it would feel to run at your dream pace.

Race sandwich. Running a short race is an ideal threshold session, so speed up your long run by running a race in the middle. Choose a local 5K or 10K race, and complete a 8–9.5km (5–6 mile) run just before – running as close to the start time as possible. After the race, stop just long enough to get through the finish procedure, then complete another 8–9.5km (5–6 mile) run.

Acceleration run. This session will be helpful if you find that you slow down at the end of long races, usually a result of allowing yourself to do the same thing in training. During any long run of 16km (10 miles) or more, promise yourself that you will run each of the last 8km (5 miles) 5–10 seconds faster than the previous 1.5km (1 mile) – so your last 8km (5 miles) might be run in 8:00 minutes, 7:55, 7:50, 7:45 then

Right: Look out for signs of overtraining and avoid killer training sessions if you are feeling too tired.

7:40 for the last 1.5km (1 mile). The idea is not to speed up drastically but to stay strong when you feel tired. It should also help you to pace the earlier miles in your run.

Skills and Drills

Many runners think of drills as being the sole preserve of the sprinter. In fact, skills and drills sessions are an essential cornerstone of sprint training as well as any sport that requires speed and agility, such as soccer or racket sports.

Drills are useful no matter what your distance for perfecting technique and giving you an edge. Research has shown, for example, that adding this kind of training improves 5K times and reduces your risk of injury.

Why practise skills and drills?
These sessions work by breaking down the running cycle into its constituent parts, slowing down the motion and improving the specific function of the muscles involved in efficient gait. The training works on your neuromuscular system, committing the movements to your memory so that when you speed up, the technique is carried through. It also trains your fast-twitch muscle fibres, which allow you to run at high speed. Your overall flexibility will be improved, which in turn lengthens your stride, and your reactions will become quicker so your leg turnover speeds up. Drilling can be as effective as conventional speedwork sessions, but without the risk of injury.

Below: Sports which require bouts of speed and direction changes, such as tennis, also use drills.

Above: Using drills gives you better running form, which should translate into faster race times.

Perhaps the best thing about incorporating these skills and drills sessions into your regular training is that these sessions are not too taxing, and so can easily be done on the same day as a harder session. You can use them as part of a warm-up for a track session or fast race – many of the moves act as dynamic stretching exercises, which will help prevent injury when you stride out fast – or you can do them a few hours after a long run, which should help to reduce any muscle soreness. Run through each drill four or five times in quick succession.

Though these exercises may look and feel strange at first, you'll be in good company if you start using them – many elite runners across all distances incorporate exercises like this into their training.

Hurdle walk

This slowed-down version of hurdling works on your hip flexibility, strength in your hip abductors and adductors (the muscles on the inside and outside of your thigh that help stabilize your pelvis and leg), and strength in your gluteals and hamstrings, which help to power you forward. Start slowly so that you get the technique right.

Hurdle skip

Once you are confident with the hurdle walk, speed up to a skip, bouncing on the balls of your feet as you go through the hurdles.

1 *Arrange six hurdles a stride apart in a straight line (use junior hurdles if you are worried about hurting yourself). Step over the hurdle confidently, keep your hips and torso square forward; push your lead foot out flat as if kicking a door open.*

2 *Plant the lead foot firmly on the ground as you bring your back leg over, trying to keep it as straight as possible. Beginners may find it difficult to stop the back leg trailing sideways so have someone else check your technique.*

This speeded up hurdle walk will improve your reaction times and use your fast-twitch muscle fibres. If you're exercising in a group (a good idea), go through in quick succession so that each person is forced to keep up the pace.

Side hurdling

1 *Keeping the hurdles in the same arrangement, a stride apart in a straight line, face them side-on and start by walking over sideways, one leg after the other.*

2 *After a couple of run-throughs, speed up to a skip, and when you reach the end of the hurdles, do not pause but skip the back leg straight back over and go back the other way.*

3 *Stay upright and tall throughout, use your arms and keep your legs almost straight. This exercise works on your hip flexibility and speed, as well as your rhythm and reaction times.*

Russian walk

You will need a flat, even stretch of ground about 20m (65ft) long for this drill. The motion is similar to the hurdle walk (without a hurdle, of course), but with greater emphasis on knee drive and arm action.

Mini hurdles

The mini hurdles used for this drill are inexpensive, but you can use any small obstacles (20–30cm/8–12in high).

1 *Lead with your knee, pushing it high and in front of you, and keeping your foot flexed and taut; extend the lead leg, using the same kicking-open-a-door action as you used in the hurdle walk.*

2 *Plant your lead foot firmly on the ground without relaxing it. Keep your back straight and strong throughout and be careful not to twist your torso or hips. Keep your heels off the floor.*

Arrange five mini hurdles in a line, 60cm (24in) apart. Run down the side of the hurdles, bringing the leg nearest them over each hurdle, planting your feet firmly on the floor. This will improve your foot speed and your arm and knee drive, so run through as quickly as you can.

Ankle walking

1 *This will improve your reaction to the ground, helping you to pick your feet up quickly. It also works on the strength and flexibility of your feet and ankles. Walk forward in small, quick, but smooth steps, staying on the balls of your feet.*

2 *Push your foot through a full range of motion as you move, from almost being on tiptoes to low down with your heel barely off the floor. Pump your arms back and forth in time to help you keep your balance and rhythm.*

Skills and drills – quick tips

• Do these sessions in a group if you can, as it will be more fun and much more challenging

• If possible, have a coach check your technique – it is easy to get it wrong and you will be teaching your body bad habits

• Inevitably, everyone trips over hurdles or ladders from time to time – treat it as a game and overcome your mental fear of the obstacles

• In all these exercises, arm drive is as important as the leg action, just as it is in running

• Make sure that you think about your entire body during drills, and don't let any part of yourself relax and drag through the movements

• Don't put too much emphasis on any particular drill, as this may result in an odd, unbalanced running style

Bungee drives

This exercise works on your knee drive and core strength. Do not set the resistance too high – this can cause injury.

Speed ladders

Again, you can buy special rope ladders to place on the floor for this exercise, or you can simply draw out a chalk ladder or place rolled-up newspapers in a ladder formation.

For this exercise you need a bungee cord and a secure post or tree to attach it to. Attach the cord around one leg just above the ankle and walk forward until it is taut (but not pulling you backward). Drive the attached leg forward as you would in the Russian walk, pushing the knee high, keeping your hips facing forward and using your arms for balance and power. Do two sets of 10 on each leg, building up to three or four sets.

1 *Place the speed ladder on the ground in an open space, where there is plenty of room. Staying on the fronts of your feet, start the exercise by running quickly through the speed ladder, placing one foot in the middle of each square and using your arms to drive the action.*

Below: Your local track should have a stock of hurdles and other equipment that you can borrow.

2 *Then run through the speed ladder, putting both feet in each square as you go. You can also run through sideways or even jump diagonally through the ladder's squares if you want to improve directional speed (for example, if you take part in any team sports).*

Skills and drills – equipment

At first it may seem as though there is a lot of equipment required for these skills and drills, however you will find that it is all relatively easy to obtain and often not too expensive.

SAQ International (SAQ stands for speed, agility and quickness) is one of the leading companies providing equipment for performing skills and drills. However, you can also perform most of these basic exercises without your own specialist equipment, by improvising. You could borrow hurdles from your local track or sports club and try using a fitness resistance band in place of a bungee. It is a good idea to set out all the equipment before you start, so you can easily do circuits of the drills, and you don't waste time between exercises.

Plyometrics or Jump Training

They may look like child's play, but the jumping and hopping movements of plyometric exercises are an essential part of many elite athletes' training plans. This type of training benefits athletes across a huge range of disciplines, from long-jumpers to football players.

Running is itself a plyometric exercise, so runners from sprint distance right up to marathon will see improvements with regular plyometric training.

Plyometrics (or jump training, as it is sometimes called) works by improving the explosive strength of the muscles, simulating running-specific actions such as accelerating or powering out of sprint blocks. These exercises recruit the fast-twitch muscle fibres used for pure speed. They also help to build overall strength, stride length, flexibility and proprioception (balance and co-ordination). The exercises don't take long and don't need to be carried out often – two short sessions a week is enough – yet they can have a huge impact on your race times. Although many amateur runners skip plyometrics, perhaps sceptical about its effectiveness, research has shown that groups who use this kind of training see greater improvements than those who don't.

One of the great things about plyometrics is that it is fun to do, but don't underestimate its effects – it is a very intense form of training, subjecting your muscles to forces many times greater than your own bodyweight. As such it is not a good idea to include plyometric training if you are new to running and exercise. The strain placed on your muscles, tendons and joints is likely to result in injury to unconditioned runners. When you do introduce plyometrics, treat it as you would intense speedwork or weight training; for example, don't do plyometric workouts on two consecutive days. A good time to do plyometrics is just before or after a speed session, ensuring you are fully warmed-up first, but if you become tired and find you can't perform the movements properly, stop and do the session another day. Poor technique will at worst result in injury, and at best have little training effect.

Quick tips for plyometric sessions

- Use a soft but even surface such as a track, lawn or mat in the gym
- Don't do plyometrics the day before a race, or two days in a row
- Engage your core muscles throughout the exercises
- Keep your landings light – land on the balls of your feet, allowing the natural rocking back on your heels to absorb force
- Perform the exercises with your absolute maximum effort, as they are designed to increase power
- Make sure that you allow at least 1 minute of rest between sets

---

Upper-body plyometrics

You can use plyometric exercises to build strength in your upper body, including your arms, chest and abdominal muscles. These exercises are used by athletes who require explosive power in their upper body, such as rowers and racket-sports players. Exercises might include plyometric push-ups, where you 'jump' up so both hands leave the ground at the top of the push-up, and throwing and catching weighted medicine balls. However, these exercises may be less effective than lower-body plyometrics, as the athlete does not use his or her full body weight during the exercise.

Below: Plyometric push-ups will build strength in your upper body.

Standing jump

1 *Stand with your feet shoulder-width apart, your knees soft and arms relaxed by your side. Jump straight up in the air, with just a slight bend of the knee so that your lower legs and ankles provide most of the force; swing your arms forward slightly as you jump.*

2 *When you land, go straight into the next jump as quickly as possible. Start with three sets of 5 and build up to three sets of 10.*

Squat jump | ## Long jump

1 Begin in a squat position, with your feet hip-width apart, back straight, knees bent and arms straight and behind you. Jump up into the air, straightening your legs and swinging your arms straight up above your head.

1 Start the exercise in a half-squat position (as for the squat jump, but slightly higher with less of a bend in the knees). Be careful if using a mat for this exercise, as the force of your landing may cause it to slip.

2 Swing both your arms behind you, then jump forward as far as you can. Bring your arms through so that they are out in front of you – the movement will help to carry you forward.

2 When you land, immediately lower back down into the squat position and repeat, without allowing your heels to stay down for more than a split second. Aim for two sets of five.

3 As you jump forward, keep your head up, looking straight in front of you rather than down at the ground. This will help you to jump a greater distance.

4 When you land, make sure you bend both knees to absorb the impact, then immediately crouch and bring your arms back for the next jump. Start with two sets of five jumps and build up to three.

Split jump

1 *Begin in a half-lunge position, with one leg in front and one leg behind you, your knees bent and hands either on your hips or by your sides. The front heel should be flat on the ground while the back heel should be raised slightly.*

2 *Lean back slightly from the hips and, pushing up from the knees, jump up into the air as high as you can. Switch your legs over while in the air, so that when you land again, your starting rear foot is in front of you. Repeat the jump, switching your legs over again.*

3 *As soon as you are back to the starting position, bend your knees and push up again for the next jump. Do two sets of four jumps on each side (so each set comprises eight jumps in total), building up to three sets.*

Jog with arm swing

Bunny hops

1 *Start the exercise on your right leg with the knee bent and your left leg bent up behind you, facing forward but with your arms out to the right (your left arm should be bent across your chest and your right arm should be straight out to the side).*

2 *Push up through your right leg to jump as high as possible, at the same time swinging your arms to the left and landing on your left leg. You can make the exercise harder by holding dumbbells. Repeat five times on each side and aim for at least three sets.*

Half-squat with your heels raised and hands on your hips. Jump up and forward, using your calves and ankles to push you. Land on the balls of your feet and keep ground contact to a minimum, hopping forward quickly. Start by hopping for 20m (60ft), then as you gain strength, rest, turn and hop back.

Depth jumps

1 *For this exercise you will need a bench or step, approximately 30cm (1ft) off the ground. Begin the exercise by standing on the bench or step with your feet shoulder-width apart and arms hanging down by your sides.*

2 *Slowly step forward so that you drop onto the floor, bringing your arms back as you go, and as soon as the balls of your feet hit the floor, spring up in the air as high as you can, swinging your arms forward and up to help.*

3 *Do three sets of five. You can make the exercise more difficult by increasing the height of your step as you become used to the impact: a higher start will build strength in your legs, while a lower start emphasizes quick reactions.*

Lateral lunge jumps

1 *Start the exercise by standing next to a fairly low step – less than 30cm (1ft) high. Bring your right foot up onto the step with your left foot on the ground parallel to it, and with both your arms out behind you. Your right knee should be bent, while your left leg remains straight.*

2 *Pushing off with your right leg, jump up as high as you can into the air, so at the highest point of the jump, both legs are straight. Look straight ahead and throw your arms up in front of you as you jump. This movement will help you to jump higher.*

3 *Land with your left foot on the step, bringing your right foot down on the ground on the other side of the step, and then push up again as quickly as you can. Complete two sets of five jumps on each side (so each set has 10 jumps in total).*

Improving Form and Cadence

Running is a completely natural activity. However, running efficiently and quickly does not come naturally to many of us, or even to elite athletes. While it is difficult to define a perfect running form, there are advantages to working on the way you run.

There are two basic elements to running faster: lengthening your stride, and increasing your running cadence (the number of steps you take in a minute). At the same time, you need to reduce wasteful movements such as side-to-side motion, or moving your head while running. There is some debate over whether it is possible, or even desirable, to radically alter your natural gait, and some of the world's fastest athletes have achieved huge success with running styles that might be considered wrong. The way you run as an adult may have become ingrained as a child, or may have been affected by years of bad habits: carrying heavy bags on one shoulder, wearing poor quality shoes, running on a camber or compensating for old injuries. To become a more efficient runner, you must retrain your brain to forget these bad habits at the same time as learning a new way of moving.

Despite all the difficulties, if you want to squeeze every bit of speed out of your run, you can try breaking your running gait down to its simplest parts and teaching your body how to run better.

Improving stride length

To work on your stride length, you must first increase flexibility in the hip joint, hamstrings and gluteals, so that your thigh can move freely up to give a good knee drive for your leading leg. Regular and diligent stretching will help. Try exercises such as sprint bounding, strides, hurdle walking and the Russian walk. You will also need good core strength to hold your pelvis and back steady while you stride forward; without this the muscles around your hips will work harder to compensate for your weak core and this will eventually lead to injury.

Left: An efficient running style takes years to develop and involves your whole body, not just your arms and legs.

> **Form guide**
> - Always start by performing drills slowly to ensure that your technique is perfect, otherwise you will teach yourself bad habits
> - Don't try to completely overhaul your running style if you are still seeing rapid improvements with your natural running style – you could do more harm than good
> - Don't overemphasize work on one particular aspect of your gait, even if you feel it is a particular weakness. Remember that your whole body works together, and working on just one movement will throw out the balance of your movement

Improving cadence

It is very difficult to alter your natural cadence. However, there is a perfect cadence: most elite runners hit the ground about 180 times a minute (recreational runners tend to have a much lower cadence). You can measure your cadence using a speed and distance monitor, or if you don't have one, simply count the number of times one of your feet hits the ground in a minute and double this figure. Exercises to try to improve your cadence include downhill running, ladder drills and ankle walking. You can also try to improve your rhythm by making a conscious effort, although it is difficult to do this without shortening your stride. Use an electric metronome on a sports watch; try to reduce up and down movement while you run, and pump your arms more quickly (your legs will usually follow).

Exercises to improve overall form

As a runner you should already be doing at least three core-strength sessions per week. If you can find 15 minutes every day to perform a few core exercises, this will make a difference over time.

1 *Strengthen your gluteus medius muscles (small muscles that help stabilize your hips and move your legs apart) by lying on the floor with one leg on top of the other, your knees bent.*

2 *Very slowly raise the top leg, making sure that you keep your feet together, and then lower the leg down again. Repeat the exercise on both sides 10 to 15 times.*

Single-leg squats, performed slowly, will also improve your core stability and help reduce any side-to-side motion; do them while looking in a mirror to ensure your knee stays straight.

Improve your arm drive by practising swinging your arms back and forth while sitting up straight on a chair. This may feel a bit silly, but it really does work.

SPRINT AND MIDDLE-DISTANCE RACING

The advice given so far has largely centred on training for distance events of 5K and beyond, which is the most accessible type of running for most people. This chapter discusses some of the specialized training necessary to become a truly great sprinter and middle-distance runner, and the athletes that have inspired generations by pushing past accepted beliefs about how fast a human being can run.

Above: Usain Bolt wins the men's 100m in the 2008 Olympic Games, earning the title 'world's fastest man'.
Left: More than any other form of running, sprinting requires sharp focus and concentration.

Sprint Form and Drills

Good form is very important for all runners, but especially so for sprinters. At speeds of up to 48 kmh (30mph), where every hundredth of a second counts, every part of the body's movement must contribute toward moving forward.

A marathon runner might be forgiven for a tight shoulder or even a lopsided arm swing, but at the other end of the spectrum technique makes a much bigger difference. In sprinting there is no room for any wasteful side-to-side movements or energy spent tensing the neck, and biomechanical problems that seem minor in slow motion are exaggerated at speed. The key to great sprinting is relaxed speed.

The best sprinters make their motion look smooth and almost effortless, and the mistake many slower runners make is to 'try too hard' – running with

clenched fists, gritted teeth and hunched shoulders, which wastes energy and prevents a full range of motion. Watch a group of well-trained sprinters, and you will see that their style is often strikingly similar. This 'perfect' sprint form is developed over years of training using drills, visualization of correct technique and, crucially, the input of an experienced sprint coach.

Right: A sprinter in her starting blocks focuses on the track ahead of her, visualizing perfect form.

Sprint form

1 The leading knee should drive high and forward, so the thigh ends up parallel with the ground. The toes of the lead foot should be pointed up, so that the foot is not allowed to 'drop' at any point during the cycle. Meanwhile, the back leg remains almost straight, not collapsing under the weight of the runner while on the ground, and extending right out behind the runner once off the ground.

2 The lead leg should land on the ball of the foot, in front of the runner but not so far forward as to produce an exaggerated stride, which leads to a braking effect. On striking the ground, the foot must pull the ground underneath the runner in a clawing action, without the heel dropping to the floor. As the other knee drives forward, the heel of that leg is brought up tucked under the runner before the lower leg is extended forward.

3 The support leg extends behind as before. Throughout the sprint, the torso should stay high and straight, the neck and face should be relaxed and the shoulders relaxed and down. The arms should both be bent at 90 degrees at the elbow, and should drive backward and forward, keeping in time with the runner's steps, helping to keep leg speed up.

Starting from blocks

1 On your marks. *You need to experiment with the blocks to find the best position for you. Many sprinters find that a distance roughly equal to that from your ankle to your knee works well. You need to get the angle of the blocks right – the back block should be steeper. Start with your feet in the blocks, crouched, and your hands just touching the line, just wider than shoulder-width apart, with your thumb and fingers forming a bridge, and your arms straight but not locked.*

2 Set. *Keeping your hands where they are, with your thumb and fingers still in the bridge position, raise your hips up so that they are higher than your shoulders and you are leaning forward slightly – you should feel quite stable, but not exactly comfortable. Your front knee should be roughly at a right angle, while your back knee should make an angle of about 120 degrees. Push your feet hard into the blocks. Your face and neck should remain relaxed.*

3 Go! *Your reaction time here is crucial, but be very careful not to react before you hear the gun go off. Push hard out with your front leg, and drive the back leg forward at the same time, pushing up and forward, and leaning almost horizontally as you accelerate out of the blocks. Don't stride too far on your first step, or take steps that are too small; you need to move as quickly as you possibly can into your perfect sprint form.*

Above: Include sprint bounds in your training sessions and you will soon see an improvement in your form.

Above: Keep your back straight and head up to get the best results from exercises like heel flicks.

Sprint drills

Practice drills are as crucial for sprinters as they are for distance runners. Add these exercises to improve your sprint action.

Sprint bounds: over a distance of 50m (164ft), practise driving your lead knee forward and fully extending your back leg, using your arms to help the action as you would while running. Bound forward, slowly at first, speeding up as you perfect the technique. Over time, aim to cover the 50m (164ft) in fewer bounds.

Heel flicks: over a distance of 30–50m, (98–164ft) run forward on the balls of your feet, kicking your heel up to almost touch your bottom as quickly as possible. Ensure that your body stays upright and straight during the drill.

Harness runs: working in pairs, one runner holds the ends of a harness while the other walks forward in the harness until he feels resistance. Run forward against the harness, trying to keep as natural a gait as possible (instead of leaning right in to the harness).

Strength Training for Sprinters

You only have to look at a group of sprinters in the starting blocks to realize that strength training plays a huge part in their success. Compared with the lean, wiry build of a distance runner, sprinters look muscular and powerful.

While strength training plays an important role in all athletes' routines, for sprinters it is essential for developing the explosive power needed to drive them along at speeds of up to 10m (30ft) per second, and the control needed to ensure no energy is wasted along the way. Generally speaking, the shorter the specialist distance, the more strength is needed.

Top-level sprinters will push themselves through two or three weight-training sessions per week up to the competition phase of their year and, as with all training, they must be careful not to overload their muscles by strength training on the same days as their more intense running workouts. In race season, sessions are cut down and resistance is reduced.

There is some debate over how much emphasis should be placed on strength training. Some coaches feel that it plays too great a part in sprinters' training, to the detriment of out-and-out speed. Even at the elite level, sprinters should not spend more than an hour at a time on strength work, and should look on it as a complement to rather than replacement for specific running sessions. Too much strength work, particularly using weights, can increase bulk and body weight to a point where the athlete's power-to-weight ratio drops. Moreover, while resistance work increases the power of large muscle groups, research has shown that type IIb fast-twitch muscle fibres, which produce 'pure speed' (as opposed to type IIa which are not quite as fast), thrive when weight training is reduced. It is therefore important to include weight training and to reduce it just before the competitive season begins.

Press-ups

Works: chest, back, arms and core

Press-ups may be performed quickly or slowly, but always take care to ensure good technique is held throughout, with the abdominals contracted, and a full range of movement down to elbows bent to right angles and up to fully extended arms. To increase intensity, perform press-ups with your feet up on a bench.

Squats

Works: This exercise trains the muscles used to drive the legs forward during a sprint, including the gluteals, hamstrings and calves

1 Increase the intensity by performing faster sets of half-squats (going down into a squat, but only coming halfway back up until the end of the set).

2 Single-leg squats work on core strength and balance. Keep your hands on your hips for balance, and lift one foot up off the ground before going into a squat.

Above: Whole-body strength plays a huge part in a sprinter's explosive power on the track.

Step-ups

Works: gluteals, hamstrings, calves, quads

1 *Use a bench high enough that the lead thigh is parallel with the floor, with the knee bent at a right angle, just before stepping up. Put your hands on your hips or drive your arms up with your legs.*

2 *With your feet shoulder-width apart, step up with one leg and use that leg to push up on to the bench, bringing your other foot up next to the first, then step back down on the same leg.*

3 *Make the exercise more challenging and sprint-specific by driving the knee of the trailing leg high into the air before planting it on the bench. As you do so, rise on to the toes of your lead foot.*

Incline sit-up

Works: upper and lower abdominals, core and back

Using an abdominals board, perform sit-ups against gravity to increase their intensity, taking care not to pull your neck. Before you begin, ensure your spine is in a neutral position and engage your core muscles to avoid over-arching or flattening your back too much as you sit up. Try not to allow your feet to leave the floor or your quads to tense during the exercise.

Bridge

Works: gluteals, core

Lie on your back with your knees bent, feet flat on the floor. Push up through your heels, until your hips are in a diagonal line with your shoulders (which stay on the floor). Keep your abdominals tense, and hold the position for 10 seconds, then pulse up and down for 30 seconds, building up to 1 minute.

Weight Training for Sprinters

When training with weights, sprinters lift much heavier amounts than distance runners, but they should not attempt this kind of training without a general background in strength and conditioning.

Strength and fitness for sprinters might be achieved through special running workouts – for example, running on hills or sand; by using core strength exercises; or with regular bodyweight exercises. Plyometric sessions are also vital for sprinters. Strength training programmes need to be tailored to the individual sprinter, with particular attention to their specialist distance and training goals, but here are some of the basic exercises they might perform. It is important to have at least one spotter – a training partner to help you catch the weight if you become unsteady – during all weighted exercises. As you become stronger and the weights you use are heavier, this is especially important since there is a real risk of serious injury if you are unable to control the weight.

Weights and repetitions

It is important to have someone work out a weight-training programme for you: getting your weights wrong could lead to injury. The weights you lift and number of repetitions you perform will vary depending on where you are in your training year. Before you start it is useful to know your Repetition Maximum or 1RM: the heaviest weight you can lift once for a particular exercise. You need a spotter to help you work this out, an exercise professional who can make an estimate from your size and training history.

Once you know your 1RM, use it as a base measurement for deciding your workouts and for progressing to heavier weights.

Dumbbell arm swings

This will improve arm drive. With light dumbbells, watching your action in a mirror, stand up straight with your feet fixed and core engaged to hold your torso steady. Bend your elbows and pump your arms back and forth as quickly as possible, as if you were sprinting for 1 minute; rest 1 minute then repeat. Complete 4–6 sets.

Power clean

Watch points: Try to keep your abdominal muscles and back tight throughout this exercise to protect your back. Try not to push the weight out in front of you, instead jump it straight up.

1 *Start the exercise with your feet hip-width apart and the barbell on the floor just in front of you. Slowly bend down to grip the barbell with both hands – you should have your hands over the bar (with your knuckles pointing down) and about shoulder-width apart.*

2 *Lift the weight at a controlled speed by straightening your knees and back, keeping the bar close to your legs. Once the barbell has passed your knees, accelerate your motion. As the bar reaches mid-thigh level, jump the weight up, taking care not to push it out in front of you, but straight up.*

3 *Flip your elbows forward so you have an under-bar grip, and bring your body under the weight, allowing it to rest on your shoulders at the top of the movement. Drop into a half-squat to take the force of the weight, before immediately straightening up. Lower the barbell back to the ground slowly.*

Snatch

Watch points: Make sure you are steady before beginning the lift. Make the final flip movement of the weight as quick and smooth as possible.

1 The start is very similar to the power clean: feet hip-width apart, bend down to grip the barbell with your hands just wider than shoulder-width. Lift the barbell in a smooth motion as before, keeping it very close to your legs.

2 When you are standing straight, continue to lift the weight, keeping the same grip and allowing your elbows to move out to the sides.

3 As the weight reaches shoulder level, quickly flip it and drop underneath the bar, extending your arms and dropping right under the weight into a squat.

4 Slowly and steadily stand out of the squat to complete the lift.

Weighted step-up

Watch point: If the weight makes you lose control of the action, use a lighter one until you are able to step up straight.

1 The step-up exercise described earlier in this section can also be performed using a barbell. Lift the weight on to the back of your shoulders, using a towel to protect your neck if necessary.

2 Ensure you are steady and in control of the weight, with your feet hip-width apart and core tense. Step up on to a strong bench, slowly bringing your lead leg up onto the bench.

3 Slowly and steadily, bring your back leg up to stand square on the bench next to your lead leg.

4 Finally, lower the same leg down followed by the lead leg, so that you are back in the starting position.

Other weighted exercises

Since general strength and good overall conditioning is very important to all sprinters, you will also find it useful to include some of the standard weighted exercises used by other types of runners in your regular training sessions.

Alternatively you may decide to use heavier weights and fewer reps. Try to include different general exercises like weighted squats, lunges, calf raises and bench presses in your regular training routine.

Sprinting: 100m and 200m

The 100m sprint is the classic athletic competition, while the more specialist 200m involves a level of technical skill that only the best sprinters can master. The best sprinters start training young but anyone can learn to enjoy running as fast as they can.

For events that are over in less than half a minute, the short sprints take years to perfect. Here are the basics of 100m and 200m training.

100m

Running the 100m is not simply a case of running as fast as you can. Good sprinters break the distance down into a series of phases. First comes the start and acceleration phase (which is sometimes called the 'drive' phase). Practising reacting to the starting gun is crucial. Coming out of the blocks, the sprinter should drive hard, looking down at the track. From 30m to 60m, they will come up slowly and smoothly into the full sprint stride, fixing their eyes on the lane ahead. This 'tunnel vision' is essential to remain relaxed and in control – you should not be thinking about the people behind you. At 60m, sprinters reach their top speed, and the aim now is to hold on

Below: The sheer determination shows on the face of Jamaican Shelly-Ann Fraser (centre) as she goes on to win the women's Olympic 100m final, 2008.

Great athletes: Carl Lewis (b. 1961, Alabama, USA)

From a young age, Carl Lewis (Frederick Carlton Lewis) was determined to be a great athlete, and by any measure he succeeded. In 1999 he was voted Sportsman of the Century by the IOC. Throughout the 1980s and early 90s, he dominated both sprint and long jump at international level. He won five Olympic gold medals for sprinting (100m, 200m and 4 x 100m relays), and was three times the world champion at 100m, the first time in 1983 and last time in 1991. Lewis openly stated his intention to match Jesse Owens' 1936 record of four gold medals at one Olympic Games, and in 1984 in Los Angeles, he succeeded, winning the 100m, 200m, long jump, and leading the 4 x 100m winning relay team. His career was not without controversy, and when he accused Canadian athlete Ben Johnson of using drugs following defeat at the 1987 World Championships, many people thought he was bitter. However, he was vindicated at the Seoul Olympics the next year, when Johnson, who had beaten Lewis to gold in the 100m, tested positive for steroids. Lewis was awarded gold. He retired in 1997.

Right: In 1999, Carl Lewis was voted Sportsman of the Century by the IOC.

100m and 200m: training examples

Date	Training phase	Theme	Weekly sessions
Oct–Dec	Conditioning	Strength and base building; less speed. Outdoor and off-road sessions	Aerobic training e.g. 3–4 mile easy runs Hill sessions (inc. sand dunes) 3 weights sessions per week: bodyweight and max weight sessions Core and flexibility work 2–3 skills and drills/plyometrics sessions
Jan–Mar	Speed endurance/indoor season (e.g. racing 60m)	Learning to deal with lactate build-up, working in speed	2–3 endurance sessions (100–200m runs e.g. 5 x 100m, 4 x 150m; Pyramids: 110m, 120m, 130m, 140m and back down with long recoveries) 3 weights sessions: slightly lower weights than in conditioning phase Hills (1 session) 2–3 skills and drills/plyometrics; greater emphasis on power moves
Apr–May	Pre-season/speed phase	Sessions move on to track; event specific practice	2–3 weights sessions: lower weights 2–3 skills and drills/plyometrics 3–4 speed and start practice sessions e.g. reaction sessions (coach starts with no warning, run 10–15m from blocks only); curve start practice; accelerations sessions e.g. 3 x 30m, each faster than last; 2–3 sets of 2–3 x 30–60m (long recoveries) 1–2 speed endurance sessions as above
Late May–Sep	Competition phase	Much lighter training volume, with races every week	Max 2 weights sessions per week with light weights 1–2 skills and drills sessions 2–3 speed and start sessions as above, but longer recoveries (12–15 minutes) e.g. 50m, 150m, 50m, 150m x 3; ladders 50m, 60m, 80m, 100m, 120m

to that speed as long as possible – usually from 60m to around 85m. From 85m to 100m deceleration is inevitable but during this 'finish' phase, the runner should relax and try to hold form. The finish is measured by the torso crossing the line, so a good lean forward is essential, but time it right: leaning too early slows you down.

Sure starts

Getting sprint starts right can help you to win races. When you are in the 'set' position you will react to the first sound that you hear.

This, however, can sometimes be a problem, as competition rules state that any reaction time faster than 0.10 seconds is a false start (because scientific research has shown that this is the fastest any human can truly react). In a race, one false start puts all the athletes on a 'yellow card', and the next athlete to commit a false start is disqualified, even if the first false start was not theirs.

200m

Most good 100m sprinters can also run a decent 200m, and vice versa, but the 200m is more technical. The first complication, which both 200m and 400m runners must deal with, is the curve start. It will take practice to find the right positions for your blocks (make sure no part of the blocks is in any other lane than your own). On the curve you cannot start at full speed, but you must learn to take it as fast as possible. Stay as far toward the inside of your lane as possible, bearing in mind that your speed will push you to the outside. As you come out of the bend, turn your right shoulder slightly to face the direction you want to run in (toward the finish), using the 'swing' effect of the curve to move up to full speed. Energy conservation is also crucial, as you have farther to run and need to limit your deceleration from 150m. Unlike in the 100m, a very small amount of lactic acid will build up, which is perhaps why 400m runners can excel at this distance.

Above: British 200m runner Linford Christie uses the curve in the track to accelerate up to full speed.

Sprinting: 400m

Running one lap of a track may not look difficult, but the longest of the sprint distances is uniquely tough. Pacing must be finely tuned as lactic acid builds up from 300m onward, resulting in heavy legs and inevitable slowing.

The special challenge of the 400m – not quite short enough to be a true sprint, not long enough to be a middle-distance run – is such that great 400m runners can come from a short sprint background (such as Michael Johnson – see box) or from a background of good 800m running.

At the elite level, the 400m is over in less than 50 seconds (less than 45 for male athletes), and there are a number of technical details to get right over that short space of time. Like 200m runners, athletes running the 400m need to practise curve starts, but they also have to negotiate a second bend at full speed (accelerating again at 200m), staying upright and not compromising form.

Endurance is another important aspect of good 400m running, and something that doesn't really come into the shorter sprints. Physical speed endurance is clearly crucial, and 400m runners need a strong aerobic base as well as plenty of lactate-threshold-level training to learn to deal with the discomfort of running with lactate build-up. Mental endurance is just as important, since athletes will have to 'dig in' over the last 100m to win the race; they need to be able to shut off from the other lanes and run their own race.

Above: Toward the end of the 400m, athletes need to stay strong and mentally focused on their own race.

Date	Training phase	Theme	400m: training examples
			Weekly sessions
Oct–Dec	Conditioning	Building aerobic base and strength	20–45-minute off-road runs 2–3 sessions weights (moderate, not as heavy as for 100m/200m training) 1–2 sessions skills and drills/plyometrics Hill and stair running session Long, slow intervals e.g. 4 x 600m, short recoveries (2–3 minutes)
Jan–Mar	Speed endurance	Learning to cope with race pace over long periods	Hill/stair running session 2 weights sessions 2–3 plyometrics/skills and drills sessions Speed sessions of 5–10 reps of 100–600m e.g. 8 x 150m, 2 x 600m; 4 x 450m close to race pace; negative split runs 200m, rest 200m x 3–4 (total distance should be not be more than 3–4 times race distance)
Apr–May	Speed/pre-season	Moving almost all training on to track	2 weights sessions, reduced intensity 2 skills and drills/plyometrics (shorter sessions) Curve-start practice sessions Pure speed sessions as for 100m/200m e.g. 50m fast, 50m relaxed fast x 6 with long recoveries Event sessions: completed at race pace, but with race distance broken down e.g. 2 sets of 3 x 350m with 50m fast, 150m relaxed, 150 as fast as possible
Jun–Sep	Competition	Regular racing, reduced training volume	1–2 weights sessions, light weights 1–2 skills and drills sessions Event sessions e.g. 200m, rest, 200m at race pace 320m as race practice; add 10–12 seconds for predicted time (used by Clyde Hart, Michael Johnson's coach)

Great athletes: Michael Johnson (b. 1967, Texas, USA)

From 1991, when he won his first World Championship title over 200m, until his last international competition at the Sydney Olympics in 2000, where he won gold at 400m and as part of the 4 x 400m relay team, Michael Johnson won a total of five Olympic golds and nine World Championship golds. His 200m world record of 19.32 seconds, set at the Atlanta Olympic Games in 1996 was the biggest improvement ever over the previous record, which he had also set earlier that year. His record was only broken in 2008 by Jamaican Usain Bolt. Johnson achieved what many thought was impossible, winning gold at the 200m and 400m in the same Olympics. His 400m world record, still standing in 2008, was set in more remarkable circumstances. Coming into the 1999 World Championships in Seville, Johnson had suffered injury problems, which meant he had barely raced that season, and only qualified by virtue of being the defending champion. He won in 43.18 seconds, and went on to lead home the American 4 x 400m team to gold. Throughout his career, Johnson's strange running style puzzled onlookers: his stiff, straight back and short strides going against ideal sprint form, but with seven of the ten fastest-ever 400m times to his name, few would argue that it worked against him.

Right: Michael Johnson was extremely talented, winning gold in 200m and 400m at the same Olympic Games.

Pace the race

Different athletes develop different strategies for pacing the 400m. As with longer races (right up to the marathon) they are faced with a choice between running out fast and 'holding on' – which is always a risky plan – or starting the race relatively slowly and gradually speeding up. When considering the second approach, it is worth bearing in mind that it will be impossible to run a negative split (the second 200m faster) in a good field, and it can be mentally very demoralizing to watch the field run away from you at the start. Ideally, athletes should train to run with as even a pace as possible. This is incredibly difficult and requires acute awareness of your own limits and your pace. The last 100m of the race is inevitably always the slowest, as your body simply cannot cope with the level of oxygen debt, but great 400m runners will learn how to minimize this slowing down – a perfect example being Michael Johnson's world-record run in 1999: he ran the first 200m in 21.22 seconds, and the second in just 21.96 seconds.

Below: Jeremy Wariner (centre) of the USA, on his way to winning the men's 400m at the IAAF World Championships in Athletics, 2007.

Hurdles

For schoolchildren trying clear them for the first time, hurdles is probably the most fearsome athletic event. Even in later life we use hurdles as a metaphor for barriers and difficulties in our lives. A good hurdler will almost literally take the hurdle in his stride.

Hurdle races should be seen as sprints with added low obstacles rather than a series of 'jumps'. In fact, much of the power, speed and strength required of a hurdler crosses over with straight sprinting, and many athletes will be proficient at both (hurdlers often start out as promising sprinters). The main differences are that a hurdler needs excellent rhythm, and advanced flexibility. Losing your rhythm in a hurdling race can cost valuable hundredths of a second. As well as building basic speed and power (using similar training to sprinters), hurdlers must learn to fix their stride rate: over 110m (or 100m for women), they'll take 8 strides from the start to the first hurdle, then 3 strides between hurdles; over 400m, 20 strides should reach the first hurdle and they'll aim for 13–14 strides between barriers. Throughout the race, the aim is to keep as close to sprint form as possible so that the forward action remains fast and smooth.

Right: The short distances between the hurdles mean that getting into a good rhythm is essential for athletes.

Great athletes: Ed Moses (b. 1955, Ohio, USA)

The career of American 400m hurdler Ed Moses started abruptly, but his incredible run of good form lasted for almost ten years. Having trained as a straight sprinter, Moses had only raced the 400m hurdles once up until March 1976, but using fewer strides between hurdles than his rivals (12–13), he was able to take his personal best over the 400m event from 50.1 seconds at the start of 1976, to 48.30 going into the Montreal Olympics that summer. He went on to win the gold medal at the Games, at the same time setting a new world record of 47.64 seconds. The following year Moses began an incredible winning streak that lasted up until 1987, winning 122 races consecutively including another Olympic gold and two World Championships titles. Moses ended his career with an Olympic bronze medal in Seoul in 1988.

Right: American hurdler Ed Moses won 122 consecutive races in just under 10 years.

Hurdle sequence

1 *At the start, the lead leg should be in the back block. The start is identical to a sprint start, driving hard out of the blocks with the body almost horizontal. However, hurdlers must come up into full sprint stance (running upright and 'tall') sooner, within four or five strides, in order to take the first hurdle well.*

2 *On take-off, the athlete drives the lead leg up and forward knee-first (as in sprinting and hurdle drills), extending but not fully straightening it. The knee should not lock, as this makes it difficult to land smoothly and keep running. At the same time she drives her opposite arm forward for balance.*

3 *Coming over the hurdle, the hurdler leans her torso forward at the hips, keeping her centre of gravity as low as possible. Remember the aim is to clear the hurdle efficiently rather than 'jump' over it. The trail leg should be tucked up and pulled through as tightly as possible, ready to drive forward for the next step after landing.*

4 *There is no pause on landing, as the lead foot touches down and 'claws' the ground (as in sprinting). The hurdler pulls upright again as she lands, to continue sprinting. As in straightforward sprinting, twisting and side-to-side movements are wasteful and disrupt running rhythm, so the aim is to keep the hips and shoulders square on to the hurdles throughout.*

Speed Endurance for Middle-distance Running

In races up to 400m, the athlete's focus must always be on speed and on 'true' speed endurance. Middle-distance track races may look pedestrian in comparison, but running a sub-2-minute 800m or a sub-4:30 mile are as much about the 'endurance' as the speed.

The first time a runner races as fast as he can around two or four laps of a track, and experiences the shattering fatigue of the last few hundred metres, it becomes clear just how important tough training is to run these distances well.

To understand this unique challenge, it is important to be aware of the different energy systems that give runners the power to propel themselves forward at different speeds. Broadly speaking there are two energy pathways: the aerobic system, which uses oxygen to produce energy from the fuel in your muscles, and the anaerobic system, which does not use oxygen. (The anaerobic system can be broken down further into the alactic or immediate anaerobic system – which

Right: Tatyana Tomashova of Russia wins the women's 1,500m race at the World Athletics Championships, 2005.

Great athletes: Maria Mutola (b. 1972, Maputo, Mozambique)

Above: Maria Mutola was a reluctant runner at first, but went on to win nine world titles at 800m.

A somewhat reluctant athlete at first, Maria de Lurdes Mutola has become one of the most successful female 800m runners ever, with 11 world titles to her name (including 7 indoors) and 2 Commonwealth golds. Mutola had been a keen footballer at school and, even when persuaded to try track running, initially found the training too intense. However, her talent for middle-distance events quickly became obvious and, at just 15 years old, she competed in her first Olympic Games (in 1988) – though she was knocked out in the first heat of the women's 800m. Mutola gained funding from the IOC and moved to the USA to train, and it was after this that she began her domination of the event. She finished fourth at the World Championships in 1991, and went on to win five Championships medals from 1993 to 2003 (including three golds). She won Olympic gold at the Sydney Games in 2000, but was beaten to the title in 2004 by her training partner Kelly Holmes. Over the next two years, Mutola suffered injury problems, but in 2006 she again won gold at the World Indoor Championships, and she competed at the World Championships in Osaka in 2007, finishing third in her semi-final. Mutola's only world-record performance was over 1,000m in 1995, but while she may not be the fastest 800m runner ever, her consistency and longevity as an athlete are matched by few.

provides intense bursts of energy for up to 4 to 6 seconds – and the lactic or short-term anaerobic system, providing energy for up to about 90 seconds of intense exercise.) While sprinting predominantly uses the anaerobic pathway, middle-distance runners make much greater use of the aerobic systems so need more aerobic training. The real difficulty, though, is getting the balance right – more than for any other running events, speed and endurance are of equal importance.

Building a base of aerobic training is essential for 800m and 1,500m runners, and during the winter months their training may not be dramatically

Below: Rashid Ramzi, 800m winner at the 10th IAAF World Championships in Athletics, knows that this race is as much about endurance as it is about speed.

Use of energy systems over different distances		
Race distance	Aerobic	Anaerobic
100m	8%	92%
200m	14%	86%
400m	30%	70%
800m	57%	43%
1,500m	76%	24%
Marathon	99%	1%

different to that of long-distance runners. Long, slow runs and relatively slow intervals with short recoveries help to condition the body ready for the serious speedwork that takes place in the lead-up to competition.

Anaerobic training could take up two or three sessions per week, though the total distance covered at this level would not amount to many miles (doing too much anaerobic training

leads to fatigue and an increased risk of illness and injury). Middle-distance runners race at or close to their maximum heart rate, and well beyond the lactate threshold, so they must train their body to adapt to these stresses. Use a mixture of very fast, fairly short reps – 200m to 400m – with long recoveries, and longer intervals at race pace or slightly slower, with shorter recoveries. The British athlete Sebastian Coe and his coach and father Peter believed that not quite allowing the heart rate to recover between intervals, so allowing lactic acid build-up, was a good way to help the body adapt. Speed endurance sessions from both sprint programmes (400m) and from 5K programmes are useful, as the middle-distance runner needs the pure power of the sprinter combined with the endurance and lactate tolerance of the longer-distance athlete.

Middle-distance Racing: 800m and 1,500m/Mile

The mile was long regarded as the 'classic' distance in athletics, a baseline measure of an athlete's speed and skill. These days, thanks to the metric system, it is rarely raced – certainly at international level – and the 1,500m has taken its place.

Sitting in between the 'metric mile' and the sprint events are the tough two laps of the 800m. Athletes who are able to compete well in one middle-distance are usually able to compete well in both distances, though they may choose to specialize in one or the other.

Both the 800m and the 1,500m require impeccable pace judgement, so participating athletes must know precisely how fast they can run each lap – the aim being to run as evenly as possible, with a 'kick'

over the last lap. However, in a race situation, of course, you may not always be able to run the race exactly as you would choose to do. Runners with a stronger endurance base might choose to push the pace early on, while those with a sprint finish might prefer to head straight to the front of the pack and try to keep the pace down.

Right: Some long-distance, easy running to develop aerobic fitness is vital for middle-distance running.

	Session one	**Session two**	**Session three**	**Session four**
		Middle-distance racing: 800m & 1,500m schedule		
Week one	4 x 400m Race Pace (RP); 6–8 mins rest; repeat	8 x 200m faster than race pace, with 200m easy between; then 2 x 600m RP with 2 mins recovery	5K/3-mile time trial or race	60 mins easy
Week two	6 x 300m just faster than RP, 3 mins recoveries	150m, 200m, 250m, 300m, faster each time, then back down, with 200m recoveries	5K time trial	60–80 mins easy
Week three	5 x 400m RP with 2 mins recoveries; 6–8 mins rest; repeat	2 x 1,000m just slower than RP, with 3–4 mins recovery	1,500m/1-mile time trial	60 mins easy
Week four	5 x 400m RP with 1 min recoveries; 6–8 mins rest; repeat	800m, 1,000m, 800m at mile pace with 2–3 mins recoveries	15–20 mins at lactate threshold pace	60–80 mins easy
Week five	4 x 400m at RP, 50 sec recoveries; 5 mins rest; repeat	150m fast, 50m easy x 6; then 2 x 800m at RP with 2 mins recovery	1,500m or 800m time trial	60 mins easy
Week six	8 x 300m at RP with 1:30–2 mins recoveries	2 x 1,000m at mile pace with 3–4 mins recovery	5K time trial	60 mins easy
Week seven	4 x 400m at RP with 1 min recoveries; 6-8 mins rest; repeat	200m fast, 200m easy x 6; then 2 x 800m at mile pace with 400m recovery	1,500m/1 mile time trial	60 mins easy
Week eight	As week 7	2 x 1,200m at mile pace, 5–6 mins recovery	15 mins lactate threshold, then 4 x 200m RP with 400m recoveries	1,500m or 800m race

Great athletes: Sebastian Coe (b. 1956, London, UK)

For British athletics fans, Sebastian Coe is an icon of a golden era of running, along with his 'rivals', Steve Ovett and Steve Cram. Though an 800m specialist, Coe's two Olympic gold medals were at 1,500m and he remains the only man to successfully defend this title at consecutive Games.

Coe won his first major competition at the 1977 European Indoor Championships, taking gold in the 800m. His first (much-hyped) race against Ovett, the European Championships 800m in 1978, was an anti-climax. Ovett won silver, Coe bronze. The next year, Coe set world records at 800m, 1,500m and the mile. In total he set 11 world records during his career.

The Moscow Olympics in 1980 saw Coe and Ovett winning each other's events – Ovett won the 800m, leaving Coe with silver; then Coe won the 1,500m, with Ovett in third place. In 1984, despite having been ill most of the previous season, Coe defended his 1,500m title, beating Steve Cram. Cram, four years his junior, eclipsed Coe the following year, beating his mile world record. In 1986 Coe was ranked number one in the 800m for the fourth time but he was not picked for the 1988 British Olympic team.

On leaving athletics, Coe went into politics but nevertheless remained heavily involved in sports. Most recently he led London's successful bid to host the 2012 Olympic Games.

Above: Sebastian Coe holds up the Union Jack after winning the Olympic men's 1,500m final, 1984.

The best way to prepare for this is to include regular time trials or low-key races in your training. Training in a group can, of course, help you to work on your speed and tactics, but only running against a group of real competitors can teach you how to run your own race.

Below: The 1,500m can be a very tactical race as competitors must decide where to position themselves in the pack.

And don't just race the distance you've chosen to specialize in: 800m runners should try the odd 400m sprint and 1,500m or even 3,000m race, while 1,500m runners should have good 800m speed and endurance up to 5,000m.

Middle-distance race schedule

Runners should have a solid base of aerobic training, hill running, weight training, plyometrics and perhaps also some cross-country racing, built up over the winter months. Note that only the four key sessions are given in the schedule, on the other days athletes should use easy aerobic running, plus some weights or plyometrics sessions if desired.

Below: Wilfred Bungei (centre-right) of Kenya wins in the men's 800m final at the 2008 Beijing Olympics.

Middle-distance Racing: 3,000m and 5,000m

The 5,000m and the less common 3,000m are a natural step up from the classic middle-distance races. For young athletes, learning real endurance on the track in these races provides a solid background for moving on to the 10,000m and on to long-distance events.

The training for 3,000m and 5,000m track races is very similar to training for a 5K race on the road (the obvious difference being that almost all sessions take place on a track). However, the difference between a 5,000m and a 5K race is marked and each setting requires a completely separate mental approach. In a road-based 5K, the front runners might not see anyone else after the first few kilometres, but on the track the athletes are never far away from each other, and this makes the whole race much more intense. Moreover, unlike a

Right: In a 5,000m event, concentration and planning are important to ensure that you don't get boxed in by other athletes.

	Monday	Tuesday	Wednesday	Thursday	Friday	Saturday	Sunday
			5K: advanced schedule				
Week one	3 easy	2 x 1,000m with 3 mins recoveries	5 easy with 4 x 100m strides at end	4 x 800m with 2 mins recoveries; 8 x 200m with 200m recoveries	Rest	6km (4 miles) inc. hills	10–13 km (6–8 miles)
Week two	4 easy	3 x 1,000m with 3 mins recoveries	5 easy with 150m hard, 50m easy x 4 at end	6 x 400m with 90 secs recoveries; 1,200m x 1	Rest	8km (5 miles) inc. hills	13–15km (8–9 miles)
Week three	4 easy	1,000m; 1,600m; 1,000m with 3 mins recoveries	4 easy with 6 x 100m strides throughout	6 x 800m with 90 secs–2 mins recoveries	Rest	6km (4 miles) inc. hills	13–16km (8–10 miles)
Week four	4 easy/ cross-train	1,200m, 1,600m, 800m with 3 mins recoveries	5 easy with 150m hard, 50m easy x 6	200m, 400m, 800m x 2 with same distance recovery	Rest	6 km (4 miles) inc. 10–15 minutes easy fartlek	13–15km (8–9 miles)
Week five	4 easy/ cross-train	1,200m x 3 with 2 mins recoveries	5 easy with 4 x 100m strides at end	6 x 400m with 90 secs recovery; 4 x 200m with same recovery	Rest	8km (5 miles) with 6 x 100m strides at end	10–13km (6–8 miles)
Week six	3 easy	3 x 1,000m with 2 mins recoveries	Rest/cross-train	6km (4 miles) with 150m hard/50m easy x 4 at end	Rest	3 easy/rests	5K race

Above: Tariku Bekele and Abreham Cherkos of Ethiopia lead the field at this stage in the 5,000m 2008 Olympic final.

road race, there are no distractions on the track: with lap after lap of running, athletes are forced to concentrate on the task in hand. A 5,000m or 3,000m runner needs to think about where he sits in the pack for most of the race; run to the front too soon, and you risk 'blowing up' in the last few laps, but stay too far back and you risk being boxed in by other athletes, unable to break away from the pack.

Track races can become quite aggressive, and runners can expect to be elbowed, tripped over and spiked as the

competition heats up. The pace is usually faster than on the road, because of the flat, smooth surface of the track, the close proximity of the other competitors, and the relatively sheltered environment. Because of this, even for the longer track distances, runners should work on leg speed, training at mile or 800m pace two or three times per week.

5,000m and 3,000m: advanced schedule

To train for these distances, follow the Advanced 5K Schedule, but do all of your speedwork on the track and aim to race once or twice a week. Even low-key races with relatively small fields will give you the competition practice you need to become accomplished at the distances.

Include some of the following sessions to build leg speed and confidence on the track:
• 6–8 x 400m at mile speed with 90-second recoveries
• 6–8 x 300m at 800m speed with 2-minute recoveries, reducing recovery if these become too easy
Longer speed ladders at 3K pace:
• 1,000m; 1,200m; 1,400m; 1,600m and down again with 2-minute recoveries
• 150m hard, 50m easy, to exhaustion.

Year-round practice
The track season is fairly short, running from May to September. In the winter, cross-country racing helps runners from middle-distance upward to keep their summer speed. Without track markings, and with the added challenge of harsh, muddy terrain and poor weather, athletes toughen up and learn to race each other rather than the clock. Find out more about cross-country running in Cross-Country and Trail Running.

Great athletes: Wang Junxia (b. 1973, Jiaohe, China)
Wang Junxia's brief career as an international runner came to an end at the age of just 23, but some of her best performances on the track remain unbeaten. Having won the 10,000m at the world junior championships in 1992, her best year was 1993, when she became the world champion at 10,000m in Stuttgart. She went on to break the world record at the distance by 42 seconds, running 29:31.78. A month later, she set a world record at 3,000m (8:06.11).

However, Wang's career was not without controversy: her then-coach, Ma Junren, was criticized for his harsh treatment of his athletes, which included forcing them to run a marathon a day at altitude; he was later (in 2000) expelled from the Chinese Olympic team after six of his athletes tested positive for illegal substances. Some have claimed that Wang's world records, in particular her 10,000m time, could not have been possible without drugs, though Wang maintains this is not the case.

In 1994, she left Ma behind, and at the 1996 Olympics she won gold in the 5,000m in 14:59.88 and silver in the 10,000m in 31:02.58. However, years of intense training had taken their toll, and Wang retired the following year on a doctor's advice.

Below: Wang Junxia's track career was brief but brilliant, with a 10,000m record of 29:31.78.

ADVANCED LONG-DISTANCE RUNNING

When you have been running for several years, the idea of covering 5K or even 32km (20 miles) in one go does not seem daunting. However, there is a huge difference between completing long distances comfortably, and actually racing them. This chapter looks at how to race long distances successfully, covering everything from perfecting your pre-training nutrition, to training your mind to deal with the loneliness that comes with long-distance running.

Above: Once you know you can conquer a distance comfortably, you'll be racing against the clock.
Left: At the front of the pack, long-distance races are fast and tactical.

Perfect Nutrition Planning

The diets of elite athletes are almost as legendary as their 240km (150-mile) training weeks. As an amateur you don't need to start eating egg-white omelettes for breakfast, but if you want to maximize your potential, then nutrition planning is as important as the training itself.

If you decide to completely devote yourself to your sport, then unfortunately you will need to accept a few difficult facts. Heavy training sessions mean that you will burn more calories than the average person, but this does not mean that you can eat whatever you want. In fact, it is more important than ever to cut out unhealthy junk food and ensure that every mouthful you eat has some nutritional benefit for your body. It is also worth noting that the best athletes are slightly underweight – research has suggested that sprinters and hurdlers are 5 to 6 per cent lighter than the average 'ideal' weight, while long distance runners should be about 15 per cent lighter. However, runners need to balance the need to stay lean with a tendency to become obsessive (which can lead to eating disorders) and the need to eat enough to fuel their training.

Below are some guidelines for planning what you eat. If you are committed to taking a detailed approach to your diet, you will need to keep a precise food diary and plan what you are going to eat each day (research has shown that people who keep long-term food diaries are more

Above: Even though sprinters like Linford Christie look bulky, they are 5 to 6 per cent lighter than the average ideal weight.

Right: Marathon runner Paula Radcliffe has a very low BMI of 18, thanks to careful nutritional planning.

Featherweight champions

There do seem to be different ideal body types for different kinds of sport, and for different forms of running – on the whole, the longer the distance, the smaller and lighter the athlete should be, but what is really important is the athlete's power-to-weight ratio. It is no good being extremely light if this means that you have no muscle. The great athletes listed below would all be considered light by average standards.

Athlete	Distance	Height	Weight	BMI
Herb Elliott	Mid distance	1.79m/5'10.5"	66.6kg	20.8
Seb Coe	Mid distance	1.78m/5'10"	54.4kg	17.2
Linford Christie	Sprint	1.89m/6'2.5"	77kg	21.6
Paula Radcliffe	Long distance	1.73m/5'8"	54kg	18.0

Above: You can work out how many calories you need to maintain or lose weight easily.

successful at losing weight and maintaining their ideal weight). Weigh and measure your portions, and check the packaging of any pre-packed foods to note what they contain. When working out how much to eat, remember to account for all the exercise you do or don't do – you may need to alter your intake if you become injured and miss sessions.

How much should you eat?

Whether you want to maintain your current weight or lose weight, you need to know approximately how many calories you burn every day. First, work out your resting metabolic rate (RMR).
For men aged 18 to 30:
(weight in kg x 15.3) + 679
For men aged 31 to 60:
(weight in kg x 11.6) + 879
For women aged 18 to 30:
(weight in kg x 14.7) + 496
For women aged 31 to 60:
(weight in kg x 8.7) + 829

Right: The men's finalists in the 2008 Olympic marathon knew the value of strict dietary planning.

Remember, your RMR is the lowest number of calories your body needs simply to function. Any activity you do during the day must also be accounted for, so if you have a sedentary job (for example you work at a desk or behind a store counter), multiply your RMR by 1.4; if you do some activity, such as walking around, multiply it by 1.7; or if you are very active (outside of your sports training), multiply it by 2. Then, add to this figure the approximate number of calories you burn during your training. You can measure this using a heart-rate monitor (you will need to input details such as your weight, age and maximum heart rate); if you work out in the gym, you can use the read-outs on the machines' consoles as a rough guide.

If you want to lose weight, reduce the number of calories you consume by 10 to 20 per cent, aiming to lose around 0.5kg (just over a pound) each week. Lose weight any faster and you risk slowing down your metabolism and losing muscle mass. You should aim to cut calories from fat – one gram of fat contains nine calories, so it is energy-dense food. Restrict your carbohydrate intake to

Above: Middle-distance runner Herb Elliott weighed just 66.6kg at the peak of his athletics career.

about 60 per cent of your calories, reduce your fat intake to around 20 per cent of your daily calories, and at the same time aim to slightly increase your protein intake to 1.6g per kg of body weight.

High Protein Diets

Running and controlling your body weight go hand in hand – running is a great way to lose weight, and losing weight is a good way to improve your running. It is no surprise that many runners will diet at some point, and high protein diets are an obvious choice.

Athletes know that they need more protein than the average person to build muscle; they may also have heard that high-protein diets are a fast and effective way to lose unwanted fat. However, to avoid having a detrimental effect on your running, you must be careful about what kind of high-protein diet you follow.

High protein vs low carbohydrate

The recent popularity of high-protein, low-carbohydrate diets such as the Atkins model stems from the idea that dieters can eat as much as they want (in terms of calories) and still lose weight fast. The theory behind these diets is that cutting down carbohydrates reduces insulin resistance, which in turn stops the body from storing energy as fat. High-protein, low-carbohydrate diets force the body into a state of ketosis, in which fat is broken down and

Below: American sprinter Carl Lewis followed a vegan diet, showing you don't need meat for protein.

chemicals called ketones are released into the bloodstream. In the initial stages of the diet, carbohydrate intake drops to around 20g (¾oz) of carbohydrate a day (remember that athletes usually get 60 per cent of their calories from carbohydrates – at least 250g/9oz a day). After the first two weeks, small amounts of carbohydrates are gradually reintroduced.

These diets are highly controversial. Some scientists say they work only by creating a calorie deficiency, largely because the choice of foods is so restricted. Others go as far as to say they are dangerous, leading to kidney and heart problems. What is certain is that these diets are not suitable for athletes. Studies have shown that people on low-carbohydrate diets have far lower endurance levels than those on diets with a high or standard level of carbohydrate. Dehydration is also a risk on low-carbohydrate diets, a clear disadvantage for runners. So, runners wishing to lose weight and gain muscle should think in terms of high protein rather than low carbohydrates.

Above: As a serious runner, you should view food as fuel, and consider the nutritional benefit of every meal.

The benefits of protein

It has been suggested that a sports person requires more protein than the average person regardless of their weight goals. An averagely active person needs around 0.8g protein per kg of body weight, but that rises to 1.2 to 1.4g/kg for middle- and long-distance runners. If you are trying to lose fat, that figure rises again to around 1.6g/kg. It is useful for several reasons. For long-distance runners, protein can be a useful extra fuel when your carbohydrate stores (as glycogen) run down. It helps build muscle, making you a more powerful, stronger athlete, and to repair damaged muscle, not only when you are injured but after any tough or long run. Protein is useful for athletes trying to lose weight, as foods that are high in protein are more difficult to digest, thus

Left: Be careful not to cut down on your carbohydrate intake, since it gives you energy for fast running.

raising your metabolism slightly. It also makes you feel full for longer: some scientists believe this is due to a hormone, PYY (peptide YY), being released into the blood by cells lining the gut when you eat protein, which tells your brain you are full. Protein also helps prevent you from losing muscle when dieting (a common side effect).

Eating enough protein

Keep a detailed food diary for a week, and work out how much protein you currently eat. The chances are you will be far short of your required amount as an athlete. It can be difficult to work out how much protein you are eating at every meal, so if you don't have time to plan every gram, try adding protein: sprinkle nuts and seeds on your breakfast cereal, or have a low-fat yogurt with your usual snack of fruit. If you need to cut calories from elsewhere, try to cut down on fatty foods rather than protein or carbohydrates.

Contrary to popular belief, vegetarians do not suffer from lack of protein or poor quality protein (the great sprinter Carl Lewis was a vegan), but you may need to plan your meals more carefully. In fact, whether you are vegetarian or not, you should aim to get your protein from a range of sources. Different foods contain different types of protein, so a combination is best.

Below: Sprinkle sunflower, pumpkin or sesame seeds on to cereals or salads to instantly increase your protein intake.

Below: A 100g (3¾oz) serving of oily fish provides one-quarter to one-third of your daily protein requirement.

Protein-rich food:	
Food	g protein/100g
Lightly roasted turkey meat	33.6
Lean grilled (broiled) beef	29.5
Grilled (broiled) mackerel	29.5
Sunflower seeds	18.8
Walnuts	14
Quorn	12
Kidney beans	8.3
Tofu	8
Medium egg (per egg)	8
Low-fat yogurt	5.5
Baked beans	5

Perfect Light Meals

Most professional sportspeople have nutritionists to carefully plan their diets, from breakfast first thing in the morning through to the smallest snacks during the day. The rest of us have limited expertise to draw on, but these simple meals should help keep you on top form.

In an ideal world you would spend hours every day training, and the hours in between planning the rest of your life around your training, including a meticulous diet. The reality for most amateur athletes is that life – and work – gets in the way, and food is often the first aspect of our lifestyles to suffer. Your light meals are often more rushed than your main meal of the day, so it's easy to grab a pre-packed salad or bagel without checking what's in it. Unfortunately these convenient meals aren't designed with runners in mind, so you'll often find them full of hidden fats and refined carbohydrates, and lacking in the essential nutrients you need to run well and stay healthy.

But it doesn't take much time or effort to make your own healthy light meals; soups can be prepared in large batches and frozen in portions so you won't need to spend time on them on busy working days. These recipes are all low in fat but high in protein and slow-release energy; serve them with wholegrain bread for the extra carbohydrates and calories you'll need for training. Each of the following recipes makes four modest portions (for which the values are given) or three more generous servings.

Lean Scotch broth

200g/7oz pearl barley
1 onion
2 carrots
1 small swede (rutabaga), peeled
*   and chopped*
1 leek, washed and chopped
115g/4oz/1 cup cabbage, shredded
75g/3oz/½ cup boiled lean gammon
*   (smoked or cured ham), cubed*
salt and pepper

Put the pearl barley in a pan with 1.5 litres/2½ pints/6¼ cups of water. Bring to the boil, cover and simmer for 45 minutes. Add all the remaining ingredients and simmer for 30 minutes.

Nutritional information per portion: Energy 280kcal/1176kJ; Protein 11.3g; Carbohydrate 50.4g; Fat 5.3g.

Hearty bean soup

15ml/1 tbsp olive oil
1 onion, finally chopped
1 clove garlic, peeled and crushed
2 large carrots, peeled and chopped
2 x 400g/14oz cans mixed beans,
*   drained and rinsed*
400g/14oz can chopped tomatoes
15ml/1 tbsp tomato purée (paste)
5ml/1 tsp dried oregano
5ml/1 tsp dried basil
1 bay leaf
150ml/¼ pint/⅔ cup red wine

Heat the olive oil in a large pan, and then fry the chopped onion and garlic together in the oil until soft. Add the chopped carrots and continue to cook gently for 4 or 5 minutes, until the carrots start to soften. Next, pour in the mixed beans and the chopped tomatoes, stirring, then add the tomato purée, dried oregano, dried basil, bay leaf and red wine, and stir well.

Gently simmer the soup for 10 to 15 minutes, then remove the bay leaf. At this stage, you can either transfer the soup to a food processor and process until smooth, or if you prefer a chunky texture, serve it as it is.

Nutritional information per portion Energy 238kcal/1000kJ; Protein 17g; Carbohydrate 52g; Fat 4.1g.

Eating on the run

In an ideal world, everyone would eat a homemade lunch every day, but life gets in the way, often forcing us to grab a pre-packed lunch. If you have to do this, make sensible choices:
• Good sandwich fillings are lean proteins such as chicken or fish, or eggs or falafel for vegetarians. These will keep you full and help to keep your muscles healthy.

• Try to avoid buying over-complicated sandwiches or those which contain an obvious dressing – this will probably contain mayonnaise and will increase the fat content
• Go for wholemeal (whole-wheat) or seeded bread rather than white for slow-release energy
• If you choose a soup or pasta dishes with sauce, go for tomato-based or cream-free varieties.

Tofu and wild rice salad

175g/6oz/1 cup basmati rice
50g/2oz/generous ¼ cup wild rice
250g/9oz firm tofu, drained and cubed
25g/1oz preserved lemon, finely chopped
30ml/2 tbsp fresh parsley, chopped

For the dressing:
1 garlic clove, crushed
10ml/2 tsp clear honey
10ml/2 tsp of the preserved lemon juice
15ml/1 tbsp cider vinegar
15ml/1 tbsp olive oil
1 small fresh red chilli, finely chopped
ground black pepper

Cook the basmati rice and wild rice in
two separate pans. Whisk together
the dressing ingredients in a bowl.
Add the tofu, stir to coat and marinate
for 20 minutes. Fold the tofu, marinade,
preserved lemon and parsley into the rice,
check the seasoning and serve.

Nutritional information per portion:
Energy 284Kcal/1185kJ; Protein 9.6g;
Carbohydrate 47.6g; Fat 5.8g.

Homemade falafel

2 x 400g/14oz cans chickpeas in water,
    drained and rinsed
1 small onion, chopped
2 garlic cloves, peeled and crushed
30ml/2 tbsp fresh coriander (cilantro),
    finely chopped
30ml/2 tbsp flat leaf parsley, finely
    chopped
5ml/1 tsp ground cumin
5ml/1 tsp garam masala
salt and pepper
10ml/2 tsp vegetable oil
sesame seeds, for sprinkling

Place all the ingredients except for the
salt and pepper and vegetable oil in
a blender and blend to a dough-like
consistency (you may need to add a dash
of oil to help the mixture stick together).
Season, making sure that you mix the
seasoning in well. Take the falafel 'dough'
out and roll it into golf-ball sized rounds,
then pat down so they are flat. Sprinkle
with sesame seeds.
    Heat the oil in a pan over a medium
heat and fry for 2 minutes on each side,
until they are crispy. Serve with a leafy
salad, tomato salsa and low-fat plain
yogurt as a dip. You can keep the falafel
for up to two days in the refrigerator
before the frying stage, fry them as
required and use them in sandwiches.

Nutritional information per portion:
Energy 183kcal/768kJ; Protein 9.7g;
Carbohydrate 22.9g; Fat 6.5g.

*Left: Wholegrain bread is a great source
of the extra carbohydrates your body
will need while in training.*

Tomato and lentil dhal

30ml/2 tbsp vegetable oil
1 large onion, finely chopped
3 garlic cloves, chopped
1 carrot, diced
10ml/2 tsp cumin seeds
10ml/2 tsp mustard seeds
2.5cm/1in fresh root ginger, grated
10ml/2 tsp ground turmeric
5ml/1 tsp mild chilli powder
5ml/1 tsp garam masala
225g/8oz/1 cup split red lentils
800ml/1½ pints/3¼ cups vegetable stock
5 tomatoes, peeled, seeded and chopped
juice of 2 limes
60ml/4 tbsp chopped fresh coriander
    (cilantro)
ground black pepper
25g/1oz/¼ cup flaked (sliced) almonds,
    toasted, to serve

Heat the oil and cook the onion for
5 minutes. Add the garlic, carrot, cumin
and mustard seeds, and ginger. Cook for
5 minutes. Stir in the ground turmeric,
chilli powder and garam masala, and cook
on a low heat for one minute, stirring.
Add the lentils, stock and chopped
tomatoes, and season with ground black
pepper. Bring to the boil, then reduce the
heat and simmer, covered, for 45 minutes,
stirring occasionally.
    Stir in the lime juice and 45ml/3 tbsp
of the coriander. Cook for a further
15 minutes until the lentils are tender.
Sprinkle with the remaining coriander
and the flaked almonds.

Nutritional information per portion:
Energy 326Kcal/1372kJ; Protein 16.9g;
Carbohydrate 43.8g; Fat 10.5g.

Perfect Main Meals

Complicated cooking is probably the last thing you feel like doing after a hard day at work or looking after your family, but let low energy stop you from eating well and you'll get caught in a vicious circle. You need to eat well to refuel no matter how long your day has been.

There is no need to spend hours and hours slaving away in the kitchen to cook the perfect main meal that will help you recover from both your chores and your training. And you certainly don't need to cook separate meals for yourself and your family; in fact children are likely to benefit from a well-balanced runner's diet, although of course you will need to make smaller portions of food for younger children.

These healthy versions of classic family main meals are low in fat, but high in protein and slow-release energy to help you recover from a hard day's work and training.

The portions in these recipes are all quite modest, but if you have worked out your nutritional requirements you can adjust the recipes to provide you with more energy if necessary.

Below: When you are training hard it is important to find the time to sit down and eat a healthy, balanced meal.

Pasta with fresh tomatoes and basil

500g/1¼lb dried penne
5 very ripe plum tomatoes
1 small bunch fresh basil
60ml/4 tbsp extra virgin olive oil
salt and ground black pepper

Cook the dried pasta in a large pan of lightly salted boiling water for 12–14 minutes, or according to packet instructions, until tender.

Meanwhile, roughly chop the tomatoes and tear up the basil leaves. When it is cooked, drain the pasta thoroughly and return it to the clean pan. Add the tomatoes, basil and olive oil, and toss to mix together thoroughly. Season with salt and freshly ground black pepper and serve immediately.

COOK'S TIP

If you cannot find ripe tomatoes, roast those you have to bring out their flavour. Put the tomatoes in a roasting pan, drizzle with oil and roast at 190°C/375°F/Gas 5 for 20 minutes, then mash roughly.

Nutritional information per portion:
Energy 552kcal/2336kJ; Protein 16.3g;
Carbohydrate 96.9g; Fat 13.8g.

Low-fat chilli con carne

15ml/1 tbsp vegetable oil
1 onion, finely chopped
1 garlic clove, peeled and crushed
300g/11oz lean beef steak, cubed
100g/3¾oz/scant 2 cups mushrooms
1 red (bell) pepper, chopped
400g/14oz can tomatoes
400g/14oz can red kidney beans
15ml/1 tbsp tomato purée (paste)
5ml/1 tsp paprika
5ml/1 tsp ground cumin
5ml/1 tsp chilli powder
500g/1¼lb sweet potatoes
200g/7oz/scant 1 cup low-fat natural
 (plain) yogurt

Heat the oil in a large pan. Fry the onion and garlic in the oil until soft. Add the beef, mushrooms and pepper and continue to cook until the meat is browned. Add the canned tomatoes, kidney beans, tomato puree and spices. Simmer for 20 minutes. Meanwhile, cut the sweet potatoes into wedges and bake in the oven at 200°C/400°F/Gas 6 for 20 minutes. Serve the chilli with the wedges, topped with the yogurt.

Nutritional information per portion:
Energy 380kcal/1596kJ; Protein 31.1g;
Carbohydrate 45.6g; Fat 9.4g.

Stir-fried prawns with noodles

130g/4½oz rice noodles
30ml/2 tbsp groundnut (peanut) oil
1 large garlic clove, crushed
150g/5oz large prawns (shrimp), peeled
15g/½oz dried shrimp
15ml/1 tbsp Thai fish sauce
30ml/2 tbsp soy sauce
30ml/2 tbsp palm sugar (jaggery) or
  light muscovado (brown) sugar
30ml/2 tbsp fresh lime juice
90g/3½oz/½ cup beansprouts
40g/1½oz/⅓ cup peanuts, chopped
15ml/1 tbsp sesame oil
chopped coriander (cilantro), 5ml/1 tsp
  dried chilli flakes and 2 shallots,
  finely chopped, to garnish

Soak the noodles in a bowl of boiling water for 5 minutes, or according to the packet instructions. Heat the groundnut oil in a wok. Add the garlic, and stir-fry over a medium heat for 2 minutes, until golden brown.

   Add the prawns and dried shrimp to the pan and stir-fry for a further 2 minutes. Stir in the fish sauce, soy sauce, sugar and lime juice. Drain the noodles, then add to the wok with the beansprouts, peanuts and sesame oil. Toss to mix, then stir-fry for 2 minutes. Serve immediately, garnished with the coriander, chilli flakes and shallots.

Nutritional information per portion:
Energy 312Kcal/1299kJ; Protein 11.8g;
Carbohydrate 35.8g; Fat 13.3g.

Chicken fried rice

30ml/2 tbsp groundnut (peanut) oil
1 small onion, finely chopped
2 garlic cloves, chopped
2.5cm/1in piece fresh root ginger,
  peeled and grated
225g/8oz skinless chicken breast fillets,
  cut into 1cm/½in dice
450g/1lb/4 cups cold cooked white long
  grain rice
1 red (bell) pepper, seeded and sliced
115g/4oz/1 cup drained canned corn
5ml/1 tsp chilli oil
5ml/1 tsp hot curry powder
2 eggs, beaten
spring onion (scallion) slices,
  to garnish

Heat the oil in a wok, and stir-fry the onion for 1 minute, then add the garlic and ginger and cook for 2 minutes more. Push the onion mixture to the sides, add the chicken to the centre of the wok and stir-fry for 2 minutes more.

   Add the rice and stir-fry for about 3 minutes, until the chicken is cooked through. Stir in the red pepper, corn, chilli oil and curry powder. Toss over the heat for 1 minute. Stir in the beaten eggs and cook for about 1 minute more. Serve in bowls and garnish with the spring onion slices.

Nutritional Information per portion:
Energy 356kcal/1500kJ; Protein 21g;
Carbohydrate 46.4g; Fat 10.9g.

Low-fat meat-free moussaka

15ml/1 tbsp olive oil
1 garlic clove, peeled and crushed
1 onion, finely chopped
1 red (bell) pepper, chopped
250g/9oz/generous 1 cup red lentils
100ml/3½fl oz/scant ½ cup red wine
400g/14oz can tomatoes
10ml/2 tsp dried oregano
2 large aubergines (eggplants)
40g/1½oz unsalted (sweet) butter
600ml/1 pint/2½ cups skimmed milk
150g/5oz/1¼ cups plain (all-purpose) flour
200g/7oz half-fat Cheddar cheese, grated

Fry the onion and garlic in half the oil until soft. Add the pepper and cook for 1 minute. Add the lentils, red wine tomatoes, and oregano and bring to the boil, then reduce the heat and simmer for 20 minutes. Slice the aubergines and brush with the remaining oil, then grill (broil) for a few minutes until soft.

   Melt the butter, then add the flour and fry for a few minutes over a low heat. Gradually add the milk, stirring. Slowly bring to the boil to thicken the sauce, then add most of the cheese, keeping a handful back. Layer the lentil mix and the aubergine in a baking dish, ending with an aubergine layer. Pour the cheese sauce over the top and sprinkle with the remaining cheese. Bake for 30 minutes at 220°C/425°F/ Gas 7 until brown on top.

Nutritional information per portion:
Energy 527kcal/2213kJ; Protein 31.1g;
Carbohydrate 57g; Fat 18.9g.

Sports-specific Fuel

Ideally, the fuel needed to run well and recover quickly would come from natural sources. However, consuming enough energy and nutrients from normal food is not practical, particularly for longer races: special energy drinks, bars and gels are designed for this.

To overcome the problems of eating on the run, manufacturers have come up with a huge range of drinks, energy gels and bars to help athletes take on food and fluids as easily as possible. Many runners struggle with these products at first, as they often taste sweet and artificial, which can be difficult to tolerate when two hours of running has left you feeling nauseous. However, it is well worth practising taking on energy foods as you run, because they will help you perform better and protect you from illness and injury afterward.

Your muscles' preferred choice of fuel is glycogen, a quickly-accessible form of carbohydrate. However, you can only store enough glycogen for between two and two and a half hours of running. For an amateur marathon runner that will only take them 29–32km (18–20 miles). At this point, as the body switches to fat for fuel, many runners

Below: Take advantage of drink stations along the race route to ensure that you don't become dehydrated.

Above: Energy bars will provide plenty of calories but are best eaten before a race rather than during.

'hit the wall' – they temporarily run out of energy as the body works to convert fat into usable energy. The aim of sports fuels is to feed your body carbohydrate so that it doesn't need to switch to fat burning (you can also help yourself by training your body to use fat as fuel – for example using long, slow runs – so that your glycogen stores are preserved for longer).

When running a long-distance race, you should aim to consume about 40 to 60g of carbohydrate per hour. It can be difficult to stomach carbohydrates on the run, so you should never try eating them for the first time during a race. Practise taking on carbohydrates in training, using whatever brand you plan to use during the race. Sports products fall into three categories:

Energy bars
These are the most energy-dense form of sports foods, but as such they are more difficult to digest. They

are best used before a race, or during long, slow races, such as ultramarathons or stage races. (However, studies have shown that eating an energy bar and taking on water with it is as effective in delivering energy as sports drinks or gels.) Typically they provide carbohydrates from rice, oats and maltodextrin. Beware of bars with high levels of glucose, which can cause a spike in your blood sugar, and fructose, which can have a laxative effect. Many bars also contain some protein (for recovery, and slow-release energy), and may also include nuts, chocolate or toffee to make them taste better. From a functional point of view, the simpler the better – more than 5g of fat, 5g of fibre and 10g of protein will make the bar difficult to digest. They usually provide 30 to 60g of carbohydrates per bar, which is enough for an hour of exercise.

Below: You can buy powdered sports drinks and add water – some races will allow you to leave these at water stations.

Above: All races must provide water, and many bigger events will also have sports drinks on offer.

Energy gels
A good compromise, energy gels are a more compact way of carrying your fuel and are easier to digest than bars. The downside is that they can be messy

Left: Practise using your chosen food and drink during training to make sure you react well to it.

to take, and you usually need to drink some water with them (to make the mixture isotonic and easily absorbed). However, they only provide around 15 to 30g of carbohydrates per portion, so you will need at least two for each hour of exercise. On a marathon that could add up to six to ten gels, which is a lot to carry and a lot to stomach. Gels usually contain fast-release carbohydrates from sugars, so it is important to take them at regular intervals (every 20 to 30 minutes) to keep your blood sugar levels steady.

Sports drinks
Faster athletes usually choose drinks over gels and bars because they are much easier to take on at high speeds. At many big races, sports drinks are available around the course so you don't have to carry anything – check which brand will be used and practise drinking it in training. Otherwise, see if you can make up your own drinks and

have them placed at water stations around the course. Most sports drinks, mixed up correctly, provide an ideal 6 to 8g of carbohydrate per 100ml – you will need to drink between 750ml and 1 litre per hour.

Preventing illness

Many athletes complain that they are more likely to catch colds and bugs in the days just after a big race. This is because the harder you train and race, the more your immune system is suppressed. Part of the reason for this is that the stress hormones which are released when your body switches to fat burning for energy block the action of some types of white blood cells, which form part of your body's defences against illness. By keeping your body's carbohydrate levels topped up, you will reduce the need for fat to be used as fuel, and also help prevent stress hormones from being released, so fuelling your run will not only help you run well on the day, but will aid your recovery afterward.

DIY Training Fuel

Runners tend to have a better awareness of what they put into their bodies than other people, so it is strange that many of them come to rely on manufactured training fuels, which can be full of highly refined sugars, especially when these recipes are so easy.

Even energy bars and drinks that contain only natural ingredients – and there are plenty of examples of these on the market – can taste artificial. For this reason many athletes prefer not to use them at all, sticking to water. In doing so they are missing out on the hugely important benefits of staying well-fuelled during tough training sessions and long races. However, if you are prepared to invest a little time, you can easily make your own energy snacks and drinks at home.

All of these recipes deliver more than 30g of carbohydrates, roughly the same as a store-bought energy gel, but because of their slightly higher fat content (in most cases), they will take a little longer for your body to digest. As such they are better for eating before you begin a training session rather than while you are out running, with the exception of the natural isotonic drink, which will provide you with an almost instant energy hit.

Above: Mixing your own natural energy drink from fruit juice and water at home is cheap and easy.

Fruit flapjacks
The oats in this bar should help to calm pre-race nerves; the sultanas and honey give a moderate-GI energy release, while the ground ginger (which is optional) should help to stave off nervous nausea.

200g/7oz/scant 1 cup butter or margarine
225g/8oz soft light brown sugar
30ml/2 tbsp clear honey
300g/11oz/2½ cups jumbo oats
150g/5oz/1 cup sultanas (golden raisins)
2.5ml/½ tsp ground ginger

Melt the butter, sugar and honey together in a large pan over a low heat, stirring constantly, until the sugar and honey have dissolved. Mix in all the other ingredients. Press the mixture into a lightly greased baking tray and bake at 190°C/375°F/Gas 5 for 15 to 20 minutes, until golden brown. While it is still hot, cut into 16 portions, but leave to cool in the tin, as the flapjack remains soft until it has cooled slightly.

Nutritional information per portion:
Energy 250kcal/1050kJ; Protein 2.5g;
Carbohydrate 34.1g; Fat 11.6g.

Banana bread
Bananas are the classic runner's fuel and this soft loaf should be easy to eat before a run. Adding cinnamon may help control your blood sugar levels, avoiding a crash after the initial burst of energy.

100g/3¼oz/scant 1 cup butter
200g/7oz/1 cup caster (superfine) sugar
2 eggs, beaten
225g/8oz/2 cups wholemeal
(whole-wheat) flour
2.5ml/½ tsp baking powder
5ml/1 tsp cinnamon
200g/7oz ripe bananas, mashed

Cream the butter and sugar together. Beat in the eggs, then fold in the flour, baking powder and cinnamon. Add the bananas and mix thoroughly. Pour the mixture into a greased loaf tin (pan) and bake at 180°C/350°F/Gas 4 for 50 minutes, until risen and golden brown on top (note the consistency of the loaf may remain soft because of the bananas; you can firm it up by refrigerating it later). Slice into ten pieces.

Nutritional information per portion:
Energy 265kcal/1113kJ; Protein 5g;
Carbohydrate 39g; Fat 10.3g.

Natural isotonic drink

This natural isotonic drink delivers the same amount of carbohydrates as a store-bought energy drink – around 6g per 100ml, so it can be absorbed easily on the run. It is very easy to make and cost effective too, as store-bought energy drinks can be expensive. To save time on early-morning runs, make up a bottle the night before and keep chilled in the refrigerator overnight.

Makes 1 litre/1¾ pints/4 cups

500ml/17fl oz/generous 2 cups
   unsweetened apple juice
500ml/17fl oz/generous 2 cups water
pinch salt

Pour the apple juice and the water into a 1-litre (1¾-pint) sports bottle, then add the pinch of salt. Shake the bottle thoroughly to mix.

Nutritional information per portion
Energy 190kcal798kJ; Protein 0.5g;
Carbohydrate 55g; Fat 0.5g.

Low-fat fruit loaf

Lack of fat in this loaf makes it easier to digest on the run. It provides enough energy for about an hour of exercise, but be careful of the high fibre content, which could unsettle your stomach.

115g/4oz/1 cup raisins
115g/4oz/1 cup sultanas (golden raisins)
115g/4oz/1 cup currants
25g/1oz/2 tbsp soft dark brown sugar
150ml/¼ pint/⅔ cup hot black tea
10ml/2 tbsp thick-cut marmalade
2 eggs, beaten
175g/6oz/1½ cups wholemeal
   (whole-wheat) flour
5ml/1 tsp mixed spice (apple pie spice)
30ml/2 tbsp skimmed milk

Soak the fruit and sugar in the tea overnight. Stir in the other ingredients and mix. Pour into a greased and lined loaf tin (pan) and bake at 180°C/350°F/Gas 4 for 1½ hours until firm.

Nutritional information per portion
Energy 249kcal/1045kJ; Protein 6.3g;
Carbohydrate 50.9g; Fat 2.7g

Above: This fruit loaf has a very low fat content and so is easy for your stomach to digest as you run.

Instant energy

If you don't have the time to spare to make your own training snacks, just grab some natural quick-release energy in the form of:

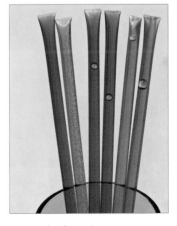

A medium banana: *this will give you enough energy for around 30 minutes of running, as well as potassium to keep your muscles from cramping. Choose very ripe bananas, which are easier to digest.*

Raisins: *this high-energy dried fruit packs a powerful 135kcal/567kJ and 35g of carbohydrates for every 50g (handful). It also contains high levels of antioxidants, which help combat some of the damage done by intense exercise.*

Honey: *clear honey in a squeezy pack (sometimes called a honey stick) makes the perfect natural energy gel. Research suggests it is just as effective as store-bought energy gels for fuelling exercise.*

5K Event: Advanced Schedule

It is a tough distance to get right, but learning how to run 5K to the best of your ability will stand you in good stead for longer distances. It's a great test of speed, stamina and strength of character and is short enough to be raced once a month.

In some ways a 5K road race is more daunting for an experienced runner than for a complete beginner. In training, there are three main areas to work on.

Style

You will need to develop a faster stride for the 5K, especially if you have become used to running farther and slower. Working on your form will help your legs to move quickly and will keep you from wasting energy during the race. Most people find that their style naturally improves when they run a bit faster, but you can work on it. Including regular skills and drills sessions to work on your flexibility, reactions and style will help, as will performing fast strides at the end of some runs.

Below: Working on your running form is important for 5K racing. Include some hill walks and runs in your sessions.

Great athletes: Paavo Nurmi (b. 1897, Turku, Finland, d. 1973)

One of the earliest examples of a strong tradition of Finnish distance runners, Paavo Nurmi won nine Olympic gold medals and three silvers and set countless world records across a huge spectrum of distances, making him a national hero in his home country. At his first Olympic Games in Antwerp, 1920, he won gold in the 10,000m, two cross-country events, and silver in the 5,000m. He was a determined athlete and his tough training is legendary. He went on to compete at two more Olympics, but in 1932 was not allowed to take part as officials ruled he had accepted too much money for expenses, breaking the strict rules on amateurism. He won his last major race in 1933. In 1952, when the Olympics came to Helsinki, Nurmi carried the torch at the opening ceremony, and there is a statue of him outside the Olympic stadium there.

Left: The Finnish great, Paavo Nurmi, lights the Olympic flame at the 1952 Games in Helsinki.

Pacing

There are two approaches to pacing a 5K. The traditional approach is the negative split – the safer option – where the first half is run slightly slower. However, recent research suggests that the best approach is actually to head out fast and try to hang on. Whichever tactic you choose, you need to develop an instinctive feel for your goal 5K pace, and longer intervals (over 1,000m) can help with this.

Coping with pain

It sounds dramatic, but if you don't feel strong discomfort for at least the last 2km of your 5K race, you are probably not working as hard as you can. Unfortunately it takes practice to learn to deal with this, which is where your mile pace and longer

Right: Running fast intervals of 1,000m and longer is a good way for you to learn pace judgement.

intervals come into play. As you get more experienced you can cut down recovery times between repetitions, which brings you closer to the race experience. For these sessions it is especially useful to train with faster athletes; if you train alone it will be very difficult to force yourself to run this fast for any length of time.

Example six-week schedule

Before starting this schedule, you should be running at least five times a week. Your long run should be at least an hour, and you should be doing one or two speedwork sessions. For longer intervals here (1,000m and beyond) you should aim to run at 3 to 5 seconds faster than a 5K pace; for shorter repetitions aim to run at your mile pace. Speed sessions should include a 10-minute warm-up jog and 10-minute cool-down. Your race goal is faster than 24:30 (8-minute miling); if you are aiming to run sub-20 minutes, reduce the recovery periods between long intervals.

Right: Train with someone slightly faster than you to make sure you push yourself hard enough.

	Mon	**Tue**	**Wed**	**Thur**	**Fri**	**Sat**	**Sun**
			5K event: advanced schedule				
Week one	3 easy	2 x 1,000m with 3 min recoveries	5 easy with 4 x 100m strides at end	4 x 800m with 2 min recoveries; 8 x 200m with 200m recoveries	Rest	6km (4 miles) inc. hills	10–13km (6–8 miles)
Week two	4 easy	3 x 1,000m with 3 min recoveries	5 easy with 150m hard, 50m easy x 4 at end	6 x 400m with 90 sec recoveries; 1,200m x 1	Rest	8km (5 miles) inc. hills	13–15km (8–9 miles)
Week three	4 easy	1,000m; 1,600m; 1,000m with 3 min recoveries	4 easy with 6 x 100m strides throughout	6 x 800m with 90 secs–2 mins recoveries	Rest	6km (4 miles) inc. hills	13–16km (8–10 miles)
Week four	4 easy/ cross-train	1,200m, 1,600m, 800m with 3 min recoveries	5 easy with 150m hard, 50m easy x 6	200m, 400m, 800m x 2 with same distance recovery	Rest	6km (4 miles) inc. 10–15 minutes easy fartlek	13–15km (8–9 miles)
Week five	4 easy/ cross-train	1,200m x 3 with 2 min recoveries	5 easy with 4 x 100m strides at end	6 x 400m with 90 secs recoveries; 4 x 200m with same distance recovery	Rest	8km (5 miles) with 6 x 100m strides at end	10–13km (6–8 miles)
Week six	3 easy	3 x 1,000m with 2 min recoveries	Rest/cross-train	6km (4 miles) with 150m hard/50m easy x 4 at end	Rest	3 easy/rests	5K race

10K Event: Advanced Schedule

For the experienced runner, the 10K has a particular draw. It is a fairly short race, so you can recover quickly from it and have several attempts at a personal best over a season, and the nice round 10 kilometres makes it perfect for pace practice.

It is a distance that eludes some of the best professional athletes, but the 10K is worth revisiting several times a year; in the winter as a means of keeping your speed up, and in the summer to ensure you can still cover a decent distance. If you're training for a 5K or for a longer event, then you should be able to run a good 10K time, but if you are training

specifically for this distance you'll need to fine-tune your sessions. The key sessions involved in running a 10K are:

Race pace

Some coaches believe that 10K race pace is the most efficient speed for most athletes. However, that is true only if you can get it right. You will use long stretches of 10K pace in your speed

sessions to get used to the pace. If you are training for a longer event, the 10K pace will stand you in good stead, as it forms the basis for faster sessions for a half-marathon and longer. If instead you are aiming to knock a huge chunk off your personal best, try these sessions at your current best pace and if they feel easy, step up to your 'dream' pace to see how you cope.

	Mon	Tue	Wed	Thur	Fri	Sat	Sun
			10K event: advanced schedule				
Week one	Rest	6 x 800m with 400m recoveries	8km (5 miles) with 5 x 100m strides at end	3 x 1.5km (1 mile) at race pace with 4 min recoveries	Rest/ cross-train	8km (5 miles) easy	13–16km (8–10 miles)
Week two	Rest	4 x 200m hard/200 easy; 10 mins easy; 4 x 800m with 400m recoveries	8km (5 miles) easy	1,000m; 1,200m; 1,600m; back down at race pace with 2 min recoveries	Rest/ cross-train	8km (5 miles) easy with 5 x 100m strides	13–16km (8–10 miles)
Week three	Rest	As week 1	6.5km (4 miles) neg split run	4 x 1.5km (1 mile) at race pace with 4 min recoveries	Rest	6.5km (4 miles) easy	16–19km (10–12 miles)
Week four	Rest	As week 2	4km (2.5 miles) neg split run	2 x 1,600m race pace, 4 min recs; then 6 x 200m hard/200m easy	Rest	8km (5 miles) easy	16km (10 miles)
Week five	Rest	6 x 800m (just faster than race pace) with 400m recoveries	8km (5 miles) easy	10K neg split run (on race course if poss.)	Rest/ cross-train	8km (5 miles) easy	13km (8 miles) with 3 x 10 mins 10K pace plus 5 x 100m strides
Week six	Rest	2 x (200m, 400m, 800m, back down); with 200m recoveries	6.5km (4 miles) neg split	5 x 1.5km (1 mile) at race pace with 2 min recoveries	Rest/ cross-train	10km (6 miles) easy	13km (8 miles) with 2 x 10 mins at race pace
Week seven	Rest	As week 5	8km (5 miles) neg split	4 x 1.5km (1 mile) at race pace with 90 sec recoveries	Rest/ cross-train	8km (5 miles) easy	16km (10 miles) easy
Week eight	Rest	6 x 800m, with 400m recoveries	8km (5 miles) neg split	8km (5 miles) easy	Rest	5km (3 miles) easy with 4 x 100m strides	10K race

Great athletes: Haile Gebrselassie (b. 1973, Arsi Province, Ethiopia)

In an international career that began in the early 1990s, Haile Gebrselassie has earned a deserved reputation as one of the greatest distance runners ever. He has set 26 world records, won two Olympic gold medals and four 10,000m golds in four consecutive World Championships.

His first real international breakthrough came at the World Junior Championships in 1992, where he won the 5,000m and 10,000m. He was not without close rivals, mainly fellow African runners, and at the 2000 Olympics in Sydney he beat the Kenyan runner Paul Tergat in the closest 10,000m in Olympic history: the margin was just 0.09 seconds. His next Olympics in Athens was a disappointment; he had hoped to retain his 10,000m title but lost to countryman Kenenisa Bekele. Since that Games,

Gebrselassie has focused on road races, with impressive wins over 10K, and world records at 10 miles and half-marathon. In 2005, he won all his road races. The one record that seemed to evade him was the marathon. Despite wins at Amsterdam and Berlin, his performances at the Flora London Marathon in 2006 and 2007 ended badly – he pulled out at 18 miles in the latter race. However, later that year, Gebrselassie was vindicated with a new marathon world record, 2:04:26. The following year proved disappointing: having decided not to race the marathon at the Beijing Olympics – he feared the city's pollution would aggravate his asthma – Gebrselassie could only reach sixth place in the 10,000m. He has now turned his attention back to road racing, and broke his own record in 2008, running 2:03:59 in Berlin. He maintains that he will run a marathon in less than 2:03 before the end of his career.

Left: Haile Gebrselassie running the London Marathon. He set a new world record at the distance in 2008.

Negative splits

A 10K event is the perfect distance to use the negative split. Practise this in slightly shorter training sessions so that you are able to get used to the feeling of running relaxed then speeding up. Gradually you will build up to a 10K 'time trial', so find a route that is as close as possible to 10K (you can use a track or a treadmill to measure the distance accurately if necessary).

Example eight-week schedule

Before beginning this eight-week schedule you should be running at least five times per week, covering a minimum of 48km (30 miles). You should be able to run for 1 hr 30 mins comfortably, and ideally you will be doing one or two speed sessions per week. All speed sessions should have a 10-minute warm-up jog and 10-minute cool down. Your target race time is 35 to 45 minutes.

Long runs

It may seem strange to run almost to half-marathon distance during a 10K schedule, but without this comfortable

level of endurance you won't be able to sustain a fast pace. It's also worth bearing in mind that the 10K can be the stepping stone to great

marathons – as it has been for many an elite athlete, such as the great Gebrselassie – so you won't regret maintaining your long-run base.

Right: Some coaches believe that 10K pace is the most efficient speed.

Half-marathon: Advanced Schedule

Half-marathon training is not dissimilar to training for the full distance, and most runners train for both concurrently. The noticeable difference is in the pace, which, if you are racing well, should be considerably less relaxed than at marathon level.

Half-marathons tend to be run just below lactate threshold pace, so you need to practise this more often in training. You can only estimate your exact lactate threshold without being tested, but for most people it is around 80 to 85 per cent of their maximum heart rate. Some of your sessions will be longer runs with periods of threshold and race pace running built in.

The mileage needed for a half-marathon almost matches that of a marathon schedule. You can run a half-marathon with fewer really long runs, but to be able to push the pace you will need to be comfortable over much longer distances. In fact, if you have

Below: Over 24,000 participants competed in the 28th Berlin half-marathon in April 2008.

time to build up to running twice a day, then you should add an extra 30 to 40 minute easy run to every day (separate from the sessions listed on the plan).

Example 12-week plan
To follow this plan you must have been running five or six times a week for several months, with one long run of 1hr 30 mins and two speed sessions per week. For intervals over a mile (5 to 8 minutes) in length, run at threshold or race pace; for one-mile repetitions use 10K pace; for 400 to 800m use 5K pace. Each speedwork and threshold session should begin with a 10-minute warm-up.

Left: To run a fast half-marathon, your mileage will need to almost equal full marathon training.

Half-marathon: advanced schedule

	Mon	Tue	Wed	Thur	Fri	Sat	Sun
Week one	5km (3 miles) easy/cross-train	6 x 800m with 400m recoveries	8km (5 miles) easy with 5 x 100m strides throughout	2 x 10 mins threshold, 5 mins recovery	8km (5 miles) easy	Rest/ cross-train	16–19km (10–12 miles)
Week two	5km (3 miles) easy/cross-train	400m, 800m, 1,200m, 1,600m then back with 400m recoveries	8km (5 miles) easy with 5 x 100m strides throughout	15 mins threshold; 10 mins recovery then 5 x 200m fast but relaxed	8km (5 miles) easy	Rest/ cross-train	19–22km (12–14 miles)
Week three	5km (3 miles) easy/cross-train	8 x 800m with 400m recoveries	10km (6 miles) easy with 5 x 100m strides throughout	15 mins threshold; 10 mins recovery then 5 x 200m fast but relaxed	8km (5 miles) easy	Rest/ cross-train	22–25km (14–16 miles) with 2 x 10 mins at race pace
Week four	8km (5 miles) easy/cross-train	4 x 1 mile with 2–3 min recoveries	10km (6 miles) easy with 8 x 100m strides throughout	3 x 10 mins threshold; 5 min recoveries	10km (6 miles) easy	Rest/ cross-train	26–29km (16–18 miles) with 3 x 10 mins at race pace
Week five	8km (5 miles) easy/cross-train	8 x 800m with 400m recoveries	10km (6 miles) easy with 8 x 100m strides throughout	2 x 15 mins threshold with 5 mins recovery	10km (6 miles) easy	Rest/ cross-train	32km (20 miles) with 2 x 20 mins at race pace
Week six	Cross-train/rest	2 x 800m, 1,600m, 2,000m with 3 min recoveries	10km (6 miles) easy with 5 x 200m fast but relaxed	2 x 15 mins threshold with 5 mins recovery	10km (6 miles) easy	Rest/ cross-train	22–25km (14–16 miles) with 3 x 15 mins at race pace; or race 10K
Week seven	8km (5 miles) easy/cross-train	2 x 800m, 1,600m, 2,000m with 3 min recoveries	10km (6 miles) easy with 5 x 200m fast but relaxed	30 mins threshold	10km (6 miles) easy	Rest/ cross-train	32km (20 miles) with 40 mins at race pace
Week eight	5km (3 miles) easy/cross-train	5 x 1 mile with 2–3 min recoveries then 5 x 150m fast/50m easy	6.5km (4 miles) easy	30 mins threshold	10km (6 miles) easy	Rest/ cross-train	29km (18 miles) with 3 x 15 mins at race pace
Week nine	8km (5 miles) easy/cross-train	10 x 800m with 400m recoveries	10km (6 miles) easy with 8 x 100m strides	2 x 20 mins threshold with 5 mins recovery	10km (6 miles) easy	Rest/ cross-train	22–25km (14–16 miles) with 2 x 20 mins at race pace; or race 10K
Week ten	8km (5 miles) easy/cross-train	5 x 1 mile with 2–3 min recoveries then 5 x 150m fast/50m easy	10km (6 miles) easy; gradually accelerate over last 2 miles	30 mins threshold	10km (6 miles) easy	Rest/ cross-train	22–25km (14–16 miles) with 2 x 20 mins at race pace
Week eleven	8km (5 miles) easy/cross-train	6 x 800m with 400m recoveries	8km (5 miles) easy with 8 x 100m strides	2 x 15 mins threshold with 5 min recovery; 5 x 200m fast but relaxed	10km (6 miles) easy	Rest/ cross-train	16km (10 miles) easy
Week twelve	5km (3 miles) easy/cross-train	Rest	Rest/cross-train	5 miles easy	Rest	5km (3 miles) easy with 5 x 100m strides	Half-marathon

Marathon: Elite Schedule

The traditional and most widely accepted method of marathon training is to run a high mileage, six or seven days a week, reaching more than 160 kilometres or 100 miles per week in training. This training is not just the preserve of top marathon runners.

Running an elite schedule is hard on your body and should not be attempted unless you have gradually built up a base fitness for this distance. However, if you can handle it, you will be using a similar schedule to the world's best marathon runners.

The key sessions for this schedule are similar to other approaches, but it requires running twice a day from Monday to Friday, with a second semi-long run halfway through the week. Your long runs are also slightly longer, reaching 37–38km (23–24 miles) at their peak.

The 12-week schedule

The easy runs are not listed in the table as they remain constant throughout: run 6–10km (4–6 miles) each morning from Monday to Friday. Remember to

Right: Following a high-mileage schedule is tough but is the surest way to reach the front of the pack.

Great athletes: Paula Radcliffe (b. 1973, Davenham, Cheshire, UK)

In the early stages of Paula Radcliffe's career, it seemed that she would be another young athlete full of never-realized potential. She broke into elite running in 1992 with a convincing win in the junior race at the World Cross-country Championships. However, a series of injuries, illnesses and – many thought – a weak sprint finish left her out of the medals in track races at major competitions. Radcliffe finally found her distance in 2002 when she ran the fastest ever debut marathon, winning the London race in 2:18:56, a women-only record. She went on to break the women's world record in Chicago later that year, then took her time down again to 2:15:25 at the 2003 Flora London Marathon.

Left: Paula Radcliffe after winning the New York City Marathon in 2007, pictured with second-placed Gete Wami.

The following year saw the lowest point of her career to date, when exhaustion and injury caused her to pull out of the Olympic marathon in Athens, where she was favourite to win. There was some consolation that autumn when she won the New York City Marathon in a sprint finish against Susan Chepkemei, and then in 2005 when she won gold in the marathon at the World Championships in Helsinki. Radcliffe took time off in 2006 and most of 2007, when she had her first child. Following victory in the New York City Marathon in 2007, more disappointment followed when her training for the Beijing Olympics was ruined by a stress fracture; she struggled home in 23rd place. She was inducted into the England Athletics Hall of Fame in 2010, and retired after running the London Marathon in 2015.

Marathon: elite schedule

	Mon	Tue	Wed	Thur	Fri	Sat	Sun
Week one	10km (6 miles)	8 x 800m with 400m recoveries	10–13km (6–8 miles)	2 x 10 min threshold, 5 mins recovery	10km (6 miles) with 6 x 3 mins hill reps	6km (4 miles)/ rest	19–22km (12–14 miles)
Week two	10km (6 miles)	800m, 1,200m, 1,600m then back with 400m recoveries	13–16km (8–10 miles)	2 x 10 min threshold, 5 mins recovery	10km (6 miles) with 6 x 3 mins hill reps	6km (4 miles)/ rest	19–22km (12–14 miles)
Week three	10km (6 miles)	8 x 800m with 400m recoveries	13–16km (8–10 miles)	2 x 15 min threshold, 5 mins recovery	10km (6 miles) with 6 x 3 mins hill reps	6km (4miles)/ rest	22–26km (14–16 miles)
Week four	10km (6 miles)	5 x 1 mile with 2–3 min recoveries	10–13km (6–8 miles)	1 x 15 mins threshold	10km (6 miles) with 5 x 100m strides	6km (4 miles)/ rest	26–29km (16–18 miles)
Week five	10km (6 miles)	10 x 800m with 400m recoveries	16–19km (10–12 miles)	2 x 15 min threshold, 5 mins recovery	10km (6 miles) with 8 x 3 mins hill reps	10km (6 miles)/ rest	32km (20 miles)
Week six	10km (6 miles)	2 x 800m, 1,600m, 2,000m with 3 min recoveries	16–19km (10–12 miles)	25 mins threshold	10km (6 miles) negative split run	10km (6 miles)/ rest	35km (22 miles)
Week seven	10km (6 miles)	2 x 400m, 800m, 1,200m with 3 min recoveries	19–22km (12–14 miles)	30 mins threshold	10km (6 miles) fartlek session	10km (6 miles)/ rest	29km (18 miles)
Week eight	10km (6 miles)	5 x 1 mile with 2–3 min recoveries then 5 x 150m fast/50m easy	19–22km (12–14 miles)	30 mins threshold	10km (6 miles) with 4 x 5 mins hill reps	10km (6 miles)/ rest	35–38km (22–24 miles)
Week nine	10km (6 miles)	8 x 800m with 400m recoveries	19–22km (12–14 miles)	35 mins threshold	10km (6 miles) with 6 x 3 mins hill reps	10km (6 miles)/rest	29km (18 miles)
Week ten	10km (6 miles)	3 x 1 mile with 2–3 min recoveries then 5 x 150m fast/50m easy	16–19km (10–12 miles)	20 mins threshold	6km (4 miles) negative split run	10km (6 miles)/ rest	26km (16 miles)
Week eleven	10km (6 miles)	6 x 800m with 400m recoveries	10–13km (6–8 miles)	20 mins threshold	6km (4 miles) fartlek session	10km (6 miles)/ rest	19km (12 miles)
Week twelve	5km (3 miles)	Rest/cross-train	5km (3 miles)	Rest/cross-train	Rest	5km (3 miles) easy/rest	Marathon

run two miles as a warm-up and cool-down for all speed and threshold sessions. You'll notice that there is the option to run every single day with this plan, but you should only run the Saturday session if you feel really strong and full of energy. Many elite runners will train every day but it takes years of conditioning to cope with this, so if you want to play it safe, stick with six days' training per week.

Try to run some of your longer efforts at race pace – perhaps just 40 to 50 minutes in the middle – to get used to how it feels. Also, if you have time, add two weight training sessions per week (on easy run days), and two Pilates sessions to maintain core strength – the higher your mileage, the more important this is to help you avoid injury.

Marathon Training the Easy Way

Logging hundreds of miles might be the best way to train for a front-of-race marathon performance, but it doesn't suit everyone. The good news is that for the average runner, great results are possible from running just three times a week, if you make the sessions count.

If you find that your training is always interrupted by impact-related injuries, or family and work commitments mean you simply don't have time to run 160km (100 miles) per week, then you can still run a good marathon with just three running sessions per week. In fact, for a marathon runner with a few years' experience, this type of training plan can bring the kind of results that win smaller races.

Sometimes high-mileage training programmes are criticized for containing too many junk miles – easy, aimless running which, some would argue, simply put you at higher risk of overtraining or picking up an injury. The key with lower-mileage training is to make sure that every run you do really counts. Your three runs per

Below: Hill training and other quality training sessions build your strength and speed without injury risk.

Low-mileage training tested

It takes a leap of faith for any marathon runner to cut down to three runs a week, but science is on your side. In 2003, a group of scientists and runners at Furman University, South Carolina, USA, formed the Furman Institute of Running and Science Training (FIRST). They trained a group of 25 volunteers using a rigid three-runs-per-week schedule. Of the 21 runners who finished the target marathon, 15 ran personal bests. Laboratory tests showed that their oxygen uptake had gone up by 4.2 per cent, their lactate threshold speed had increased by 2.3 per cent, and their body fat had gone down by an average of 8.7 per cent. For further details of their programme visit their website at www.furman.edu/FIRST.

Above: In this type of schedule, your long runs should be quite fast – at target marathon pace.

week are a speed run, a tempo or hill run, and a long run. In addition to the three runs per week, you should aim to cross-train for two sessions a week to keep your fitness levels high and weight down. Some runners even find that they gain fitness using this method; you can train harder on your cross-training days than you would running, as the change of activity uses different muscles and usually has no impact, so your running muscles get the rest they need. Your overall fitness should improve, your body fat should reduce (making you a more efficient runner), and your risk of injury should be lower, putting you in great shape to tackle the marathon.

Marathon: easy schedule

	Day one	Day two	Day three	Day four	Day five
Week one	6 x 800m with 400m recoveries	Cross-train 30 mins	2 x 20 mins tempo with 5 mins recovery	Cross-train 30 mins	16–19km (10–12 miles)
Week two	3 x 1,600m with 3–4 min recoveries	Cross-train 30 mins	5 miles with 6 x 2 mins uphill effort	Cross-train 30 mins	19–22km (12–14 miles)
Week three	3 x (400m, 800m) with 400m recoveries	Cross-train 40 mins	40 mins tempo run	Cross-train 40 mins	22–26km (14–16 miles)
Week four	6 x 800m with 400m recoveries	Cross-train 30 mins	40 mins tempo run	Cross-train 30 mins	16–19km (10–12 miles)
Week five	4 x 1,200m with 600m recoveries, then 4 x 400m with 200m recoveries	Cross-train 40 mins	5 miles with total 10–15 mins uphill effort	Cross-train 40 mins	26–29km (16–18 miles)
Week six	8 x 800m	Cross-train 40 mins	50 mins tempo run	Cross-train 40 mins	29–32km (18–20 miles)
Week seven	4 x 1,600m with 3 min recoveries	Cross-train 45 mins	1hr tempo run	Cross-train 45 mins	32km (20 miles)
Week eight	4 x 1,200m with 600m recoveries	Cross-train 45 mins	5 miles with 4 x 2 mins uphill effort	Cross-train 45 mins	19km (12 miles)
Week nine	10 x 800m	Cross-train 45 mins	1hr 10 mins tempo run	Cross-train 45 mins	29km (18 miles)
Week ten	4 x 1,400m with 600m recoveries, then 4 x 400m with 200m recoveries	Cross-train 40 mins	1hr 10 mins tempo run	Cross-train 40 mins	26km (16 miles)
Week eleven	6 x 800m	Cross-train 40 mins	50 mins tempo run	Cross-train 40 mins	16–19km (10–12 miles)
Week twelve	Rest	Cross-train 30 mins	5km (3 miles) easy/ easy cross-train	Cross-train 30 mins/rest	Marathon

The 12-week schedule

There are only three runs a week in this schedule, but you must complete them all (if you like you can add a fourth easy run) and you must put effort in. On your long runs, stay close to your target marathon pace, even adding bursts of half-marathon pace running. Do your tempo runs at 10K pace (just faster than threshold pace), long intervals (1,000 to 1,600m) at 5K pace and 800m or less at mile pace. Choose an activity you enjoy for your cross-training and treat your cross-training sessions as high-quality workouts, adding faster intervals and higher resistance for extra fitness gains. Scientists (see box opposite) have found that runners can see much greater improvements in marathon times when they take the cross-training sessions as seriously as they would a speed workout or long run, so decide before each session what kind of training you will do and make the sessions progressively harder as the weeks go by.

Right: You can cross-train hard once or twice a week, building fitness and reducing body fat.

Marathon: Heart-rate Training

It can be difficult to tell how hard you are training, as your mood, the weather and even illness all have an effect on your perception of effort. What's more, until you are experienced at racing over a range of distances, it can also be hard to judge your pace.

Above: When you first begin heart-rate training, you may find it frustrating running slower than usual.

be able to stay below your lactate threshold, which in turn means you are less likely to hit the wall.

Finding your target zones
You can choose to have laboratory tests to find your different heart-rate training zones, but if you don't have the time or money for that, use these simple sums.

First of all, you need to find out your maximum heart rate (MHR). You can do this using the formula 214 − (0.8 x age) for men, or 209 − (0.9 x age) for women. For a more accurate figure, however, use this test (which you should not attempt if you are very unfit or new to exercise): warm up, then run for 4 minutes as fast as you can on a treadmill; take a 2-minute recovery jog, then repeat the hard run. You should hit your MHR toward the end of your second fast interval.

Below: A basic heart-rate monitor is enough to tell you when you're in the right training zone.

This is where introducing objective science, in the form of heart-rate training, can be useful. Switching to heart-rate training can be frustrating for runners used to pushing themselves as hard as they can. Running at your target heart rate feels incredibly slow at first. Your body – and your willpower – allow you to train much harder than is beneficial, often leading to overtraining or injury. To begin heart-rate training from scratch, you will need to spend a period building a base, training at

less than 60 per cent of your working heart rate (WHR, see below) and excluding speedwork. You will gradually be able to run faster at the same heart rate, and after this you can add speedwork and tempo runs. The advantage of training this way is that your heart rate should be lower in marathons, so you should

Find your resting heart rate (RHR) by wearing the heart-rate monitor to bed. In the morning it will tell you the minimum heart rate achieved during sleep.

Work out your WHR like this:
1 MHR – RHR = x
(for example 205 – 44 = 161)
2 Take the effort level you need to achieve, say 60 per cent, and multiply this by your WHR
(for example 161 x 0.6 = 97)

Left: Once you've found your working heart rate, use it to plan sessions.

3 Add this figure to your RHR to find your target heart rate
(for example 97 + 44 = 141 bpm).

Applying zones to training: 12-week schedule
Follow this schedule after building up your base using a heart-rate monitor. You can use the alarm on your monitor to tell you when you have hit your target rate. Figures are percentage WHR. Before and after each speed session (Days Two and Four) do 10 minutes at 60 per cent WHR.

	Day one	Day two	Day three	Day four	Day five
Marathon: heart-rate training					
Week one	40 mins at 60%	5 mins at 70%; 4 mins at 85%; 3 mins at 85–90%; then run all-out for 1 min; then back down	40 mins fartlek at 70%	2 x 10 mins at 80% with 3 mins recovery	1:30 at 60–70%
Week two	40 mins at 60%	2 x 10 mins at 85–90%, recovering to 55% in between	40 mins fartlek at 70–85%	15 mins at 80%	1:45 at 60–70%
Week three	40 mins at 60%	As week 1	40 mins fartlek at 70–85%	3 x 8 mins at 80% with 3 mins recovery	2:00 at 60–70%
Week four	40 mins at 60%	3 x 5 mins at 85–90%, recovering to 55% in between	50 mins fartlek at 70–85%	20 mins at 80%	2:15 at 60–70%
Week five	40 mins at 60%	As week 1, but repeat sequence	50 mins fartlek at 70–85%	25 mins at 80%	2:30 at 60–70%
Week six	40 mins at 60%	8 x run up to 90%, recover to 55%	1 hour fartlek at 70–85%	30 mins at 80%	3:00 at 60–70%
Week seven	40 mins at 60%	4 x 4 mins at 85–90%, recovering to 55% in between	40 mins fartlek at 70–85%	20 mins at 80%	2:30 at 60–70%
Week eight	40 mins at 60%	As week 5	1 hour fartlek at 70–85%	35 mins at 80%	3:00 at 60–70%
Week nine	40 mins at 60%	10 x run up to 90%, recovering to 55%	1 hour fartlek at 70–85%	40 mins at 80%	2:45 at 60–70%
Week ten	40 mins at 60%	6 x 4 mins at 85–90%, recovering to 55%	50 mins fartlek at 70–85%	40 mins at 80%	2:30 at 60–70%
Week eleven	40 mins at 60%	As week 1	40 mins fartlek at 70–85%	20 mins at 80%	1:45 at 60–70%
Week twelve	40 mins at 60%	Rest	30 mins fartlek at 70–85%	Rest	Marathon

Key Race-training Sessions

Every workout you do helps you to reach the start line of your race in peak condition. But just as specific running training is the only way to become a better runner, putting in a few race-specific sessions is the best way to be competitive on the big day.

Race training sessions are not the same as speedwork; though many are fast, the point of these workouts is always to replicate race-day conditions in some way. The following workouts will help you feel confident and ready to race.

Race-day warm-up

You'll need a thorough warm-up before your race, and you should practise this before some of your training sessions. Run gently for 5 minutes. Then, find some flat, even, soft ground and do 20–30m (65–98ft) of high knees (skipping

Below: Group fartlek sessions, where you take it in turns to dictate pace, are great race practice.

forward, on the balls of your feet, kicking your knees high in front); cover the same distance with some heel kicks ('running' forward kicking your heels right back to your bottom). Use your arms throughout, pumping them back and forward. Finish the warm-up with a few more minutes' light running.

Race pace practice

Even if you've chosen to do most of your long runs at a slow pace, you should add a couple of race-pace sections during the hardest point of your training (usually 6–8 weeks before the race). Work out your mile pace based on your target race time, but be flexible – if you can't talk after 30–40 minutes at this pace in training, or if your heart rate

is consistently above 85 per cent MHR, it's too fast (if you're aiming for a marathon or half, your race pace should feel very comfortable over a short distance). You can find your ideal training pace, and work out a predicted race pace, using the tables at the end of the book.

At the sharp end of a race, there are likely to be several surges in pace as different people try to establish a lead. Sometimes people may even deliberately slow the pace, which can be off-putting (and is meant to be!). Learn to cope with this using group fartlek sessions. Gather a group of friends of different paces and abilities, and draw numbers out of a hat. Don't tell anyone else which number you have. After 10 minutes of easy

Above: It's impossible to know how you'll feel on race day but visualizing the event will help.

jogging, the person with number one goes to the lead, running as fast as they like for any length of time from 1 to 5 minutes, then shouts "End!" The group jogs to recover and regroup for 2 or 3 minutes, then the next person takes the lead without warning; and so on until everyone in the group has led an interval.

Negative split
This is by far the safest approach to pacing long events (10K or more), so it makes sense to practise it in training (it features strongly in our 10K Schedules). The simplest way to do this is to find a short, fairly straight out-and-back route and run the return leg faster, but remember you're aiming for a very close split, so don't crawl the first half and sprint the second. Go for a time that is just a minute or two faster over the second leg.

Right: Try running hard at the end of sessions, when you're already tired, to toughen yourself up.

Fast finish
Even if you're not a naturally fast finisher, you can train to develop a good final kick, which will often put you at an advantage, especially in races of 10K or less. Short, sharp speed sessions will develop the basic leg speed you need for this, but you should also try sprinting when you're already tired. At the end of a threshold or race-pace section, without a recovery break, accelerate smoothly into a 200m sprint. Recover for 30 seconds, then repeat. Build up to three or four sprints over a few weeks.

Dress rehearsal
Try to visit your race course before race day. If you can, have a run out over the course the week before, practising your pace and fuelling strategy (but relaxing toward the end of the route). If you can't get to your course, then choose a route with similar characteristics (e.g. gradient and surface), and run it at the same time of day as your race will be.

Races are perhaps the best kind of specific race training you can do. Up to 16km (10 miles), you can even race the same distance in your build-up, but treat it as a practice run so you don't wear yourself out. For the marathon or half, shorter races are a good progress check and help you to cope with race-day nerves, practise your warm-up and nutrition strategies, and even find out which kit you're most comfortable in.

Above: When you're running well, hold on to the feeling for race day.

Try to set aside some time in the few weeks before your race to think through your race day and visualize everything going according to plan, right up to crossing the line in your target time. You can also use training sessions: when you feel you're running smoothly and strongly, tell yourself 'I will run this well on race day.'

Race Tactics

You might think race tactics are only for athletes at the very front of a race, but a little planning is useful for anyone hoping to perform well. Well-rehearsed tactics can shave seconds off your time or just boost your confidence with a higher placing.

The most important decision you will have to make is how to pace your race. Confident and well-trained runners run as evenly as they can. However this is a difficult approach to take, as other runners will try to influence your pace. Runners who have a strong sprint finish will try to hold the pace slow to keep something for the end of the race, while those who don't have this strength may force the pace early on to create a gap between themselves and the rest of the field. Paula Radcliffe uses this tactic to good effect in most of her marathons. Forcing surges in pace also exhausts sprint finishers, so they are unable to use their end kick.

Assessing the competition

Your choice of pacing strategy may depend on who else is running. If you are at the sharp end of a race and know some of the other fast athletes, try to discover who are the main threats beforehand, working out what kind of runners they are, what times they have run recently, and how they are likely to respond to your tactics.

You can use other runners to help you through your race, particularly in longer road events. Psychologically it is difficult to run alone for long periods of time: you will become too focused on your own discomfort and may lose perspective and find it difficult to judge your pace. Staying with a group of runners means you can use them as pacers, and you can use them either to distract yourself (perhaps by chatting as you run if they are willing and able to talk), or to help focus you on the race pace. You can also draft behind groups of runners, effectively using them as a windblock to minimize resistance to your own forward motion. For this to work, you need to stay close behind the other runners.

Above: You can use the other runners taking part to help you stick to your pace in crowded events.

Using earphones

Earphones have become an increasingly common feature at long-distance road events, and it is true that music can be useful to help keep you on pace as you run. However, the running community is divided over whether they should be allowed at large events, some feeling that it is rude and anti-social to wear them, others arguing that it is simply a safety issue. If you choose to run wearing your earphones, don't put them on until you have started so that you don't miss any announcements. Keep the volume low enough so that you can hear someone if they are trying to get your attention.

Race etiquette

Emotions can run high on race day, so try not to tread on anyone's toes – literally or figuratively – by following these six simple guidelines on race day etiquette:

1 Start in the right area for your predicted finish time, not in front of faster runners. If there are no start pens, ask a few runners what time they are aiming for to help you gauge where to stand.

2 During the race, don't side-step, stop suddenly or start walking unexpectedly. Call out to those behind you first so they don't trip over you.

3 Don't over-draft. Staying behind someone all the way then dashing out to beat them at the finish is very bad form. If you're running at the same pace as someone else, take it in turns to lead so you can both conserve energy, up to an agreed point. Then race them!

4 Help people who are in distress. If another runner has collapsed, don't assume that someone else will find them soon.

5 Make sure that you thank volunteers around the route.

6 Try to stay for the medal presentations and to cheer on the slower runners, finishing after you, even if you have had a bad race yourself and just feel like going home.

Above: Take it in turns to lead a pack of runners, as it's harder to run at the front all the way.

Crowd control

Ensure the crowd doesn't work against you. Don't waste energy weaving in and out of others to move forward – run to the outside and sprint around the group. Water stations are prime spots for losing places, so be prepared. If possible, have your friends and family hand out drinks to you slightly apart from the official water station, so you

don't end up in a scrummage, and have your water in bottles rather than cups. Also, don't be pushed into running on the outside of a group, as courses are measured along the shortest route possible (in big races this is sometimes marked by a line painted on the road).

Whatever your race plan, it will be effective only if you stick to it. Don't allow yourself to be distracted by others' tactics – after all, this may be precisely what they are relying on to gain an advantage.

Below: Be courteous to runners around you and if you need to change pace, warn them by calling out.

Below: Over longer distances your race tactics may not come into play until the final few miles.

Mental Training: Long-distance Strategies

Any sports event requires as much mental strength as physical fitness, but the mind plays a far greater role for long-distance runners. In a marathon, whether a first-timer or about to set a world record, your body will be aching and your instincts telling you to stop.

The last few miles in any long-distance event are extremely gruelling. At this point, the only thing that will keep you going is a strong mind.

Disassociation vs focusing

There are two main approaches to getting through long-distance events. The first, disassociation, is where the athlete tries to distract himself from the discomfort, fatigue and sometimes boredom of the race. For recreational runners, listening to music while racing is a good example of this (some experts also believe that music can help you run

faster). Other techniques might be playing mental games – trying to remember a list of past winners of the race, or something completely unrelated such as your top ten favourite films.

Focusing is the opposite approach, and is tough to do in a marathon – it takes practice. With this approach, you concentrate intently on the task in hand. Be careful not to focus on the negative (aches and pains, loss of confidence) and instead focus on your breathing, your style, and the feel of the pace. Think about all the training you have put in and the goal you have for the race.

Below: Focusing on the positive, perhaps by remembering good training sessions, helps to keep you strong.

Left: Some scientists believe that listening to music while you run can actually make you faster.

Above: When you are competing in a race, learn to focus on your tactics and competitors to stay on target.

If you are at the competitive end of the race, think about your tactics and the opponents around you. Research has shown that the focusing approach is more successful, so it is worth practising, however unpleasant – try it in shorter races first.

Motivation

To train for a long race, you will have had strong motivation. Keep that in mind as you race. Remind yourself what you want to get from it, whether it is a specific time, to beat a particular opponent, or to win. Studies have shown that people who race for intrinsic

rewards (to feel good about themselves, to achieve a new personal best) are more successful than those who compete for extrinsic rewards (their coach's approval, prize money). Whatever your goal was, it should be strong enough to push you to the finish when the going gets tough.

Visualization

This technique is widely used by elite athletes and can be applied to your life in general. The idea is to visualize running a successful race over and over again and in as much detail as possible. Think about your smooth, strong running style, hitting each mile bang on target pace, and finishing strongly and in your desired time. Just thinking about these actions produces the same effect on your brain

as if you had actually done them, and so creates a pattern of success. Practise visualization two or three times a day, in a quiet, calm space, and run through your success just before your race and when you hit bad patches.

Enjoyment

Toward the end of your race, it is easy to feel tired and grumpy, particularly if you have missed a mile time by 30 seconds and start to believe you are failing. Try to focus on your enjoyment of the sport: appreciate the strengths of your body and the success you have had in training. Try not to count down the miles; if it helps, slip into your race pace, trust yourself to stay on target by intuition, and promise yourself not to look at your watch for three or four miles.

Central Governor Theory

For years it has been generally accepted that long-distance athletes become fatigued because their body runs out of fuel or is not strong enough. However, the Central Governor Theory, supported by the respected sports scientist and runner Professor Tim Noakes, opens the possibility that this fatigue is all in the mind. The theory goes that our ancient ancestors had to keep back some of their energy for emergency situations, and our bodies still hold on to this legacy, so that when fuel stores are running low, a central governing mechanism in the brain tells the muscles to slow down to conserve energy. If you can show your brain that you are not going to die from excessive effort, the theory goes, you can keep running.

Supporters argue that this theory is proven by the fact that so often runners feel they have nothing left to give, only to put in a final spurt when they know they are about to stop. You can retrain your brain with race-specific, stressing sessions, such as very long runs for marathons, or 5 x 1,000m at 5K pace for a 5K event. In theory, surviving the stress should show your brain that it is feasible to go the distance.

Mental Training: Winning Strategies

In any race, at any distance, it could be argued that essentially, winning comes down to mental toughness. Two competing athletes who have exactly the same ability and training must use all their mental powers to gain victory.

The elite athlete is often portrayed as an aggressive opponent, 'destroying' other competitors, but there is far more to winning than fighting talk, and whether you are aiming to win or just to perform to your very best, these strategies can help you.

Toughness

Mental toughness is an important quality for endurance runners in particular, but there is a great deal of debate over whether runners are born with it or learn it. The truth is probably somewhere in between. You can help yourself to become mentally strong by using 'character building' workouts: run at race pace in training, pit yourself against faster athletes, train in difficult

Below: Try to think like a winner, no matter what your speed, to help you to achieve your goals.

conditions. Coaches will sometimes teach their athletes to cope with stress by arranging for interruptions to training, or changing plans at the last minute. This helps runners deal with unexpected problems and stay focused on their race.

Self-confidence

There is a fine line between self-confidence and unfounded arrogance, but it is an important distinction: the latter will lead to complacency, disappointment and ultimately loss of confidence. Self-confidence is crucial, however, as positive 'self-talk' is a valuable tool in helping you to maintain your pace through rough patches in a race. Use affirmations in training that you can call on again on race day – say out loud, 'I am strong', 'I can achieve my target', or train yourself out of weaknesses (for example 'I will run smoothly' if you know you have a problem with erratic style).

Above: Sprinters are known for their focus, but relaxation techniques will help runners over any distance.

You can also build up your confidence by thinking about past successes, by going through your training diary to reassure yourself that you have done all you can, and by asking other people (such as your coach or training partners) what they feel are your strengths.

Focus

Watch top-class sprinters before a 100m race, and you will see them go through their own rituals to help them focus on the task ahead. Focus and 'getting in the zone' is also crucial for longer-distance runners. You need to calm any pre-race nerves without becoming so calm that you breeze through the race without putting full effort into it. Relaxation techniques such as deep breathing, or energizing techniques such

Left: If a race is going to be physically tough, you will also need to be mentally tough and should train for this.

can do to prevent it from happening again, and move on. Otherwise the memory of your disappointing race will spoil future performances.

Analyse your performances

If you have a coach, he will be able to give you feedback, but it is also useful to become more self-aware so that you're constantly assessing your own strengths and weaknesses. Sports psychologists sometimes teach athletes to use a technique known as performance profiling. The runner draws up of a list of traits they think are important in their sport (for example relaxation, focus, enjoyment); rates the relative importance of each trait for a 'perfect' athlete; and then rates their own performance for each of the attributes. This is a good way of objectifying yourself to determine which areas you need to work on.

as thinking intently about your target or an opponent, can be useful in achieving the right balance.

Think like a winner

You may have heard gold medallists saying that if they didn't think they would win, they wouldn't race. You may not

Below: Events with different elements, such as triathlon or adventure racing, require renewed focus for each stage.

expect to come first, but you can adopt this approach. Instead of heading to a race and thinking 'I'll see what happens' or 'I'll do my best', be determined to achieve your target time or the position you want. Do not allow doubt to take over your mind at any time. However, if your race does not go to plan, don't waste time punishing yourself. The best athletes make mistakes sometimes, and sometimes conditions are against them. Work out what went wrong, what you

Below: Your training partner can build your confidence by reminding you of your strengths.

Advanced Racing Kit

At the start of any running race, it is clear which people are going to be the front runners. The difference can be seen not just in their lean, muscular physiques, but also in the pared-down clothing they wear.

Choosing special kit for a race may not take much off your finish time, but it could give you an extra edge. Light, comfortable kit should be barely noticeable, enabling you to fully focus on the clock and your opponents as you run. Wearing the right kit is about more than the science of running faster, however: racing kit should make you feel confident, strong and psyched up, and this psychological benefit will be more noticeable to you than any reduction in weight or drag.

If you buy special kit for a race, make sure that you have worn it beforehand (especially your shoes); this is not the time to test new styles, as something as seemingly innocuous as a badly placed seam could chafe and ruin a good run. At the opposite end of the spectrum, if you have been wearing the same

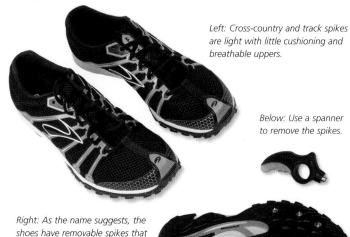

Left: Cross-country and track spikes are light with little cushioning and breathable uppers.

Below: Use a spanner to remove the spikes.

Right: As the name suggests, the shoes have removable spikes that add traction.

'lucky' T-shirt for five years, perhaps it is time to treat yourself to something better suited.

Performance shoes

Most shoe manufacturers now make a range of shoes especially designed for fast training and racing. These typically weigh less than 300g (for a men's UK size 8/US size 9), and have been stripped of most of the technical features found in standard training shoes. They have less cushioning, fit more snugly, and may have a more curved shape for faster running.

Heavy runners or those with serious gait problems should avoid these shoes. For track and cross-country races, you can wear 'spikes' or 'racing flats', which look like old-fashioned running slippers. As the name suggests, some have spikes that screw into the outer sole for better traction on the ground.

Left: Good technical kit can give you a powerful psychological edge when it comes to your race day.

Above: These track shoes have shorter spikes and are made for middle-distance running.

Shorts and tights

In a race situation, you want to carry as little weight and bulk as possible, so many people go for traditional, very short, vented shorts, which allow your legs a fuller range of movement (although they are not for the self-conscious!). Tight shorts are another good option as they minimize the risk of chafing on the insides of your legs. In winter, it is worth wearing full-length tights to keep your muscles warm and to avoid cramp. Whichever you choose, unless you are on a very long race, keep pockets to a minimum – you need only a small internal key pocket.

Tops

Fast runners tend to opt for sleeveless tops, but be careful that the armholes don't chafe. Sleeveless tops not only reduce the weight of your outfit but keep you cool, which is essential at the front-end of a race. Loose-weave tops are a good choice as you will need to use safety pins to attach your race number.

It is not really worth wearing a jacket to a race, even on a cold day. It is very difficult to pin your number to it, it becomes too hot after a few minutes' running, and the extra bulk can slow you down. If the weather is poor, stay inside as long as possible before the start or wear a bin-liner (trash bag), which you can throw away once you get going. Make sure you have some warm clothes to put on straight after the race.

Compression kit

This is a fairly new phenomenon in sportswear, but one which has quickly become popular. Compression kit is always very tight, and some types have plastic webbing to support muscles. Originating in team sports and power sports (such as sprinting), the idea behind this kit (worn as a base layer) is that it increases bloodflow and therefore oxygen delivery to your working muscles. As such, it is also said to help with recovery. The best compression kit has graded pressure to help keep blood circulating. Research suggests that good compression kit is genuinely effective at improving endurance and aiding recovery, but it is more likely to give an edge to a good athlete than to transform an average runner. In fact, one of its biggest selling points is that it gives you a psychological boost by making you more aware of your muscles.

Left: Compression kit is very tight to support the muscles.

Above: Traditional racing vests are the lightest, coolest option and will keep you comfortable.

Left: Tight shorts minimize chafing – these trail shorts also have handy loops to hold energy gels.

Above: Compression kit boosts bloodflow to your muscles and makes you aware of your body.

Advanced Equipment

While top-end apparel and shoes are essential for fast racing, investing in some essential equipment will give your training an edge – and having splashed out a week's wages to buy a new watch, you will certainly feel motivated to use it.

Once you've started measuring your training it's easy to find plenty of gadgets to help you out, from simple stopwatches to the most advanced GPS speed and distance monitors.

Watches

Time is very much of the essence for runners. The more you run, the more detail you will want to know – which is why that old plastic watch you have had since you were 12 will no longer be good enough. Sports watches can have a bewildering array of functions, but the ones you need to look out for are:

Chronograph. The chronograph or stopwatch mode is the most basic requirement for a sports watch. Most will be capable of recording far longer times than you will ever be running in one go, but make sure the display is detailed enough: if you enjoy doing fast sprints on the track, you will want to know your time down to hundredths of a second.

Lap timer. Recording your lap times or mile splits is a useful way of tracking your progress and training yourself to pace runs evenly. Some watches store up to 300 split times, which sounds excessive – but if you want to review a few weeks' training, it is surprisingly easy to use up the watch's lap memory.

Interval and countdown timers. If you can, buy a watch with two interval timers – this is especially useful for speedwork if you don't have access to a track. You can set one timer to countdown 3 minutes for a hard 800m, then the other for 90 seconds' recovery time. An alarm will sound every time you need to change pace, and you can usually record splits and total time as well.

Pacing alarm. Some top-end watches have an alarm that beeps to keep you on pace, which is especially useful if you are trying to work on your cadence.

Above: Few advanced runners train without a basic chronograph (or stopwatch) to time themselves.

Basics. Make sure your watch has a big, clear display – some are angled to make them easier to read when you are running; a durable strap; scratch-proof glass; a backlight for running in the dark; and is a good fit on your wrist (women may need to look for a female-specific watch, as men's watches may slip).

Heart-rate monitors

Once a tool for obsessives only, heart-rate monitors are now a fairly standard piece of kit for runners. Monitors range from a basic model that shows your heart rate and has a stopwatch, to top-end versions with 'virtual coaching'. Heart-rate monitors consist of a chest strap with electrodes (you need to wet these for the monitor to work well) and a transmitter, and a wrist unit, which picks up the signal and tells you your heart rate. Functions might include:

Left: The bigger and clearer your watch display, the more useful you will find it.

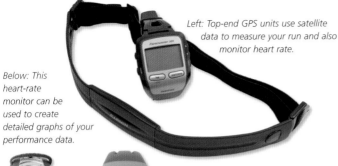

Left: Top-end GPS units use satellite data to measure your run and also monitor heart rate.

Below: This heart-rate monitor can be used to create detailed graphs of your performance data.

Left: Smaller units still offer a wide range of functions, the most basic being current heart rate.

with heart-rate data to give an estimate of how many calories you have burned during a session.

Memory. Some monitors can store information about several workouts at once, including total time, splits, time in each pre-set heart-rate zone, average, minimum and maximum heart rate.

Heart-rate zones. You will be asked to set up heart-rate zones for different levels of activity (for example lower than 60 per cent of your maximum heart rate; 61 to 75 per cent; 76 to 90 per cent). The monitor then sounds an alarm to let you know how hard you are working, and you can use this to plan your interval training.

Calories burned. You can usually input personal details such as your weight and gender, and the monitor will combine this

Software. Top-end models come with software for your home computer, which enables you to download and analyse information from your monitor, creating graphs and charts of your heart-rate data. This can be useful for evaluating and planning your training.

Above: Non-GPS speed and distance monitors use footpods like this one to give accurate measurements.

Speed and distance monitors
Often combined with a heart-rate monitor, speed and distance monitors (SDMs) fall into two categories. The less expensive models work with a footpod that attaches to your shoes, which sends information to the watch unit – you need to calibrate these models to get a more accurate reading, and they can lose accuracy on hills or uneven ground when your stride changes. The second type uses global positioning system (GPS) technology to give an accurate pinpoint of where you are and how fast and far you are running. The disadvantage with GPS-based monitors is that, in urban areas especially, you can lose contact with the satellite and be unable to take any measurements. SDMs usually come with the same features as a heart-rate monitor, but can combine this with data on your average speed, maximum and minimum speed, distance travelled, and sometimes cadence (on footpod models).

Left: They may be cumbersome, but GPS monitors are the easiest way for you to gauge your pace.

Periodization and Self-coaching

Great running performances always involve a little bit of luck. Weather conditions, catching a bug or tripping over could all spoil what would have been a perfect race. What really matters is the condition of the athlete on the day of the race.

The goal of runners at any level or distance is to be in their absolute peak condition – highly trained, but not overtrained – and that is the result of careful long-term planning or 'periodization'.

Track athletes almost always use periodization, as sprinting and middle-distance running have distinct seasons, but it is also a useful concept for long-distance runners, and one widely used by those at the top of the sport. The idea is to divide your training into different periods. First, the whole training year (sometimes called a macrocycle) is divided into broad phases lasting from a few weeks to a few months. Within this big picture are mesocycles of three to

four weeks and microcycles of one or two weeks. Specific sessions don't need to be planned a year in advance, but the general theme is decided and, as you approach a particular period, specific days can be allocated to work on different areas of your training. The idea behind this planning is to allow your body to adapt to hard training, to bring yourself to a peak of fitness and speed in time for a particular race goal, and to recover and progress your training. Learning how to plan your own training year is essential if you are coaching yourself (as many recreational athletes do).

Successful self-coaching

A coach is a valuable asset for any runner (see box), but sometimes time and money mean we have to plan our own training. In this case,

Above: A training diary enables you to plan ahead and is a very valuable self-coaching tool.

Below: Dividing your training sessions into cycles ensures that you reach a peak when it comes time to race.

you must learn to be as objective as possible about your running. A good coach will not simply hand you a training schedule. He will look at your lifestyle, how factors such as your career, family life or even your personality will affect the kind of training that is realistic for you. He will be able to listen to your problems and worries and adapt your training as necessary. If you are coaching yourself, you need to be aware of this and have the confidence to go with your instinct – for example if you have been feeling tired for weeks on end, recognize the need for a recovery week.

Planning, patience and progression
The secret to successful self coaching is the 'three Ps': planning, patience and progression. If you don't plan your training, you will become aimless and either do too much, too soon, or you will have the opposite problem and find that you never run any faster, which

Above: It's vital to plan progressive training so that you continue to see improvements in your running.

Finding a coach

There is no doubt that any athlete will run better with than without a coach. The question is which coach, because working with someone who does not understand your needs is more likely to have a negative effect on your training.

A good coach should have an understanding of elite training – he may have been an international athlete himself – but should also be confident and happy coaching people at all levels and appreciating their individual limitations. When choosing a coach, remember that each one will have his own individual approach: some coaches favour lots of long, slow running; some believe in training with very high mileage; while others put an emphasis on cross-training. Make sure that you are happy with your coach's approach before you start training together. If you are looking for a coach for the first time, a good place to start is your local running club, or the athletics governing body in your area.

saps your motivation. Lack of patience is the quickest route to injury and frustration. Any lack of progression in your training means you are unlikely to achieve your long-term goals.

If you are coaching yourself and are serious about improving your running, your training diary takes on a new level of importance, too. Instead of simply writing down your achievements at the end of each day, work out your training periods: when planning the year, write themes across the top of each week in

pencil. Then map out your three to four-week cycles (for example, weeks one and two might be moderate, week three hard, week four easy) and your short-term goals. Plan your specific sessions a week or two in advance, so that you can be flexible and adapt your training if something isn't working (or working better than you expected!).

Planning your Training Year

Planning your training a long time in advance should, in theory, make your training easier and more successful. With a clear plan to follow you will be less tempted to throw yourself into last-minute training for a race or, on the other hand, to avoid stepping up your training.

Above: You can run short 'practice' races in your sharpening phase to fine-tune race speed.

The basic concept of periodization is built around the idea of training for a particular event, so before you plan your year, you will need to decide on your primary goal.

Setting a goal
For many distance runners the goal will be a marathon, which you can only race well once or twice a year;

Left: Before planning your training periods, you need to prioritize races for the coming year ahead.

if your goal is a shorter distance you may be able to race it several times over, but should aim to peak at a particular race. In order for periodized training to work well, you should choose a goal more than six months away so that you have time to build the foundation of your fitness (see below). Once you have chosen your goal race, you can work your planning backward from that date. You should also think about setting mini-goals – these might be shorter races (for example a half-marathon four to six weeks before a full marathon), or simply realistic time and distance targets for training.

Single and double periodization
If you have been running for several years, your body will have adapted to exercise and will not need such a long base phase. Some runners choose to have a double peak in their training year. This is normal for track and field runners, who want to peak for the indoor season in winter then the main season in summer; long-distance track runners might also aim to peak for the winter cross-country season. For road runners, especially those whose main event is the marathon, there are usually two peaks, in spring (March–April) and autumn (September–October). The training year might look like this:

January	Strength
February	Speed end/speed
March	Speed
April	Peak 1
May	Recovery
June	Base/strength
July	Speed endurance (inc. short races)
August	Speed
September	Speed
October	Peak 2
November	Recovery
December	Base

Training phases
Typical training phases over a year might be:

Base or foundation phase. There is no intense running during this phase. You are simply building up the number of miles you do slowly. The aim of this phase is to allow your body to make the physiological changes it needs to support the demands of more intense training: your muscles and tendons become stronger and your body becomes more efficient at transporting oxygen. The length of time spent in this phase is probably the most variable: a beginner or someone returning from injury could spend up to six months base building, while someone with many years of healthy running behind them could spend six to eight weeks in this phase.

Strength and conditioning phase. This is an important stage to go through to avoid injury and build the power of your muscles ready for faster running. You will maintain moderate mileage built up during your base phase, but start to add hill training, weight training and training on soft ground. Your stronger muscles will propel you forward faster, stabilize your joints and help alleviate fatigue in the late stages of a long race. You might spend one or two months in this phase.

Speed endurance phase. This phase can be incorporated into your strength phase, and experienced runners do some sort of speed endurance work all

Below: Running on soft ground during your strength and conditioning phase helps stabilize your joints.

year round. It is worth spending some time working on this area; think of it as a mini base-building phase for your shorter, quicker speedwork. During this period you will introduce threshold runs and long intervals once or twice a week, and you should spend anything from four to six weeks in this phase.

Speed or sharpening phase. This is when you bring all your preparations together, adding the leg speed that will make you a faster racer. You will add two or three faster speed sessions – ideally on a track – and reduce the amount of strength work you do, while maintaining a high mileage. During this phase you might also run some short races as a guide to your progress. This is the phase covered by most training schedules – the 8 to 16 weeks of true race preparation, and your goal race comes at the end of this period.

Recovery phase. Too often overlooked by runners, who may feel guilty about skipping training, this phase is crucial to racing well in your next training year. After your race, you might take a few days off running altogether, then ease back in with short, easy runs and cross-training.

Above: In the base or foundation phase, you'll work on building volume without intensity.

Below: Your fastest speed sessions, on a track, will take place just before you complete your goal race.

Race Recovery

We have all heard stories about how hard elite runners train, but perhaps the most common mistake made by recreational athletes is thinking this means training as hard as you possibly can, as often as you can. Sometimes, not running is just as important.

Top athletes work just as hard at not running when necessary as they do at putting in 240km (150-mile) weeks. Missing out on essential recovery time will, at best, leave you exhausted and unable to run as fast as you would like; and at worst, ill or seriously injured. Taking easy weeks or weeks off should be part of your training on a cyclical basis (periodization), and it makes sense to put your longest recovery period after your hardest race of the year. There is a great deal of debate about the best way to recover from a race, but no doubt at all that it is necessary. Ideally, race recovery begins before you even reach the start line.

Before your race
The work you put in before a race, especially when that race is a marathon, is crucial to recovering well. If you have planned your training carefully and have had a long build-up with no interruptions from injury, then your muscles will be much better

Above: If weather conditions are tough on race day, you'll need to take longer to recover.

Below: In the weeks immediately before a race it's important to cut down on your training.

Above: When your training session hasn't gone to plan, sitting down and reconsidering your race goals will help.

prepared to cope with the demands of the race. Damage will be limited and recovery much quicker. It follows that if your training has not gone according to plan, you should revise your race goals to avoid placing undue stress on your body. Failure to do so leads to a downward spiral: your training goes badly, so the race goes badly, you skip recovery to get back into training and race better next time; then you become injured again and your next race is even worse. Treat your race as a high-quality training run, take some time out afterward and start from the beginning again.

The training you don't do is also very important. Before taking part in any race it is important to have a period of 'tapering', where you cut down your training to around 30 to 40 per cent of your highest workload for between one and three weeks

Left: Research has shown that the right nutrition and hydration before and during your race improves recovery time.

stress hormones that lower your immunity, and potentially causing damage to your undertrained muscles.

Nutrition is also essential to keep you well after the race. Countless studies have shown that marathon runners in particular report far higher than average rates of illness (usually colds) than the rest of the population (even athletes who have trained but do not complete a race). There are no definite explanations for this, but some studies have shown a link between carbohydrate consumption during the race (from sports drinks) and risk of illness afterward. One theory is that when your body switches to using fat for fuel, the stress hormone cortisol is released during the process; this blocks the actions of some immune responses. If you can keep your glycogen stores topped up throughout by drinking about one litre per hour of sports drink, then your body will not need to use as much fat for fuel, so less cortisol is released.

Below: Fit in extra time for rest and relaxation before you race, to reduce the impact of stress hormones.

before you race. The longer your goal distance, the more important the taper, so the week before a marathon you barely need to train at all. This taper period ensures your muscles have time to repair any minor damage from your intense training, and they can store enough fuel for your run. Some runners don't believe in tapering, but research has shown that runs of more than 16km (10 miles) two weeks or less before a marathon are detrimental.

Eating, drinking and sleeping well will also help your body meet its race demands. The female marathon world-record holder, Paula Radcliffe, eats around 3,000kcal (12,600kJ) per day and sleeps for 12 hours. You may not have time for 12 hours of sleep, but the principles that work for her will also work for you.

During the race

Try not to get carried away when you race. If you have put in the training, you should have an idea of the fastest pace you can realistically

aim for; stick to that. Running beyond your limits will ultimately lead to a poor race performance, which could take months to recover from psychologically. It also puts you at greater risk of injury and illness, raising your heart rate too high, releasing

After your Race

You may just feel like collapsing on the ground as soon as you finish a race, but try hard to resist the temptation. What you do in the first few minutes and hours afterward can have a real impact on your recovery.

When your race is finally over, however tempting it might be, don't stop moving. Walk around for at least 10 minutes immediately after finishing your race, staying tall and stretching out your arms and legs as you walk. This will help to keep your circulation up, starting the process of removing waste products that have built up (such as lactic acid). It is also a good way of gently stretching out your muscles – static stretching after a long, fast race is a bad idea, as your muscles will be riddled with tiny tears that could be worsened by intense stretching.

While you're walking around, start the process of refuelling your body with a light snack. It is not uncommon to feel nauseous after a race, but try to force some carbohydrates and protein down now and you will reap the benefits later. The ideal ratio for recovery is to eat 4g of carbohydrates for every 1g of protein, and recent

Above: Fight the urge to collapse after a race; have a gentle walk and try to refuel as quickly as possible.

research suggests that the protein will be used by the body more effectively if it is eaten immediately rather than a few hours later. The good news is that when your appetite returns later in the day, you can keep eating – you will have burned around 2,500kcal and used up 30 to 70g of protein during a marathon so you need to replenish those stores.

Reducing inflammation in your legs early on could also help with your recovery. You can take anti-inflammatory drugs to help with any aches and pains you have. Another (much-debated) treatment is ice baths, an idea popular with elite athletes. The obvious benefit is cooling and numbing your sore legs, and some say that the icing boosts circulation, again helping to remove

Mental recovery

Many athletes have a sense of anticlimax after taking part in a big race, and taking time off running can make matters worse. Try to use the time off positively – remind yourself that you worked hard for your race and deserve some time to yourself. You can use the time to refresh your training; review your training diary and analyse your performance in the race. Look at areas of your training that you think could be improved – perhaps if you had done more strength training, for example, you could have stayed more upright at the end of the race.

When you are training again, use the recovery period as a chance to try new activities or start work on an area of weakness, such as core strength. This will keep you feeling positive and give you a strong basis for your next training period.

waste products from the body. A massage might seem like a tempting prospect after 26.2 hard miles, but save it for a few days later – your legs will be too sore to be handled, and you risk causing further damage to your muscles.

Returning to running
Different athletes have very different approaches to returning to training after a race. Some jump straight back into speedwork, while others wait for weeks before pulling their trainers (sneakers) on again. The best path is somewhere between these extremes.

You might start to get itchy feet a few days after your race (especially if the result was good), but refrain from any running for a week after your race. At this stage there is no such thing as 'active rest' (cross-training to give your body a break); your muscles need to rest and refuel. After that, you can start to reintroduce gentle running and cross-training.

Below: Your body will cool down quickly after a race, so make sure that you wrap up warm.

Post-race problem-solving			
Here are some of the most common post-race problems, and possible solutions			
Problem	**Before race**	**During race**	**After race**
Muscle tears and sprains	Train well, taper well; work on strength and flexibility	Keep to your steady, pre-planned pace	Do not stretch; ice; rest
Colds	Taper	Take on 60–70g carbs per hour	Rest, sleep well, avoid sources of infection
Feeling down	Set realistic race goal, plan activities for the weeks after	Stick to your race plan and trust in it	Be proactive: analyse your race, then plan ahead
Poor, slow running	Taper	Keep to your planned pace; take on carbs	Eat carbs and protein; take a full weeks rest; sleep well

Treat the three or four weeks after your race as a reverse of your taper, starting at 30 to 40 per cent of your highest workload, and building

Below: Some runners have a sense of anticlimax after their goal events, but planning ahead helps with this.

back up slowly to what you would consider a full but light week of training. Avoid racing again until you are completely recovered – a good rule of thumb is to take a day off racing for every mile raced (so that is around a month off for a marathon).

BRANCHING OUT

Running quickly becomes a way of life. That
doesn't mean that you should restrict yourself
to training on the track or road for the standard
distances; there is much more on offer if you want to
take your sport further. You can head off-road for
incredible views that can only be seen on foot; challenge
yourself by running a race that lasts five days; or try
your hand at multi-sport races. This chapter gives you a
general introduction to some of the ways you can
freshen up your running repertoire.

Above: As a general rule, the harder the run, the better the views!
Left: Mountain running is one way your fitness can take you to explore new heights.

Cross-country and Trail Running

Running off-road is very different experience to pounding out miles on the road. The exhilaration of coming back from a run, windswept, covered in mud and with lungs full of fresh air is matched only by the pain of slogging through miles of soggy ground.

Cross-country and trail running are at once closely related and miles apart. Both involve running through the countryside, often without markers, but the quick, fearless mindset of the cross-country racer could hardly be more different to the relaxed and enjoyment-focused approach of the trail runner.

Since both sports involve running on soft ground, they place special demands on your body. The impact on your joints is lessened, as the ground naturally absorbs more shock than the road, but the flip side is that your muscles have to work harder to push off, which can result in strained muscles and tendons in untrained off-roaders. Once you are used to the surface, however, it is an excellent form of training for all kinds of running, strengthening your legs (and your character) and improving your balance and core strength.

Below: Off-road running works on your balance and core strength but it takes a lot of practice.

Above: Cross-country races often start much faster than road events and will help build your racing skills.

Cross-country running

This has unpleasant associations for many of us: memories of being forced across muddy fields whatever the weather at school puts many people off trying again. However, cross-country races, which often form local leagues with fierce competition between clubs, are a great way to train fast and build strength through the winter, in preparation for the next year's road and track seasons. Cross-country racing is notoriously fast and cut-throat, taking place over short distances (usually 5–9.5km/3–6 miles).

Proper preparation

Off-road running can strengthen your core muscles and improve your balance and proprioception (your spatial awareness and ability to negotiate uneven ground). However, if you go into trailing or cross-country after years of road running you will probably injure yourself before you feel any benefits, as these areas are so untrained. Before you go off-road for the first time, work on your core strength, and improve the balance and strength in your ankles using single-leg squats and wobble-board work – a coach or personal trainer will be able to show you how to use this.

Off-road kit

Try to run off-road in your usual trainers (sneakers) and you will soon be forced to give up. You need better grip and less cushioning on soft ground. Cross-country runners usually wear extremely light 'spikes' – slipper-like shoes with spikes in the soles to claw through mud. Trail runners can choose from a huge range of shoes depending on the surface they intend to run on. For long-distance or fairly hard surfaces, bulkier trail shoes with cushioning are the best, while trail-racing shoes are closer to the cross-country model. The outer sole of the shoe should have deeper lugs for grip, the tongue should be gusseted to keep stones and water out, and the upper of the shoe may be waterproofed. Most trail shoes also include rock plates in the midsole to protect your feet from the hard ground and stones underfoot.

Left: Trail shoes have more protective outsoles than road shoes and are sometimes waterproof.

Above: There are not always distance markers in off-road races so you're racing others rather than the clock.

To stand a chance of running well, you must be prepared to go out fast from the gun – bottlenecks over stiles or through hedges are inevitable, and the farther forward you are the less these will delay you. To be successful you will need to develop a shorter, quicker stride than that for road running, striking the ground with your mid- or forefoot, since landing on your heel can make you sink into the ground or slip over. It can also be difficult to pace: there are usually no mile markers, so you are racing the other runners and not the clock – a skill that transfers well to road and track racing.

Trail running

As the name suggests, trail running is distinguished from other off-road running by the fact that it is run over public footpaths and marked trails. However, there is more to this type of running than waymarks. Trail races are usually more beginner friendly, and often take place over longer distances (some marathons and ultra-marathons are trail races). The ground, although soft, is usually slightly easier going as it is generally used for walking. The pace is easier going too – as in any race, the front runners are out to win, but this doesn't have the same fast start as a cross-country race. Overall times are inevitably slower than on the road, so you can relax and forget about your personal best.

Most people find that trail running is better for relaxing the mind than toughening it up. Races take place all year round, so if cold mud doesn't appeal, you can race on trails when summer is in full bloom and enjoy the scenery. Many coaches advise that all runners should do their long runs on trails wherever possible, because of the reduced impact on your joints and the distraction of the setting.

Right: Trail races are more relaxed than cross-country events and often offer beautiful surroundings.

Mountain or Fell Running

If you've tried road running and off-road running, and have started to find that flat races are a little dull, or that your hill training sessions have started to feel easy, the only way is up. Literally – up a mountain.

The sport of mountain running (known as fell running in the UK) at its purest involves running up a mountain and back down the other side, though in the USA and continental Europe there's a great deal of crossover with trail races,

Below: In many mountain or fell races runners choose their own route, often over the most difficult ground.

so runners are more likely to keep to marked paths. Of course, fitness, strength and agility are all key attributes of mountain runners, but what really sets them apart is their courage: there is no time to apply the brakes as you hurtle down a 1,000m slope in a fell race.

The actual running involved in mountain races clearly needs to be very different to running on the flat

Above: Mountain running is not for the faint-hearted – here a fixed rope helps runners stay safe.

ground, or even on good trails. Even the best mountain runners accept that it's not usually possible to 'run' all the way up a mountain (fell races don't necessarily involve any scrambling or climbing, though the

Fell running categories

The Fell Runners Association classifies fell races to show their difficulty:

Ascent	Category A	Minimum 76m (250ft) climb per 1.5km (1 mile); minimum 1.5km (1 mile) long; maximum 20% road
	Category B	Minimum 38m (125ft) climb per 1.5km (1 mile); max 30% on road
	Category C	Minimum 31m (100ft) climb per 1.5km (1 mile); max 40% on road
Distance	Category L	Long: minimum 19km (12 miles)
	Category M	Medium: minimum 9.5km (6 miles)
	Category S	Short: maximum 9.5km (6 miles)
Other	Category O	Orienteering-style race with checkpoints
	MM	Mountain Marathon

Rock of ages

In the UK, fell running originated in small, local races that were often part of fairs. The term fell is, strictly speaking, specific to the mountains and steep hills of the Lake District in Cumbria, north-west England, although it has been adopted in the UK to cover all mountain events. A popular challenge for fell runners now is to 'bag' as many Lake District peaks as possible inside 24 hours, the record being 77, while the classic test is the Bob Graham Round, a circuit of 42 peaks first completed by fell runner Graham in 1932.

In the USA, mountain running is a younger sport and is perhaps less visible thanks to the greater crossover with trail racing, but from the mid-90s onward the USA has had its own national mountain racing team, which competes internationally. In continental Europe and beyond, due in part to the different scale of the mountains, races tend to be longer and higher, with some held over a day or more (such as the annual Tour du Mont Blanc). These often follow paths and the routes are partly marked out, so they differ from British fell races. From these events, a new sub-category called 'skyrunning' has emerged, which is basically long-distance events at high altitude.

Above: Even at the front of a mountain race it's rare to see people actually running up the ascents.

fastest runners might choose routes that do if they're the shortest). By the time they reach the top of the mountain, most will have slowed to a controlled climb. In training for fell races, runners need to build up their climbing muscles, using the kind of terrain and gradients expected in the race. However, the real skill comes on the descent, when the ability to allow yourself to 'fall' down the mountain comes into play. Quick feet, strong ankles and good balance and proprioception are essential if you are to get down in one piece. Near the top of mountains especially, there may be no trail, and the ground might consist of loose stones, so you need a light touch on the ground to avoid slipping. It goes without saying that the only way to get better

at mountain running is to practise running over mountains, but beginners should always keep safety in mind, training with an experienced mountain runner if possible, and starting with lower, gentler slopes.

Fell racing falls into a number of categories depending on steepness and distance. In its simplest form it bears some resemblance to cross-country running or orienteering: apart from the start and finish, the route is often unmarked and part of the skill of racing well is choosing the fastest route (which is rarely the easiest!). If it sounds scary, that's with good reason, as the remoteness of the route and added risk of injury from the steep, uneven ground can leave runners open to hypothermia if they become immobile. As such, fell runners

need to be able to navigate over mountainous ground, and have a basic knowledge of mountain safety. Though like all runners they dress as lightly as possible, they should carry basic safety kit such as a light layer of clothing to keep warm.

Below: Races are won and lost on the descent, with the most agile and fearless runners coming first.

Adventure Racing

As the name suggests, adventure racing is a sport for people who are tired of trudging around the block or obsessing over splits on the track. Adventure racing is an 'anything goes' multi-sport that gives you the chance to test yourself with new activities.

The fundamentals of adventure racing are off-road running and cycling, navigation, and often kayaking. Added to that list could be any number of physical and mental challenges: abseiling, ball games, archery, inline skating – whatever the organizers see fit to put you through. Adventure racers generally compete in mixed teams, and must complete the challenges while navigating around a set of check points as quickly as possible. Though often set in remote, rough countryside, some adventure races are staged in big cities: you may find yourself abseiling off a landmark building, or navigating through hidden alleys.

The beauty of adventure racing is that it is unpredictable and encourages you to take part in sports that you may never have considered. As such it is difficult to train for them too specifically. As a runner you will be at a clear advantage, since this and the bicycle are the main modes

Below: Adventure races can go on for days and some are deliberately staged at night for a dramatic atmosphere.

Above: Don't expect an easy running route during adventure races – you'll need to get your feet dirty!

of transport between challenges. However, the surprise element of some races is such that it is more about having a go than becoming incredibly proficient at an activity. This, with the difficulty of navigation, means that surprise wins are not uncommon in adventure racing, where being fit and fast is not always the key to coming first.

Developing team spirit

Unlike more standard running events, which are almost always individual pursuits, adventure racing is all about working together as a team. Ideally your team mates will have a good mix of skills so that you can help each other with your weakest tasks: one runner might do most of the map-reading, while a big, strong runner might carry more of the kit. Adventure racers sometimes use 'towing' to help less strong runners and cyclists: slower team members are literally 'towed' along using a bungee cord so they can go faster without tiring. If you are racing as a team, it is crucial that you stay together as there are usually penalty points for losing your team and reaching checkpoints separately.

Being part of a strong team is also crucial for the psychological side of adventure racing. Although

Kitted out

Don't panic, you are unlikely to need your own bow and arrow to start adventure racing, but some different running kit, plus a bike, are essential. Your bike should be a mountain-type bike – if you are only trying adventure racing there is no need to invest heavily, but tyres that grip and good suspension are essential (you will also need a helmet to race). Padded Lycra shorts, which reach below the knee (even for men) are a better choice than standard running shorts because they don't ride up, and you should opt for a light, long-sleeved top for both warm and cool conditions. Depending on the length of your race, a running backpack (with a hydration bladder, a plastic pouch with a straw for carrying large quantities of water), a waterproof jacket or cape, gloves and a headtorch may all prove useful.

these events are designed to be fun – and they are – they can often go on for more than 24 hours, sometimes without any breaks for sleeping. You will need to be able to keep each other's spirits up when both your body and sense of humour inevitably start to fail.

Below: You won't know exactly what's in store until the race briefing, so be prepared to try anything.

Above: Team members must stick together to help each other both physically and mentally.

Benefits

If you do decide to give adventure racing a go, it can work wonders for your running when you return to normal events. It may not be suitable for those who want to win road races, but for the mid-pack runner, the different disciplines build your endurance, fitness and overall

strength. Like triathlon, your risk of injury is lower because you tend not to use the same muscles in every training session, and your reduced running lowers the risk of impact-related injuries. Perhaps most importantly, taking part in one or two of these races each year gives you a mental break: since it is impossible to judge your performance against existing personal bests, you can enjoy instead the fitness you have built up through years of running.

Above: Kayaking is a regular feature of adventure racing so you'll need whole-body strength.

Navigation Basics

Anyone who spent their youth hiking and camping will be at a distinct advantage in off-road races. Map-reading is a skill that some people pick up very easily, but even if the idea frightens you, you can at least learn to find out where you are if you become lost.

The ability to run fast over difficult terrain is only part of off-road racing. All your training could go to waste if you lose hours on needless diversions caused by poor navigation. But it's not just about fast times: being able to find your way to the next checkpoint or the finish could be crucial for your safety.

Navigating fell races

A basic level of skill in navigation is essential for most adventure races and fell races (as well as orienteering events, which are entirely based around your ability to navigate). In fell races, navigation is secondary to running, as there are usually no checkpoints – you just have to get up and down a mountain as quickly as possible. Being able to use a map and compass simply enables you to find the quickest and safest route and to be able to get off the mountain if visibility becomes poor.

Above: Use the map to find out what kind of terrain you should be running on and use landmarks to stay on course.

Below: On adventure races you'll usually have to work in teams for safety.

Using a map and compass

Although it may sound daunting, in its simplest form, using a map and compass is straightforward. However, it is much easier to understand if you have a demonstration, and you can go on courses lasting a few hours to make you comfortable with the process. This is the basic procedure:

1 Holding your map as flat as possible, line up the edge of your compass with the direction in which you wish to travel (it doesn't matter which way you hold your map).

2 Turn the ring of your compass so that the guidelines are aligned with the north–south lines on the map. (N on the ring should be pointing north on the map.)

3 Hold the compass straight and flat in front of you and turn around until the north arrow is aligned with N on the compass ring. You are now facing in the direction you wish to travel.

4 Look in front of you for a feature that is marked on the map in your direction of travel (for example a boulder, building, or stream) and head toward it.

Left: Basic map-reading using a map and compass is a simple process.

Right: Once you've become a skilled navigator you will find that it is easier to cover courses much more quickly.

Navigating adventure races

In adventure racing your aim is much more complicated: you must visit as many plotted checkpoints as possible in the shortest time to win. Like fell races, there is no set route, so part of the skill is plotting a viable but direct route between checkpoints. You are given a dibber – an electronic tag – at the start of the race to record the checkpoints you have visited, and you will usually be given a map of the race area, as well as a detailed description of where the checkpoints are (giving grid reference and a description of the surroundings of each checkpoint).

In this type of race you will have to use your head constantly – there is no time to admire the beautiful scenery or you may find that you become lost. Help yourself by practising map-reading before your event using a standard walking map (the map you are given at the event will usually be a much larger scale, more detailed version). If at all possible, find out what kind of map you will be given at the event and practise using the same type, so that

Below: Clear running terrain may not always be easy to find – memorizing map symbols before your race will help.

you can learn the symbols for fences, streams, pits and other structural features, and how to determine the shape of the land. Unless you are in a very tough race, your checkpoint should be next to a feature, so you can find it with relative ease.

Plotting your course

At the start of your race, you should plot a course (by drawing on your map if possible) between checkpoints. Note which features you expect to pass on the way and where your significant changes of direction are. Before you reach each checkpoint,

know in which direction you will need to set out for the next one, as working it out at the checkpoint could help other teams find it, giving them an advantage. Most importantly, every time you set off again, look for a landmark or feature to check that you are going in the right direction – even after only a couple of minutes at the checkpoint you may become disoriented.

Of course, the safest way to approach your first navigational race is to run it as a team with a more experienced map-reader, who can show you the ropes as you go along.

Ultrarunning

If you thought marathon running was as much of a mental as a physical challenge, then ultrarunning is even more so. At 80km (50 miles) or more in length, ultra races are tough. But it's worth it – these can be some of the most dramatic, beautiful races in the world.

Although the idea of running farther than a marathon may seem daunting, if you have ever trained for this event you might be surprised by how little extra effort it takes to train for a 50K, 100-mile race or even a superhuman feat such as crossing the USA.

The ultrarunning scene has been dominated for a long time by slightly older runners – athletes whose natural speed is dropping off but whose endurance and mental strength are higher than ever. However, this is now changing and, as with all types of running, it is becoming more popular, as runners of all ages and abilities look for new challenges.

Going the distance

If you are still a competitive marathon runner you will need to put your usual running speed out of your mind. Patience is a virtue at these longer distances, and at 80km (50 miles) or more you can expect to add a couple of minutes per 1.5km (1 mile) to your usual marathon pace. That's

Below: Be prepared to run much slower than your usual race pace during longer ultrarunning events.

Above: Ultrarunning is tough but can take you to some of the most dramatic races in the world.

not to say the fastest ultrarunners in the world are slow – most would complete 50K faster than a fairly good runner could race a marathon – but unless you're at the very top, your aim will be completion rather than competition. Regular walk breaks are also a staple of ultrarunning strategy, even for sub-3-hour marathon runners. Typically you run for 15 to 20 minutes followed by a 3- to 5-minute walk break, taking care not to slump down or lose momentum.

Since your overall speed is slower during an ultramarathon, your speedwork is also longer and slower. You can forget about 400m repetitions on the track; your shortest intervals will be miles, run at around your half-marathon pace. If you are used to long threshold or tempo sessions, you will run those same longer intervals at your usual marathon race pace. In an ultra race, you will remain well below your lactate threshold unless you decide to run a sprint finish. If you have never carried out any strength training for shorter distances, then you should reconsider for ultra training. Spending hours on your feet often leads to a hunched posture and poor running style, which can eventually cause serious injuries. During an ultra race there is a greater need to carry more weight in the form of a fuel belt or backpack. Developing the muscles in your core, back and upper body will help you to stay strong and comfortable through the entire race.

Example schedule

Training for the beginners' ultra distance, 50K, is not that different to training for a marathon. The schedule below is a rough guide to how a 12-week plan could work. This assumes that you already have a base of fitness and have trained for a half or full marathon in the last year. Since this distance is only 8km (5 miles) longer than a marathon, the speed sessions are still fairly fast, although short intervals and leg-speed sessions are not included.

Right: It's crucial for ultrarunners to gain core strength to keep themselves in good form over the distance.

	Mon	Tue	Wed	Thur	Fri	Sat	Sun
			Ultrarunning schedule (HMP = half-marathon pace)				
Week one	Rest	9.5km (6 miles) with 2 x 1.5km (1 mile) at 10K pace	8km (5 miles) easy	9.5km (6 miles) with 15 mins at HMP	Rest	9.5km (6 miles)	19km (12 miles)
Week two	Rest	9.5km (6 miles) with 3 x 1.5km (1 mile) at 10K pace	8km (5 miles) easy	9.5km (6 miles) with 20 mins at HMP	Rest	9.5km (6 miles)	22.5km (14 miles)
Week three	Rest	As week 2	2 x 5km (3 miles) easy (am/pm)	As week 2	Rest/6.5km (4 miles) easy	9.5km (6 miles)	25.5km (16 miles)
Week four	Rest	11km (7 miles) with 3 x 1.5km (1 mile) at 10K pace	2 x 6.5km (4 miles) easy	9.5km (6 miles) with 25 mins at HMP	Rest/6.5km (4 miles) easy	9.5km (6 miles)	29km (18 miles)
Week five	Rest	11km (7 miles) with 4 x 1.5km (1 mile) at 10K pace	2 x 6.5km (4 miles) easy	As week 4	Rest/6.5km (4 miles) easy	9.5km (6 miles)	32km (20 miles)
Week six	Rest	As week 5	1 x 5km (3 miles); 1 x 9.5km (6 miles)	11km (7 miles) with 30 mins at HMP	Rest/6.5km (4 miles) easy	13km (8 miles)	29km (18 miles)
Week seven	Rest	13km (8 miles) with 4 x 1.5km (1 mile) at 10K pace	1 x 5km (3 miles); 1 x 9.5km (6 miles)	As week 6	Rest/6.5km (4 miles) easy	13km (8 miles)	35km (22 miles)
Week eight	Rest	9.5km (6 miles) with 3 x 1.5km (1 mile) at 10K pace	8km (5 miles) easy	8km (5 miles) with 15 mins at HMP	Rest/6.5km (4 miles) easy	9.5km (6 miles)	22.5km (14 miles)
Week nine	Rest	As week 7	2 x 8km (5 miles) easy	11km (7 miles) with 30 mins at HMP	Rest/6.5km (4 miles) easy	13km (8 miles)	29km (18 miles)
Week ten	Rest	9.5km (6 miles) with 3 x 1.5km (1 mile) at 10K pace	2 x 6.5km (4 miles) easy	As week 9	Rest/6.5km (4 miles) easy	9.5km (6 miles)	25.5km (16 miles)
Week eleven	Rest	As week 10	9.5km (6 miles) easy	9.5km (6 miles) with 25 mins at HMP	Rest/6.5km (4 miles) easy	6.5km (4 miles)	19km (12 miles)
Week twelve	Rest	8km (5 miles) easy	Rest	8km (5 miles) easy	Rest	Rest	50K race

Ultrarunning: Longer Events and Stage Races

Once you begin to think about training for distances greater than 80km (50 miles), your training mileage to race distance ratio alters hugely. It is impossible to run this distance in a single training run, as your body would not be able to recover in time for your race.

When training for longer events, you have to push the mileage as high as you can, breaking the distance into manageable chunks, and have faith that on the day your mind will make up the rest. Despite this apparently impossible task, plenty of average people with busy lives find time to train for 100K races and beyond.

Long-distance training

To train for this kind of race, you can use the basic schedule from the previous page, but slow down your speed intervals further: for mile repetitions, use your half-marathon pace, and for the Thursday sessions use your normal marathon pace. You will also need to

Food supplies

In a normal road race you may rely on energy gels or drinks for food, but while these will play a big part in your ultra race, you obviously won't be able to live on them for hours or days on end. Experiment with different foods to see what your body can cope with. Remember that, as you are running quite slowly, digestion will be easier than during a marathon, but you may still find that you become nauseous after a long period of running.

Choose bland foods that are dense in calories, such as cold new potatoes, cheese sandwiches or plain potato crisps (chips). If your race is staged abroad, try to find out what food will be available and if it is unfamiliar, take some contingency supplies.

increase the mileage, which you can do in two ways: by increasing your Saturday run so that you do two long runs back to back, and by running twice most days. Obviously you will need to do this very slowly, so you can add another six to eight weeks building up mileage at the start of the training period.

Building up the distance

To build up your long runs, start with a run of around 9.5–13km (6–8 miles) on the Saturday (1 hour) and 16–19km (10–12 miles) on Sunday (90 minutes). Add 3km (2 miles) a week to the Sunday run until you reach 29km (18 miles), then gradually build up the Saturday run until both match. You can then take

Left: When training for races longer than 80km (50 miles) you should work toward having two long runs per week.

Above: Very long races and stage races can be gruelling, so work on your mental strategy beforehand.

Below: As you'll be increasing your mileage, you should try to run off-road more to reduce impact on your legs.

both runs up to 32km (20 miles). Don't exceed 3 hours running on either day, as your body will not be able to recover, and remember that your pace should be much slower than marathon race pace. Avoid any other activity (such as strenuous housework or gardening) on these days, and try to keep your runs off-road as much as possible to reduce the impact on your joints.

To run twice a day through the week, try using your run to commute to work (or part of the way). Some stage races require twice-a-day running, so this is good practice; while other stage races typically require 16–32km (10–20 miles) of running each day. Running to work also has the advantage that you will need to carry a backpack, which will help keep your pace down and teach you to run with extra weight if this is a feature of your race.

Mental preparation

You will know from your experiences racing shorter distances how powerful the mind can be in helping your running performance. While focusing on your race is the best approach for most shorter races, disassociation is definitely the best approach for the endless miles of an ultrarun. The race will be as much of an ordeal for your mind as your body, and you can expect at least two or three rough patches over a 100K race that will be bad enough to make you want to stop.

In a stage race, the second and third days are often the hardest, as you will have run hard but still have plenty to do. Expect these low points and prepare for them. If you can, take an MP3 player to pick you up, or join forces with a runner at a similar pace and chat (your slower pace allows you to do this). If all else fails, try repeating a mantra to yourself: 'I can do this', or 'I am strong and fit'.

Triathlon

If the growth of running as a mass participation sport has been rapid since the 1970s, the triathlon's emergence from relative obscurity has been astonishingly fast. Triathlons are races where competitors must swim, then cycle, then run.

Many runners change to triathlon because they have suffered impact injuries from high-volume running training; others simply enjoy the new challenge. It is certainly a good way to build all-over fitness, and you may find that your running times improve as a result of the more varied training.

Although the three sports of swimming, cycling and running have been combined for years, the modern sport of triathlon is widely accepted to have started in California in the 1970s, created

Below: Swimming with hundreds of other people is one of the skills you need to master for triathlon.

by friends who trained together in the different disciplines and decided to hold a race. The first event, the Mission Bay Triathlon in San Diego, California, was held in 1974. A few years later, the first Ironman or full-distance triathlon was held in Hawaii, following a debate between runners, swimmers and cyclists over who had the greater endurance fitness. Three races already in existence on the island – the 4km (2.4-mile) Waikiki Roughwater Swim, 185km (115-mile) Around Oahu Bike Race and the Honolulu marathon – were combined, with 5km (3 miles) taken off the bike course to create a continuous route. Only 15 athletes took part, but the Ironman distance – now held all

Above: The right kit can help you to achieve faster times in triathlon, especially during the cycling phase.

over the world, with championships in Hawaii – now attracts tens of thousands of runners every year. A shorter triathlon became an Olympic event in 2000 and, although the sport is still young, there are now athletes specializing in this combination sport.

Don't be fooled into thinking that because you are a good runner, you will make a good triathlete. Everyone can ride a bike, but racing on one is a different skill, while few adults are good swimmers. Even if you have some background in these sports, you will need to change your approach and technique to ensure a comfortable transition from one to the next. Swimming, cycling and running in triathlon are geared toward moving as quickly as possible with the least amount of energy expenditure, with minimum upset when switching from one set of muscles to the next. The time taken to change kit between each stage (called transition – the first change is T1, the second T2) is also recorded to give the final time. Triathlon kit is geared toward making this process as smooth as possible.

Standard triathlon distances			
	Swim	**Bike**	**Run**
Super sprint	400m	10K	2.5K
Sprint	750m	20K	5K
Olympic/Short	1,500m	40K	10K
Middle/Half Ironman	1.9K (1.2 miles)	90K (56 miles)	21K (13.1 miles)
Long/Full Ironman	3.8K (2.4 miles)	180K (112 miles)	42k (26.2 miles)

Above: Transition – where triathletes change from one discipline to the next – is sometimes known as 'the fourth discipline of triathlon'.

All the gear

If you like running for its simplicity and lack of expense then triathlon, along with adventure racing, is probably not for you. Race entry is two or three times that of a running race, but the real cost is the kit needed to train and compete. If you are trying out triathlon, consider buying some

kit (such as the bike) second hand, or look out for triathlon packages from specialist shops. Your biggest purchases will be:

Triathlon suit. An all-in-one or two-piece technical suit, designed to be worn through the whole race to avoid the need for changing. It is quick drying, and has padding for the cycle stage.

Wetsuit. Most triathlons involve an open-water swim, and wetsuits are often required. A wetsuit will keep you warm and help with buoyancy.

Bike. You don't need to spend a fortune on a bike, but the more you pay, the lighter and more efficient your bike will be. Triathlon-specific bikes have a different fit to traditional road bikes to preserve your running muscles and aid efficiency. They are often fitted with tri-bars or aerobars,

Left: Wetsuits are often compulsory in open-water swims.

Right: Special lightweight triathlon shoes help you make the most of your strongest discipline.

which enable you to lean forward with your forearms pointing ahead, making you more aerodynamic.

Bike shoes and pedals. Special clipless pedals with corresponding shoes allow your feet to clip on to the pedals, so you can pull them up as well as pushing down, generating more power.

Triathlon shoes. Of course, you can use your standard running shoes, but triathlon shoes are lighter, dry quicker, and are easier to pull on and fasten.

Triathlon: Training Sessions

For many runners, coming to triathlon after years of focusing on putting in running miles, swimming and cycling are distant childhood memories. Consequently the runner either dreads getting back into the pool or on the bike, or remembers these sports as simple fun.

Cycling and swimming are fun, but they're certainly not simple. You will need to go right back to basics in order to learn how to swim and cycle effectively, and more importantly, how to combine them with your 'first' sport.

Swimming

Freestyle (front crawl) is by far the most commonly used stroke in triathlon, but it is difficult to get right. You need to achieve as efficient a stroke as possible to conserve energy for the later stages of the race, while at the same time learning how to 'sight' (raise your head to check you are on course), and survive the rough-and-tumble of the triathlon swim. Triathletes aim to use their legs less than usual in the swim, to save the muscles for the bike and run sections, but you will need to practise kicking harder toward the end of your swim to force blood into the muscles you are about to use.

If it has been years since you swam, or you never learned, attending adult classes will be useful. There are four basic components to good freestyle stroke:

Body position. You should be lying horizontally at the top of the water, face down; your feet should break the surface when you kick without bending excessively at the knee.

Breathing. Learn to breathe on both sides. Most people find it easiest to breathe every third stroke. Don't lift your head, but turn with the motion of your body as your arm comes out of the water.

Kick. Move your legs from the hip, toes pointed and feet close together, and without bending your knees too much.

Stroke. Reach ahead of you and curve your hand to 'catch' the water. Pull right through, keeping your arm straight through the stroke, past your hip, and only bending the elbow to return the arm to the front.

Swim sessions:

Sets. Use sets of ten laps of the pool with rests in between, first to build up your endurance, then to do speed intervals as you become more confident.

Above: Taking swimming lessons will make you more efficient in the water, saving energy for the bike and run stages.

Below: You'll need to kick harder at the end of the swim so you're ready to stand, run and cycle.

constant, and practising taking on sports drinks as you go, since in a triathlon this will be your best opportunity to do so.

Hills. Try hill sprints or longer drags to build power in your legs, but remember to keep your action smooth and steady – if your pedalling slows right down, change gear.

Spinning. Triathletes use easy 'spinning' on an easy gear to help flush lactic acid out of their legs and prepare for the run section of the race. Try a few minutes of this at the end of your rides.

Running

If you decide to commit to triathlon training, you will need to cut down to three or four runs per week, and your long run probably won't be as long as you are used to. All of your run sessions are quality sessions, however, so you might do a speedwork session, threshold run, long run and a triathlon-specific session called a brick. This involves alternating cycling and running and is more easily done in the gym. The idea is to become used to the sensation of running after cycling, when the blood will have pooled in your cycling muscles and will take time to shift to your running muscles.

Below: This hands-on-top steering position helps beginners to feel in control – and elite triathletes to climb hills.

Above: Use bike/run 'brick' sessions to get used to running fast straight after a period of cycling.

Stroke count. Count the number of strokes you use to swim one lap. Aim to reduce the number of strokes.

Catch ups. This works on your stroke. Instead of moving your arms continuously, keep your right arm out in front of you until the left arm meets it, then as soon as your hands are side by side, stroke with your right arm, and so on.

Cycling

You may not be used to using a road bike, so take time to get used to the fast feel and more responsive steering. If you

are using clipless pedals for the first time, practise in a traffic-free area first. When you buy your bike, get fitted in a specialist shop – this could save hours of agony later on, or at the very least make you a more efficient cyclist. When you are starting out, hold the handlebars at the front, on top of the brakes, so that you can use them if necessary; when you are ready, start using the 'drops' (the underneath, curved part of the handlebars). Invest in a cycle computer so that you can monitor your cadence.

Bike sessions:

Long rides. Endurance cycling needs hours of training, so include one long ride in your training each week, learning to use the gears to keep your effort

Triathlon: Olympic Distance Training

Running makes you incredibly fit. There is no doubt about that, but if you have been feeling smug about your improved athleticism, you may be in for a shock when you start triathlon training, which involves a much higher level of overall fitness.

Aside from the technical difficulty of learning new sports, triathlon requires a level of whole-body strength and fitness that running, with its very specific gains, does not. If you are new to triathlon, Olympic distance (1,500m/40K/10K) is a good place to start: it is not so long as to wear you out with high-volume training, but long enough to test out your new-found swimming and cycling skills.

Fitness levels

As with any race you will need a base of fitness. If you have not been swimming or cycling for a few years, spend two or three months building them into your training schedules, starting with just one swim and bike ride a week. You will also need to cut down the number of runs you do, since you will be

Above: Even after reducing training sessions for triathlon, running is likely to remain your strongest discipline.

Left: Don't jump straight into a triathlon training plan as you'll need to build up your cycling and swimming fitness first.

Finish times

If you are new to competing in triathlons it is difficult to know what kind of finish times you can expect.

At the fast end of an Olympic distance race, male competitors will finish in under 1hr 45 mins (<20 mins swim; <2 mins T1; <55 mins bike; <30 secs T2; <33 mins run). Top female athletes complete in well under 2 hours in total. For an average competitor, a sub-2:30 time is considered fast, while anything below 3 hours is a very decent effort.

Triathlon: beginners' 10-week schedule

	Mon	Tue	Wed	Thur	Fri	Sat	Sun
Week one	Swim: 10 WU; 2 x 10 fast; 10 CD	Run: 4 miles easy	Cycle: 1hr easy	Swim: 40 easy	Rest	Brick: 3 x 15 mins bike, 5 mins run	Run: 1hr, 9.5–13km (6–8 miles) easy
Week two	Swim: 10 WU; 10 SC; 10 CD	Cycle: 1hr with 2 x 10 mins faster	Run: 8km (5 miles) easy	Swim: 40 with 10 CU	Run: 6.5km (4 miles) with 4 x 2 mins fast	Rest	Brick: 45 mins bike, 30 mins run
Week three	Cycle: 1hr over hills, using gears	Swim: 10 WU, 2 x 10 fast; 10 CD	Run: 8km (5 miles) with 4 x 2 mins fast	Swim: 50 easy	Rest	Run: 1hr15	Brick: 4 x 10 mins bike, 5 mins run
Week four	Swim: 30 easy	Cycle: 45 mins flat and fast	Rest	Run: 8km (5 miles) with 15 mins threshold	Rest	Cycle: 1hr easy	Run: 1hr easy
Week five	Swim: 10 WU; 10 CU; 2 x 8 fast; 10 CD	Brick: 5 x 10 mins bike, 5 mins run	Run: 8km (5 miles) easy	Swim: 50 easy	Rest	Run: 1hr30 16–7.5km (10–12 miles)	Bike: 1hr20 with steady hills
Week six	Swim: 60 easy	Run: 10 mins warm-up, 3 x 1.5km (1 mile) at 10K pace; cool-down	Bike: 1hr easy	Swim: 10 WU; 500m timed; 10 CD	Rest	Bike: 1hr45 steady	Run: 1hr30
Week seven	Swim: 10 WU; 10 SC; 10 fast; 10 SC; 10 CD	Brick: 4 x 15 bike, 5 run	Run: 8km (5 miles) with 3 x 1.5km (1 mile) at 10K pace	Swim: 50 with 20 faster	Rest	Run: 1hr with 6 x 2 mins faster	Bike: 1hr on hills using gears
Week eight	Swim: 10 WU; 10 SC; 300m fast; 10 CD	Run: 9.5km (6 miles) with 6 x 3 mins fast, 2 mins easy	Bike: 1hr15 mins steady	Swim: 10 WU; 3 x 8 fast; 10 CD	Rest	Run: 1hr15 easy	Swim: 500m, change, bike: 45 mins; run 20 mins
Week nine	Rest	Swim: 10 WU; 500m timed;10 CD	Run: 8km (5 miles) easy	Bike: 16–24km (10–15 miles) flat, timed	Swim: 60	Rest	Bricks: 3 x 10 mins bike, 5 mins easy
Week ten	Rest	Swim: 40 easy	Run: 6.5km (4 miles) easy	Bike: 45 mins steady	Rest	Bricks: 2 x 10 bike, 5 run, easy	Triathlon

Swim sessions: CU = catch-ups; SC = stroke count; WU = warm-up; CD = cool-down. Figures represent 25m laps.

unable to fit in more than three runs a week once you start triathlon training. Work on your weakest discipline most to build up your confidence.

Keeping records

Your training diary will be more important than ever when you start triathlon training, as the training is much more complex and you will probably do more sessions per week than with straight running training. This will help you to make sure you are doing enough in each discipline, and to chart your progress in your less familiar sports.

Right: Practising swim drills will improve your stroke and gradually help you to speed up in the water.

Taking Your Running Further: Destination Events

Combining your love for running and the hard-won fitness it has brought with a trip to an exotic location is the perfect way to see more of the world. Here are some of the most spectacular must-do events for runners of all abilities.

Himalayan 100 Mile Stage Race, Darjeeling, Mirik, India

The best race in the world for a true runner's high, this 'undulating' five-day race is tough, but perfectly accessible. Every October/November, in stages ranging from 16–48km (10–30 miles), although officially the longest stage is marathon distance, about 100 runners climb and drop thousands of feet at altitudes between 1,980m–3,600m (6,500ft–11,800ft). Starting in Darjeeling, they run over rough tracks, past tea plantations and pine forests and through remote villages, where the welcome is always warm. It is a difficult race, but with marathon-level fitness you should be able to complete it – and it will be worth the hardship for the race's main selling point: stunning panoramic views of four of the world's five highest peaks, including Mount Everest. www.himalayan.com

Right: Mount Kanchenjunga watches over runners on day two of the Himalayan Stage Race.

Below: Running at altitude for five days is tough, but there is a huge support team on hand and, of course, constantly stunning views.

Hood to Coast Relay, Oregon, USA

If you find running to be a lonely sport, then this race is for you. It's the world's biggest relay, running 315km (197 miles) from the awe-inspiring Mount Hood to the Pacific coast in Oregon – home to one of world's biggest running shoe manufacturers, Nike, and to American running legend Steve Prefontaine. The race began in 1982 with just 8 teams, and now every year in August 1,000 teams of 12 make the journey with the slower teams starting out first. There are 36 legs ranging from just over 6km (3½ miles) to just under 13km (8 miles) and to take part, and you need to average a pace of about 14 minutes per kilometre. But don't think this race is about running fast: the emphasis is on fun and teamwork, with competitions for best decorated vans (teams are allowed two each to carry all their supplies) and best team names. Teams work together to support each other, handing out food, drink and moral support to fellow members along the way. If you would like to be one of them next year, you will need to be quick off the mark: the race tends to sell out in a day. www.hoodtocoast.com

Above: The spectacular Mount Hood provides an impressive backdrop to the start of the Hood to Coast Relay.

Below: Competitors cross the start line as they prepare to complete a distance of 315km (197 miles) in 36 stages.

Boston Marathon, Boston, USA

This historic marathon in a historic city is one that every runner should aim to add to their list, for one simple reason: Boston Marathon has strict qualifying times for entry, which means that running it puts you firmly in the faster than average category. In fact, those times are not too intimidating: 3:10 for men and 3:40 for women, slowing down with age category. Apart from the prestige of gaining an entry, runners enjoy the sense of tradition. The marathon started in 1897, making it the oldest annually held marathon in the world. Like the city's history, it has not been without conflict: in 1967, before the Amateur Athletic Union allowed women to run in long-distance events, Kathrine Switzer entered the race without giving her gender. Officials tried to remove her from the course, but other runners surrounded her so that she could finish. These days, more than 20,000 entrants of both sexes enjoy the slightly downhill, point-to-point run, finishing in Boston's Copley Square. www.baa.org

Above: Officials try to remove Kathrine Switzer from the Boston Marathon in 1967; women are now very welcome!

Below: The race's entry conditions help ensure its popularity, as qualifying marks you out as a 'real' runner.

Above: The relentless icy white of the landscape provides a unique backdrop to the race.

Left: You can't be overdressed for this race – snow shoes are essential.

Below: Competitors in the North Pole Marathon run laps of a temporary camp on the shifting ice.

North Pole Marathon, Arctic Circle

If crowded big-city marathons are not for you, then this relatively new race could be the answer. Running on sea ice near the North Pole, there is not actually much to look at: you will run laps of a temporary camp on the ice, but sheets of white stretching into the distance give the event a surreal and unique atmosphere. Naturally, there is no need to worry about overheating, but participants should consider revising their usual personal bests, since the addition of snow shoes, layers of clothing and temperatures well below freezing can slow you down considerably. Running is all about seeing different places, and this is certainly one of the more unusual.
www.npmarathon.com

Sun Herald City to Surf, Sydney, Australia

For a race that feels more like a giant street party, you can't do better than this 14K event, held in August. Said to have been inspired by San Francisco's Bay to Breakers event, it began in 1971 with a respectable 2,000 competitors. It has gone on to become one of the biggest road races in the world with more than 63,000 finishers in 2006. Starting in the city's Hyde Park and running down to the famous Bondi Beach, it is one of the friendliest, liveliest races on the planet, full of costumes and characters. For most of the people who participate in City to Surf, the finishing time is not important, but the lead runners still complete the race in little more than 40 minutes.

www.city2surf.com.au

Left: Tens of thousands of runners crowd the streets of Sydney in one of the world's biggest road races.

Below: The emphasis of the City to Surf, for most of the participants, is on fun and celebration.

Above: Competitors in the Great Wall Marathon wind their way through the beautiful Tianjin Province.

The Great Wall Marathon, Tianjin Province, China

Marathons are rarely much tougher, nor the rewards more spectacular, than this annual run along the Great Wall of China, which takes place in May. Participants must conquer the winding stone course, which includes many steep ascents and descents, as well as over 5,000 stone steps. Race organizers suggest that one of the best ways of preparing for this marathon is to run up and down the stairs of a 20-storey building! Aside from the main marathon, a half-marathon, 10K and 5K runs are also held each year. This is a popular event: in 2008 over 1,700 runners conquered the Wall over the four different distances. Competitors are treated to breathtaking views of the surrounding Tianjin Province as they explore one of the world's most famous landmarks in this truly unique event.
www.great-wall-marathon.com

Above: Though without doubt an arduous climb, the views along this course are spectacular.

Below: Exhausted runners literally crawl up some of the 5,000-plus stone steps which form part of the course.

Marathon des Sables, Morocco

This six-day event, which started in 1986 and is held in April, is billed as the toughest foot race on earth for good reason. Drawn by the other-worldly beauty of the Moroccan sand-dunes and the lure of the challenge, most competitors come to regret entering this event at some point while running through 225km (150 miles) of heat and sand, which includes a single stage of 78km (52 miles). Runners have to carry all their own belongings (the organizers supply water and tents) throughout the race. Medical attention for dehydration and ruined feet is in high demand. However, it is the formidable reputation of this event, and the satisfaction and experience of completing it, that keeps it selling out more than a year in advance every time.
www.darbaroud.com

Right: Over 15km of plaster (Band-Aid) is used in every Marathon des Sables race.

Below: Competitors must carry all their own kit for the whole 225km (150 miles).

Above: A suitably dressed runner in the Marathon du Medoc crosses through Pauillac vineyards.

Below: Spectators look on as a competitor samples some of the local wine on offer around the course.

Marathon du Medoc, Pauillac, France

It is difficult to imagine a greater contrast to the arduous Marathon des Sables than the Marathon du Medoc, run in September each year, even though it sells out almost as quickly.

Bizarrely, the main attraction at this marathon is not the glorious countryside scenery, the jolly atmosphere or the slick organization; it is the aid stations. However, these are no ordinary tables laid out with sorry half-full cups of water or energy drinks. This unique race runs through France's most famous wine-producing region and samples of local wine are on offer at 21 different stops through the race, along with other fuels ranging from freshly baked French bread to delicacies such as foie gras and oysters. Fast times are more than possible on this course, but to attempt one really is to miss the point of the event.
www.marathondumedoc.com

Monaco Marathon,
Monte-Carlo, Monaco

Established in 1997, this unique marathon takes its 3,000-plus competitors through three different countries, as Monaco itself is too small to host the whole distance. The route starts in Monte-Carlo, follows the coast into France and then Italy before it turns back, taking competitors back through France again, finally finishing with a lap around Monaco's Louis II Stadium.

Runners are given a special 'marathon passport' which they must get stamped in each country. With its glamorous location, spectacular views of the Côte d'Azur, and almost guaranteed sunshine, it is not hard to see why this race becomes more and more popular each year.
www.fma.mc/mcrun

Right: Competitors run through the famous harbour in Monte-Carlo before crossing the border into France then Italy.

Below: Runners can expect clear weather and wonderful views of the stunning Côte d'Azur.

Old Mutual Two Oceans Marathon, Cape Town, South Africa

Calling itself 'the world's most beautiful race', the Two Oceans Marathon is a 56km (35 mile) ultramarathon held annually in Cape Town, South Africa, on the Saturday of the Easter weekend.

The race begins in Newlands, and follows a circular route through Muizenberg, Fish Hoek, over Chapman's Peak and Constantia Nek, and eventually finishes at the University of Cape Town campus. The route covers open road and more challenging mountain climbs, with stunning views of both the Indian and Atlantic oceans, the two oceans that give the race its name.

A popular half-marathon, which has become the biggest in South Africa, is also held on the same day as the ultramarathon.
www.twooceansmarathon.org.za

Below: Competitors race on open road before tackling the more difficult mountain climbs.

Above: The race is run against a backdrop of spectacular scenery through the Cape Peninsula.

Resources

Books

Austin, Michael, *Running and Philosophy: A Marathon for the Mind*, Blackwell, 2007

Bean, Anita, *The Complete Guide to Sports Nutrition*, A&C Black, 5th edition, 2006

Bingham, John, *No Need for Speed: A Beginner's Guide to the World of Running*, Rodale, 2004

Burfoot, Amby, *The Runner's World Complete Book of Running for Beginners*, Rodale, 2005

Daniels, Jack, *Daniels' Running Formula*, Human Kinetics, 2nd edn, 2004

Dick, Frank W., *Sports Training Principles*, A&C Black, 4th edn, 2002

Fee, Earl, *The Complete Guide to Running: How to be a Champion from 9 to 90*, Meyer & Meyer Sports Books, 2005

Fitzgerald, Matt, *Brain Training for Runners*, New American Library, 2007

Hamlett, Alison, *Need to Know? Running*, Collins, 2007

Jackson, Lisa & Whalley, Susie, *Running Made Easy*, Anova, 2nd edn, 2008

Kowalchik, Claire, *The Complete Book of Running for Women*, Simon & Schuster, 2000

McConnell, Kym, and Horsley, Dave, *Extreme Running*, Pavilion Books, 2007

Noakes, Tim, *The Lore of Running*, Human Kinetics, 2002

Smith, Mike, *High Performance Sprinting*, Crowood Press Ltd, 2005

Websites

www.runnersworld.com
www.runnersworld.co.uk
www.runningtimes.com
www.mapmyrun.com
www.marathonguide.com
www.aimsworldrunning.org

Metric/imperial conversions for popular race distances

Race distance	Conversion
100m	109.3 yards
1km	0.62 miles
1 mile	1.6 km
1,500m	1,640.4 yards
5K	3.1 miles
10K	6.2 miles
10 miles	16.1 km
Half-marathon	13.1 miles/21.1 km
Marathon	26.2 miles/42.2km

Useful Contacts

American Running Association
4405 East-West Highway
Suite 405, Bethesda, MD 20814, USA
www.americanrunning.org

Berlin Marathon
Sport-Club Charlottenburg e.V.
Glockenturmstr. 23
14055 Berlin, Germany
www.berlin-marathon.com

European Athletic Association (EAA)
Avenue Ruchonnet 18
Lausanne, CH 1003, Switzerland
www.european-athletics.org

International Association of Athletics Federations (IAAF)
17 Rue Princesse Florestine
BP 359, MC98007 Monaco
www.iaaf.org

Komen Race for the Cure
5005 LBJ Freeway, Suite 250
Dallas, TX 75244, USA
www.raceforthecure.com

London Marathon
115 Southwark Street
London SE1 0JF, UK
www.virginmoneylondonmarathon.com

New York City Marathon
9 East 89th Street
New York, NY 10128, USA
www.tcsnycmarathon.org

Paris Marathon
A.S.O. Athlétisme
2 Rue Rouget de Lisle, TSA 61100
92137 Issy-les-Moulineaux Cedex
France
www.parismarathon.com

Race for Life
Cancer Research UK,
Angel Building, 407 St John Street,
London EC1V 4AD, UK
raceforlife.cancerresearchuk.org

Road Runners Club of America
1501 Lee Hwy, Suite 140
Arlington, Va. 22209, USA
www.rrca.org

UK Athletics
British Athletics, Athletics House,
Alexander Stadium
Walsall Road, Perry Barr
Birmingham B42 2BE, UK
www.britishathletics.org.uk

USA Track & Field (USATF)
132 East Washington Street
Suite 800
Indianapolis
USA
www.usatf.org

World Association of Veteran Athletes
www.world-masters-athletics.org

Race time predictor

Use a recent race performance to predict your finish time over another distance. The closer the two distances, the more accurate the prediction will be.

Mile	5K	10K	Half-marathon	Marathon
4:00	13:18	27:43	1:01:05	2:07:21
4:10	13:51	28:52	1:03:37	2:12:38
4:20	14:24	30:01	1:06:09	2:17:55
4:30	14:58	31:12	1:08:46	2:23:22
4:40	15:31	32:21	1:11:18	2:28:39
4:50	16:04	33:29	1:13:48	2:33:52
5:00	16:37	34:38	1:16:20	2:39:08
5:10	17:11	35:49	1:18:56	2:44:34
5:20	17:44	36:58	1:21:28	2:49:51
5:30	18:17	38:07	1:24:01	2:55:10
5:40	18:50	39:15	1:26:30	3:00:20
5:50	19:24	40:26	1:29:07	3:05:48
6:00	19:57	41:35	1:31:39	3:11:05
6:10	20:30	42:44	1:34:11	3:16:21
6:20	21:03	43:53	1:36:43	3:21:38
6:30	21:37	45:04	1:39:20	3:27:06
6:40	22:10	46:12	1:41:50	3:32:18
6:50	22:43	47:21	1:44:22	3:37:35
7:00	23:17	48:32	1:46:58	3:43:01
7:10	23:50	49:41	1:49:30	3:48:18
7:20	24:23	50:50	1:52:02	3:53:34
7:30	24:56	51:59	1:54:34	3:58:51
7:40	25:30	53:09	1:56:09	4:02:09
7:50	26:03	54:18	1:59:41	4:09:31
8:00	26:36	55:27	2:02:13	4:14:48
8:10	27:09	56:36	2:04:45	4:20:05
8:20	27:43	57:47	2:07:22	4:25:33
8:30	28:16	58:56	2:09:54	4:30:49
8:40	28:49	1:00:04	2:12:34	4:36:23
8:50	29:22	1:01:13	2:14:56	4:41:19
9:00	29:56	1:02:24	2:17:32	4:46:44
9:10	30:29	1:03:33	2:20:04	4:52:01
9:20	31:02	1:04:42	2:22:36	4:57:18
9:30	31:35	1:05:50	2:25:06	5:02:31
9:40	32:09	1:07:01	2:27:43	5:07:58
9:50	32:42	1:08:10	2:30:15	5:13:15
10:00	33:15	1:09:19	2:32:47	5:18:32

Index

Acknowledgements

Picture Credits

l=left, r=right, t=top, b=bottom, bl=bottom left, br=bottom right, c=centre, tr=top right.

2:09 events: 126b, 194t, 201tl, 207br, /Dave Gratton: 98, 130. **Across the Divide (www.adventure-racing.org)**: 230t, 233t. **Alamy**: /brt PHOTO: 10t, /Peter Widmann: 17b. **Aquajogger**: 63tr. **Banayote Photography**: 107b. **The Boston Marathon**: FAYFOTO/ BOSTON: 100b. **Bridgeman Art Library**: /Musee Municipal Antoine Vivenel, Compiegne, France, Lauros/ Giraudon: 132b. **Peter Bull illustration**: 22, 23, 35, 71, 82, 83, 84, 85, 87. **MHFS 10k for Men**: /James Clare: 106b. **Corbis**: /Bettmann: 10b, 11b, 133t, 134t, 135tr, 135b, 137tl, 137b, 177tr, 188t, 242t, /Fabrizio Bensch/ Reuters: 192b, /S. Carmona: 176t, /Duomo: 137tr, 165t, /Rick Friedman: 242b, /Li Ga/ Xinhua Press: 177b, /Andrew Gombert/epa: 109t, /Frederic Haslin/ TempSport: 43tr, /Gary Hershorn/ Reuters: 168t, /Karl-Josef Hildenbrand/ dpa: 155, /IMANE/ Image Point FR: 17t,/Dimitri Iundt/TempSport: 12, 168b, /Gilbert Iundt/TempSport: 162t, /ALFRED CHEN JIN/ Reuters: 245tr, 245b, /Mike King: 123t, 166t, 166b, /Justin Lane/epa: 206b, /LWA-Stephen Welstead: 64, /Wally McNamee: 173b, /Peter Macdiarmid/ Reuters: 99, /Leo Mason: 102b,108t, /Phil Noble/Reuters: 105t, /Kerim Okten/epa: 169, /Neal Preston: 178b, /Jerome Prevost/ TempSport: 102t, /Reuters: 43tl, /Franck Robichon/epa: 218, /Anne Ryan/ NewSport/Corbis: 13b, /Sampics/:172, /Tobias Schwarz/ Reuters: 13t, /Stapleton Collection: 133b, /Shannon Stapleton/ Reuters: 109b, /René Shenouda: 206t, /Roberto Tedeschi/epa: 219br, /Underwood & Underwood: 134b, /SUSANA VERA/ Reuters: 164, /Allana Wesley White: 94t, /Adam Woolfitt: 11t, /Chen Xiaowei/ xh/Xinhua Press: 2, /Li Yue/xh/ Xinhua Press: 162b, /How Hwee Young/ epa: 165b, /Jeff Zelevansky/epa: 194b. **Detail Events**: 226 (all), 227 (all). **The Flora London Marathon**: 108b. **Getty Images**: /Allsport Hulton/Archive: 136t, /Allsport UK/Allsport: 248t, 248b, /PIERRE ANDRIEU/AFP: 247t, 247b, /Daniel Berehulak: 244b, /Julian Finney: 173t, 217t, /Stu Forster: 171br, /Gallo Images: 249t,/John Gichigi: 139b, /Paul Gilham: 171bl, /IOC Olympic Museum/ Allsport: 135tl, /Ross Kinnaird/Allsport: 163, /Matthew Lewis: 107t, /David Madison: 106t, /Leonard Mccombe// Time Life Pictures:136b, /Chris McGrath/ ALLSPORT: 244t, /Ethan Miller: 105b, /STAFF/AFP: 171t, /Michael Steele: 132t, /Touchline Photo/ALLSPORT: 249b, /PIERRE VERDY/ AFP/ Getty Images: 246t, 246b. **Pete Hartley**: 97t, 214t, 220, 221, 222t, 222b, 223b, 224b, 225t, 228t, 228br, 229t, 229b, 240t. **HoodtoCoast.com**: 241t, 241b. **Elizabeth Hufton**: 240t. **iStockphoto**: 34br, 49t, 53t, 53br, 62br, 63tl, 63b, 75b, 90t, 91t, 92b, 144b, 147b, 158bl, 184bl, 186b, 201tr, 232, 233b, 245tl. **Philip O'Connor**: 7, 8, 9, 15t, 16b, 20t, 21br, 26 (all), 27 (all), 28b, 30t, 31tl, 31tr, 32, 33tl, 33tr, 34l, 36 (all), 37 (all), 38, 39, 41t, 41b, 42b, 45tr, 46t, 47b, 48t, 48b, 49b, 52t, 56 (all), 57 (all), 58 (all), 59 (all), 65, 68b, 73bc, 73br, 80, 83tr, 85br, 86, 88t, 100t, 101t, 103b, 110, 114, 115t, 119t, 120, 124t, 125bl, 125br, 126t, 128br, 129t, 138, 139b, 140, 143t, 143b 144t, 148 (all), 149 (all), 150 (all), 151 (all), 152, 153 (all), 158t, 158bc, 158br, 159 (all), 160 (all), 161 (all), 170, 174, 179t, 184t, 185b, 188bl, 189, 191br, 192t, 196t, 196b, 198, 200, 201b, 204t, 204b, 205, 208 (all), 209bl, 209bc, 209br, 210t, 211tc, 211tl (x 2), 212b, 213, 216b, 217b, 223l. **Mike King**: 14bl, 14br, 16b, 18bl, 18bc, 19, 24l, 24tc, 24tr, 25t (3 pics), 25bl, 25bc, 28t, 30b, 31bl, 31br, 33tr, 40, 42t, 44br, 44bl, 45b, 46b, 47t, 51t, 51b, 52b, 53bl, 54 (all), 55 (all), 60 (all), 61 (all), 66b, 68t, 73br, 84tl, 84tr, 88b, 89tl, 89tr, 94bl, 96b, 97b, 119b, 121br, 141t, 141b, 142b, 145 (all), 146 (all), 147tl, 147tc, 147tr, 154, 156 (all), 157 (all), 167 (all), 184br, 188br, 206t, 210b, 211tr, 215br, 216tr, 228bl. **Race for the Cure**: 101b, 104t. **Runner's World Magazine**: 14t, 15b, 18t, 24tr, 25br, 45tl, 50, 69tl, 69tr, 71b, 75t, 96t, 103t, 104b, 111, 112, 113, 115b, 116t, 117, 122, 123br, 176b124b, 129b, 131, 142t, 175, 185t, 191t, 198b, 199, 202, 203t, 203bl, 203br, 207t, 207bl, 209t, 211b, 212t, 214b,215t, 215bl, 216tl, 219bl, 223tr, 224t, 225b, 230b, 231, 234 (all), 235 (all), 236 (all), 237 (all), 238t, 243 (all).

Models: Emily Crompton, Michael Egbor, Jo Freeman, Christophe Fromont, Chanelle Garnett, Suzi Hall (www.innovatefitness.com), Elizabeth Hufton, Sharon Knight, Mark Leary, Catherine Lee, Cressida Lorenz, Freddie Lorenz, David McCombes, Sophie Meer, Amber Milligan, Andrew Milligan, Jay Milligan, Russ Peake, Rebecca Rideout, Jessica Rideout, Oliver Stafford.

With thanks to Greenwich Leisure Ltd (GLL) for photography locations.

The author would like to thank: Keith Anderson, Mike Gratton, Suzi Hall, Steven Seaton and Steve Smythe for their expertise; Rupert Elkington-Cole for picture research; Brooks for kit; and Karen, Sarah, Helen, her family, and the staff of *Runner's World* magazine (UK).